Staff Favorites
Potluck

FOOD & WINE BOOKS EDITOR **Anne Cain**

PROJECT EDITOR **Tara Stewart Hardee**

DESIGN DIRECTOR **Melissa Clark**

PHOTO DIRECTOR **Paden Reich**

SENIOR PRODUCTION MANAGER
Greg A. Amason

ASSOCIATE MANAGER FOR PROJECT
MANAGEMENT AND PRODUCTION
Anna Riego Muñiz

COPY EDITOR **Donna Baldone**

PROOFREADER **Jacqueline Giovanelli**

INDEXER **Mary Ann Laurens**

CONTRIBUTORS **Margaret Monroe Dickey, Anna
Hampton, Mindi Shapiro Levine, Lindsey Lower**

FELLOW **Holly Ravazzolo**

ISBN-13: 978-0-8487-5938-4

ISSN 2471-643X

Library of Congress Control Number:
2018942068

First Edition 2018

Printed in the United States of America

10 9 8 7 6 5 4 3 2 1

FOOD & WINE MAGAZINE

EDITOR IN CHIEF **Hunter Lewis**

EXECUTIVE EDITOR **Karen Shimizu**

MANAGING EDITOR **Caitlin Murphee Miller**

EXECUTIVE WINE EDITOR **Ray Isle**

SENIOR FOOD EDITOR **Mary-Frances Heck**

CULINARY DIRECTOR **Justin Chapple**

We welcome your comments and suggestions
about Time Inc. Books.

Time Inc. Books
Attention: Book Editors
P.O. Box 62310
Tampa, Florida 33662-2310
(800) 765- 6400

Time Inc. Books products may be purchased
for business or promotional use. For information
on bulk purchases, please contact Christi
Crowley in the Special Sales Department at
(845) 895-9858.

FRONT COVER FROM TOP LEFT, CLOCKWISE
**Antipasto Chopped Salad (page 81); Roman
Pizza (page 152); Lemony Zucchini-Fregola
Salad (page 85); Grilled Skirt Steak with Green
Sriracha (page 201)**

BACK COVER FROM TOP
**Pumpkin Layer Cake with Mascarpone Frosting
(page 207); Caramel Layer Cake with Caramel-
Buttercream Frosting (page 204)**

PHOTOGRAPHERS **Antonis Achilleos, Victor
Protasio**

For additional photo contributors,
see page 287.

Cold Fried Chicken,
p. 168

FOOD & WINE

Staff Favorites
Potluck

FOOD & WINE
BOOKS

Caraway Rolls with Garlic-Parsley
Butter, p. 45

CONTENTS

GF GLUTEN-FREE

v VEGETARIAN

GF GLUTEN-FREE

V VEGETARIAN

Mustard Greens with Apple
Cider-Dijon Dressing, p. 62

From top: Harissa-
Spiced Cassoulet, p. 187;
Grilled Skirt Steak with
Green Sriracha, p. 201;
Oma's Green Mountain
Salad, p. 53

FOREWORD

One of the easiest and most fun ways to throw a party is to make it a potluck. When guests contribute dishes, it takes the pressure off the host, and gives guests a chance to shine—everybody wins.

The editors of FOOD & WINE are pleased to bring you this collection of contemporary dishes for your next potluck. These elegant recipes, shared by our favorite chefs or created by the F&W Test Kitchen, feature fresh ingredients and bold flavors in crowd-pleasing fare like Rosemary Chicken with Corn and Sausage Fricassee (p. 176), Hummus and Salad Pizza (p. 151), and Rye and Crème Fraîche Strata with Smoked Salmon (p. 157). You'll also find plenty of upgrades to potluck classics. (Because who doesn't love a knockout pasta salad?)

Each dish has been selected for its potluck-friendliness, and is easy to make, easy to transport and serve, and guaranteed to please. (And to help you set out an inclusive spread, we've flagged the recipes that are Gluten Free and Vegetarian.)

The right bottle of wine can elevate a potluck into a dinner party, so we've invited our wine experts to share their favorite potluck-friendly wine pairings (p. 246). We've also included some "big batch" beverages that are perfect when you're entertaining a crowd.

Join us as we reimagine the potluck!

—The Editors

THE EATERS

Hunter Lewis
Editor in Chief

Chapel Hill native and UNC graduate, Hunter is a passionate cook and journalist. He worked at *The Herald Sun* as a crime reporter, eventually putting his passion for food to work as the newspaper's restaurant critic. He moved to New York to work for Chef Jonathan Waxman's restaurant Barbuto, then at *Bon Appétit* and *Saveur.*

Last meal on earth Oysters (from New England, the South, and the Pacific Northwest), caviar crème fraîche and potato chips, grilled quail, simple vegetables, a bottle of Champagne, a glass of rye on the rocks, and a slice of chocolate cake.

Melanie Hansche
Deputy Editor in Chief

Melanie works with our print, marketing, digital and test kitchen teams to manage key projects, including our inaugural chef mentorship program. An Australian of German descent, she's a self-confessed food nerd, persistent baker, and co-owner of an Aussie café. Melanie has spent over a decade editing food magazines, cookbooks, and reviewing restaurants.

Dream food vacation Mel is itching to taste the vibrantly spiced vegetables, grilled lamb and seafood, and pistachio-spiked pastries of Turkey—from its seaside villages to the banks of the Bosporus in Istanbul.

Karen Shimizu
Executive Editor

Karen grew up with parents who both worked, but also made food a priority: a California-born mom who always got dinner on the table for her four kids, and a Japanese dad who liked to take her out for sushi. Karen worked at *Saveur* and *Organic Life* before joining *Food & Wine.* A mom herself, these days she loves recipes that marry you-can-do-it-on-a-weeknight simplicity to bold, fresh, palate-expanding flavors.

Tools of her trade A Griswold cast-iron skillet, stainless-steel fish spatula, and Microplane (for zesting citrus and grating garlic) are kitchen essentials for Karen.

Ray Isle
Executive Wine Editor

Ray spends an inordinate amount of time cooking, to ensure that he has enough interesting food to pair with all the wine he "has" to taste. It's very important, he likes to point out, to try at least 20 different Syrahs with a leg of lamb you just roasted.

Travel essentials A cushioned suitcase for his wines and a delicious sandwich.

Justin Chapple
Culinary Director

As the star of F&W's Mad Genius Tips video series, Justin spends much of his time developing oddball cooking hacks in addition to testing and creating hundreds of recipes a year for the magazine.

Go-to potluck dish Justin opts for something simple, yet bursting with flavor—a big bowl of farro salad packed with briny green olives, golden raisins and lots of parsley.

An avocado a day He enjoys one of these creamy, green fruits daily. His guarantee for the perfect soft, ripe avocados: Wrap dark, firm avocados in foil and put them in a 200 degree-heated oven for ten minutes.

Mary-Frances Heck
Senior Food Editor

A graduate of the Culinary Institute of America, and the author of *Sweet Potatoes,* Mary-Frances's knowledge of all things edible expands far beyond the humble root vegetable. Her writing and recipes have appeared in numerous cookbooks, *Lucky Peach, Cooking Light,* and in the pages of *The Wall St. Journal.*

Indulgent breakfast Sitting on the porch with her wife, sipping hot, black coffee while enjoying a plate of soft scrambled eggs on homemade English muffins topped with fresh snipped chives, fresh fruit or a simple green salad, followed by a bottle of cold rosé Champagne.

Jordana Rothman
Restaurant Editor

Holding the title for the most envious role of all, "professional eater," Jordana traveled some 37,000 miles in a tiny span of six months, seeking out and uncovering the 10 best new restaurants in America. She never once ate fast-food along the way, but she did eat a lot of sour gummies.

Meal of the year Every June, Jordana hosts a themed dinner party (AKA "The Memory Palace"). Last year's "Mystery Cult" theme included 750 grams of Ossetra caviar served spooned into Bugles with sour cream and parsley stems—she called those "horns of plenty."

Anne Cain
Books Editor

An experienced cookbook editor with over 35 titles under her belt, Anne is also a registered dietitian. When it comes to eating, she lives by the philosophy of "all things in moderation." Except, perhaps, when it comes to cheese where overindulgence is unavoidable.

Proudest food moment Making my grandmother's recipe for a raisin-laden, sherry-soaked nut cake last Christmas. My brother announced to our family that it was "better than Mama's."

Caitlin Murphree Miller
Managing Editor

Starting out in copy and production departments, Caitlin has been fascinated by the mechanics of making magazines from the very beginning. With five magazines and hundreds of difficult issue closes behind her, her passion is getting well-planned and beautifully high-quality magazines out the door on time, on budget, and with as little stress as possible.

Guilty pleasure Boxed Mac 'n' Cheese. The first thing she learned to "cook" as a kid, the nostalgic flavor brings her back to her childhood.

Winslow Taft
Creative Director

Formerly the art director for *Mental Floss* and a gardener for The Winslow Gardens, Winslow is a lover of all things design. Find him sipping old-fashioned cocktails and relaxing with his pups in his retro-inspired, renovated cottage from the 1920s.

A change of taste Growing up, Winslow couldn't understand why his grandmother loved tomato sandwiches. Now he can't imagine summer without Duke's mayo spread thickly between two slices of bread, salt, pepper and his homegrown Black Krim tomatoes.

Nina Friend
Editorial Assistant

Prior to starting at *Food & Wine,* Nina obtained her masters in journalism from Columbia University. Growing up, her family's obsession with food shaped her love for it. When she isn't Instagramming mouthwatering cookies from her mom's Chicago-based cookie company (Big Fat Cookie), Nina can be found rapping the Hamilton soundtrack and re-reading the Harry Potter series.

Recent baking feats Marbled banana bread—gooey because of her impatience—but still delicious!

Alison Spiegel
Deputy Digital Editor

Alison got into food media when she realized she was spending more time bookmarking recipes, mapping out her dining plan for the week, and suggesting restaurants to her friends than anything else she did. When her day doesn't revolve around her 4 p.m. treat, it's pegged to a 5 p.m. aperitif.

Most likely to Be seen with a huge, flaky croissant (or any other relative of the delectable pastry) in hand at all times.

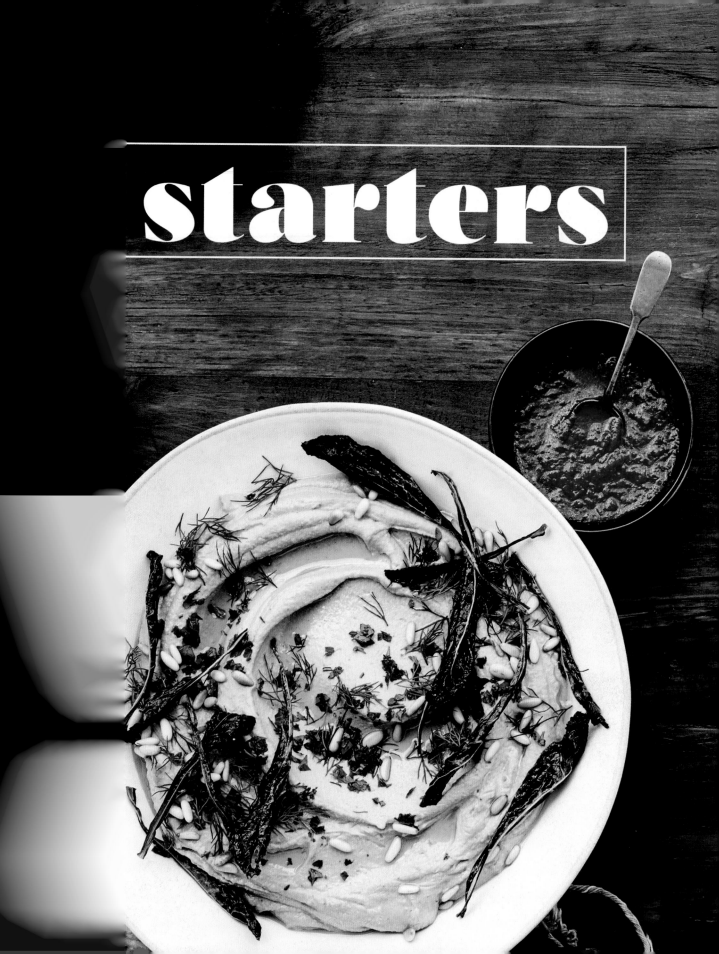

starters

CLASSIC HUMMUS

(v)

MAKES **About 6 cups**

TIME **1 hr 30 min plus overnight soaking**

📷 PAGE 13

2 cups dried chickpeas

2 tsp. baking soda

1 cup tahini

¼ cup plus 2 Tbsp. fresh lemon juice

3 large garlic cloves, minced

1 tsp. ground cumin

Kosher salt

Extra-virgin olive oil, sumac, pomegranate seeds, roasted chickpeas, thinly sliced radishes and fresh mint, for garnish

Pita chips, radishes, baby fennel and carrots, for serving

1 In a medium bowl, cover the dried chickpeas with 2 inches of water and stir in 1 teaspoon of the baking soda. Refrigerate the chickpeas overnight. Drain the chickpeas, then rinse them under cold water.

2 In a medium saucepan, cover the chickpeas with 2 inches of fresh water. Add the remaining 1 teaspoon of baking soda and bring to a boil. Simmer over moderate heat for about 1 hour, until the chickpeas are very tender. Drain, reserving ¾ cup of the cooking water. Rinse under cold water.

3 In a food processor, combine the chickpeas with ½ cup of the reserved cooking water. Add the tahini, lemon juice, garlic and ground cumin; season with salt and puree until creamy (add more cooking water if necessary). Transfer to a serving bowl. Garnish with olive oil, sumac, pomegranate seeds, roasted chickpeas, thinly sliced radishes and mint. Serve with pita chips, whole radishes, fennel and carrots. —*Susan Spungen*

MAKE AHEAD

The hummus can be refrigerated overnight.

VARIATION

Spinach-and-Herb Hummus Blanch 6 ounces of curly spinach in boiling salted water until wilted, about 10 seconds. Drain well and cool under running water. Squeeze the spinach dry and coarsely chop. Using a blender and working in batches, if necessary, add the spinach and 1½ cups mixed fresh herbs (parsley, cilantro or dill) to the other ingredients in Step 3 above. Garnish with olive oil, toasted pine nuts, chopped herbs and kale chips. Serve with harissa. —*SS* 📷 PAGE 13

BEET HUMMUS

MAKES **6 cups**

TIME **2 hr 30 min plus overnight soaking**

📷 PAGE 13

- **2 cups dried chickpeas**
- **2 tsp. baking soda**
- **3 medium beets**
- **1 cup tahini**
- **¼ cup plus 2 Tbsp. fresh lemon juice**
- **3 large garlic cloves, minced**
- **1 tsp. ground cumin**
- **Kosher salt**
- **Toasted sliced almonds, crumbled feta, dukka, thinly sliced scallions and sliced watermelon radishes, for garnish**
- **Pita chips, radishes, baby fennel and carrots, for serving**

1 In a medium bowl, cover the dried chickpeas with 2 inches of water and stir in 1 teaspoon of the baking soda. Refrigerate the chickpeas overnight. Drain the chickpeas, then rinse them under cold water.

2 Preheat the oven to 425°. Wrap the 3 medium beets loosely in foil and set them on a baking sheet. Roast at 425° for 1 hour, or until tender. Let cool, then peel and chop.

3 In a medium saucepan, cover the chickpeas with 2 inches of fresh water. Add the remaining 1 teaspoon of baking soda and bring to a boil. Simmer over moderate heat for about 1 hour, until the chickpeas are very tender. Drain, reserving ¾ cup of the cooking water. Rinse under cold water.

4 In a food processor, combine the chickpeas with ½ cup of the reserved cooking water. Add beets, tahini, lemon juice, garlic and ground cumin; season with salt and puree until creamy (add more cooking water if necessary). Transfer to a serving bowl. Garnish with toasted almonds, crumbled feta, dukka, thinly sliced scallions and sliced watermelon radishes. Serve with pita chips, whole radishes, fennel and carrots. —*Susan Spungen*

MAKE AHEAD

The hummus can be refrigerated overnight.

CURRIED ONION AND CAULIFLOWER HUMMUS

Ⓥ

MAKES **About 5 cups**

TIME **1 hr 30 min plus overnight soaking**

2½ **cups dried chickpeas, soaked overnight and drained**

8 **garlic cloves, peeled**

1 **tsp. baking soda**

½ **cup tahini**

½ **cup fresh lemon juice**

⅓ **cup extra-virgin olive oil plus more for drizzling**

½ **tsp. ground cumin**

Salt

Canola oil, for frying

½ **lb. cauliflower, cut into ½-inch florets**

2 **tsp. curry powder**

1 **large onion, halved and thinly sliced**

1½ **tsp. finely crushed pink peppercorns**

Chopped parsley, for garnish

Pita or naan, for serving

1 In a saucepan, cover the chickpeas, garlic and baking soda with 2 inches of water and bring to a boil. Cover and simmer over moderately low heat, stirring every 15 minutes, until the chickpeas are tender, 50 minutes; if necessary, add water to keep them covered.

2 Drain the chickpeas and garlic and transfer to a food processor; puree until very smooth. With the machine on, gradually add the tahini, lemon juice, ⅓ cup of olive oil and the cumin; season the hummus with salt.

3 In a skillet, heat ¼ inch of canola oil. Add the cauliflower and fry over moderately high heat, stirring, until tender and deeply browned, 8 to 10 minutes. Transfer to a paper towel-lined bowl to drain. Add 1 teaspoon of the curry powder and toss well. Season with salt and toss again.

4 Pour off all but ¼ cup of the oil from the skillet. Add the onion and a big pinch of salt and cook over moderately high heat, stirring, until just starting to soften and brown in spots, about 5 minutes. Add the pink peppercorns and the remaining 1 teaspoon of curry powder and cook, stirring, until fragrant, about 3 minutes. Season with salt.

5 Spoon the hummus into a bowl and top with the onion and cauliflower. Drizzle with olive oil, garnish with parsley and serve with warm pita or naan.
—Alon Shaya

MAKE AHEAD

The hummus can be refrigerated overnight. Top with onion, cauliflower and olive oil just before serving.

Pimento Cheese

WHITE BEAN DIP WITH HERBS Ⓥ

MAKES **3 cups**

TIME **10 min**

- ¼ cup plus 2 Tbsp. extra-virgin olive oil
- 3 garlic cloves, very finely chopped
- 1 tsp. finely chopped sage
- ½ tsp. finely chopped rosemary
- Two 19-oz. cans cannellini beans, drained
- 2 Tbsp. water
- Salt
- Cayenne
- Pita chips, for serving

1 In a medium skillet, heat ¼ cup of the olive oil until shimmering. Add the garlic, sage and rosemary and cook over moderately high heat, stirring, until fragrant and the garlic is just beginning to brown, about 1 minute. Add the beans and toss to coat.

2 Transfer the cannellini beans to a food processor. Add the water, season with salt and cayenne and process to a fairly smooth puree. Transfer the dip to a small serving bowl, drizzle the remaining 2 tablespoons of olive oil on top and serve with pita chips. —*Grace Parisi*

MAKE AHEAD

The dip can be refrigerated overnight. Drizzle with olive oil just before serving.

PIMENTO CHEESE

MAKES **1 quart**

TIME **20 min**

- 4 oz. cream cheese, at room temperature
- 2 oz. mayonnaise
- 1 roasted red pepper, peeled, seeded and chopped (about ¾ cup)
- 2 garlic cloves, minced
- 1 tsp. cayenne
- 1 tsp. salt
- 8 oz. sharp cheddar cheese, shredded
- 8 oz. Monterey Jack cheese, shredded
- Crackers, for serving

1 In a stand mixer fitted with the paddle (or in a medium bowl), beat the cream cheese and mayonnaise until smooth. Add red peppers, garlic, cayenne and salt. Mix just until combined, then stir in the cheeses. Chill. Serve with crackers. —*Angie Mosier*

MAKE AHEAD

The pimento cheese can be made ahead and refrigerated for up to one week.

CRUDITÉS WITH RANCH DRESSING

MAKES **12 servings**

TIME **25 min**

- 2 Tbsp. extra-virgin olive oil
- 1 cup finely chopped yellow onion
- ½ cup unseasoned rice vinegar
- 2 cups mayonnaise
- ½ cup sour cream
- 1 Tbsp. garlic powder
- 1 Tbsp. onion powder
- 1 Tbsp. agave
- Kosher salt
- Freshly ground pepper
- Crudités, for dipping (radicchio leaves, sliced radishes, multicolored carrots, blanched green beans, snap beans, cherry tomatoes)

1 In a small nonstick skillet, heat the olive oil. Add the onion and cook over moderate heat, stirring occasionally, until golden brown, about 10 minutes. Scrape the onion into a blender, add the rice vinegar and puree until smooth. Transfer the puree to a medium bowl and stir in mayonnaise, sour cream, garlic powder, onion powder and agave. Season with salt and pepper and serve with crudités. —*John Besh; Chris Lusk*

CRUDITÉS UPGRADE

Best New Chef alum Grant Achatz shares his secrets to making a majestic crudités platter.

Season the vegetables like meat Achatz dresses carrots and blanched green beans in a basic vinaigrette to add dimension.

Break out your mandoline Vary the chopping style—wedges, matchsticks, slices—to add visual and textural interest.

Embrace the fruidité "There's only so much raw broccoli you can eat," says the chef, who advocates for fruit on every crudité platter.

Turn up the plumage "It's cliché, but you eat with your eyes first," says Achatz. Garnish your platter with bushy bouquets of herbs like tarragon, chive and chervil bundled up with lettuce.

"This classic ranch is the perfect creamy dip for crisp vegetables but is also light enough to use as a salad dressing. Serve crudités and dressing along with pickled shrimp and deviled eggs for a gorgeous appetizer platter. —ANNE CAIN, BOOKS EDITOR

Crudités with Ranch Dressing;
Deviled Eggs with Crab and Caviar
(page 22); Pickled Shrimp with
Red Remoulade (page 23)

DEVILED EGGS
WITH CRAB AND CAVIAR

(GF)

MAKES	24 servings
TIME	Active 35 min; Total 1 hr

📷 PAGE 21

1 dozen large eggs

¾ cup mayonnaise

2 Tbsp. Dijon mustard

2 Tbsp. minced shallot

2 Tbsp. thinly sliced chives
plus more for garnish

1 Tbsp. finely chopped parsley

1 Tbsp. capers, rinsed and finely
chopped

1 tsp. finely chopped thyme

1 tsp. sherry vinegar

¼ tsp. Tabasco
Kosher salt

3 oz. crabmeat, picked over
Caviar, for garnish

1 Fill a large bowl with ice water. In a large saucepan, cover eggs with water by 1 inch and bring to a boil. Cover and remove pan from the heat. Let stand for 10 minutes. Drain eggs and transfer to ice water bath to cool completely.

2 Peel and halve the eggs lengthwise. Transfer the yolks to a medium bowl and mash with the back of a spoon. Arrange the egg whites on a platter. Add the mayonnaise, mustard, shallot, 2 tablespoons of chives, the parsley, capers, thyme, vinegar and Tabasco to the bowl with the egg yolks and whisk until smooth. Season with salt. Transfer the mixture to a piping bag and fill the egg whites (or use a small spoon). Top each deviled egg with some of the crabmeat and garnish with caviar and chives. —*John Besh; Chris Lusk*

MAKE AHEAD

The deviled eggs can be assembled and refrigerated overnight. Top with crabmeat and garnish just before serving.

"Deviled eggs can go high or low. Here, we opt for the former and add a touch of elegance with fresh crabmeat and caviar. Serve them with Champagne. Heaven!" —HUNTER LEWIS, EDITOR IN CHIEF

PICKLED SHRIMP
WITH RED REMOULADE

MAKES **12 servings**

TIME **Active 25 min; Total 1 hr**

 PAGE 21

PICKLED SHRIMP

- 1 **small onion, quartered**
- 1 **qt. distilled white vinegar**
- 1 **cup sugar**
- ¼ **cup kosher salt**
- 3 **thyme sprigs**
- 2 **garlic cloves, crushed**
- 1 **Tbsp. crushed red pepper**
- 2 **tsp. mustard seeds**
- 2 **tsp. fennel seeds**
- 2 **whole cloves**
- 24 **jumbo shell-on shrimp (2¼ lbs.)**

REMOULADE

- 1 **celery rib, finely chopped**
- 1 **cup mayonnaise**
- ½ **cup Creole or stone-ground mustard**
- ¼ **cup ketchup**
- 2 **Tbsp. jarred horseradish**
- 2 **Tbsp. hot sauce**
- 2 **tsp. celery salt**
- 1 **tsp. finely grated garlic**
  Kosher salt
  Lemon wedges, for serving

1 MAKE THE PICKLED SHRIMP Fill a large pot with ice water. In a large saucepan, combine onion, vinegar, sugar, salt, thyme, garlic, red pepper, mustard seeds, fennel seeds and cloves with 2 cups of water and simmer for 10 minutes. Add the shrimp, remove from the heat and let stand for 5 minutes. Transfer the shrimp and the cooking liquid to a large bowl. Set the bowl in the ice water bath and let cool completely.

2 MAKE THE REMOULADE In a medium bowl, whisk all of the ingredients and season with salt.

3 Drain, peel and devein the shrimp and arrange on a platter. Serve with the remoulade and lemon wedges. —*John Besh; Chris Lusk*

MAKE AHEAD

The shrimp and the remoulade can both be prepared ahead and refrigerated overnight. Arrange on the platter just before serving.

Lima Bean and
Ricotta Crostini

LIMA BEAN AND RICOTTA CROSTINI

(v)

MAKES **16 servings**

TIME **30 min**

- **1 cup fresh ricotta cheese**
- **½ tsp. finely grated lemon zest plus 2 Tbsp. fresh lemon juice**
- **¼ cup extra-virgin olive oil**
- **Kosher salt**
- **Freshly ground black pepper**
- **One 10-oz. package frozen lima beans**
- **2 Tbsp. each finely chopped parsley and chives**
- **1 Tbsp. finely chopped tarragon**
- **1 dried chile de árbol, finely chopped with seeds, or ½ tsp. crushed red pepper**
- **Sixteen ½-inch-thick slices of baguette, toasted**

1 In a medium bowl, mix the ricotta with the lemon zest, 1 tablespoon of the lemon juice and 2 tablespoons of the olive oil. Season with salt and pepper.

2 In a medium saucepan of salted boiling water, blanch the lima beans until tender, 2 to 3 minutes. Drain and cool under running water, then slip off the skins and transfer to a medium bowl. Add the parsley, chives, tarragon, chile and the remaining 2 tablespoons of olive oil and 1 tablespoon of lemon juice. Season with salt and pepper.

3 Spread the ricotta mixture on the crostini, spoon the lima bean salad on top and serve. —*Justin Chapple*

MAKE AHEAD

You can make the ricotta mixture and the lima bean salad ahead and assemble the crostini just before serving.

COUNTRY HAM AND PICKLE CROSTINI

MAKES **8 servings**

TIME **15 min**

- **Eight ¾-inch-thick, diagonally cut baguette slices**
- **Extra-virgin olive oil, for brushing**
- **Kosher salt**
- **8 oz. thinly sliced country ham, preferably Edwards**
- **Sliced pickled vegetables, such as cauliflower, carrots and cucumbers, for garnish**

1 Preheat the oven to 350°. Arrange the baguette slices on a baking sheet. Brush the tops with oil and season with salt. Toast until golden and crisp, about 8 minutes. Transfer to a serving platter and let cool slightly.

2 Top the toasts with the ham, then garnish with pickled vegetables. —*Justin Croxall*

MAKE AHEAD

You can assemble the crostini 1 to 2 hours ahead, cover and let sit at room temperature until you are ready to serve.

HERBED SALMON TARTARE WITH CHIPS

MAKES   **8 servings**

TIME   **Active 15 min; Total 45 min**

- 1 **English cucumber—peeled, seeded and cut into ¼-inch pieces**
  Fine sea salt
- 8 **oz. skinless salmon fillet, finely chopped**
- 8 **oz. skinless hot-smoked salmon fillet, finely chopped**
- ½ **cup finely chopped chives**
- ½ **cup finely chopped dill sprigs**
- 12 **cornichons, finely chopped**
- 1 **small shallot, finely chopped**
- 1 **Tbsp. fresh lemon juice**
- ¾ **cup crème fraîche**
  Freshly ground pepper
  Potato chips or crostini, for serving

1 In a colander set over a bowl, toss the cucumber with 2 teaspoons of sea salt and let stand for 30 minutes. Rinse the cucumber well and pat dry with paper towels.

2 Transfer the cucumber to a medium bowl and stir in the fresh salmon, hot-smoked salmon, chives, dill, cornichons, shallot and lemon juice. Gently fold in the crème fraîche until just incorporated. Season with salt and pepper and serve with potato chips or crostini. —*Nadine Levy Redzepi*

MAKE AHEAD

You can make the salmon tartare ahead and refrigerate 2 to 3 hours.

DEVILED CRAB DIP

MAKES   **8 to 10 servings**

TIME   **Active 20 min; Total 40 min**

- 8 **oz. cream cheese, softened**
- ⅓ **cup crème fraîche**
- ¼ **cup packed tarragon leaves, chopped**
- ½ **cup packed parsley leaves, chopped**
- 1 **Tbsp. toasted benne or sesame seeds plus more for garnish**
- 2 **tsp. finely grated lemon zest plus 4 tsp. fresh lemon juice**
- 2 **tsp. kosher salt**
- ½ **tsp. smoked paprika**
- ¼ **tsp. freshly ground pepper**
- 1 **lb. lump crabmeat, picked over**
  Saltine crackers and crudités, for serving

1 Preheat the oven to 350°. In a stand mixer fitted with the paddle, beat cream cheese, crème fraîche, tarragon, parsley, benne seeds, lemon zest, salt, paprika and pepper on low speed until smooth. Using a spatula, gently fold in crab. Transfer to a 1-quart baking dish and bake until heated through and the edges are bubbling, 20 minutes. Garnish with more benne seeds and serve with crackers and crudités. —*Joe Kindred*

MAKE AHEAD

The unbaked crab dip can be refrigerated overnight. Take the unbaked dip to your gathering and bake for 20 minutes after you arrive.

Deviled Crab Dip

VEGETABLE-CHICKEN SUMMER ROLLS

(GF)

MAKES **8 rolls**

TIME **40 min**

- ¼ **cup Asian fish sauce**
- ¼ **cup fresh lime juice**
- 2 **Tbsp. water**
- 1 **tsp. sugar**
- 1 **Thai chile, stemmed and very thinly sliced**
- **Eight 8-inch round rice paper wrappers**
- 4 **baby Chioggia or golden beets, scrubbed and very thinly sliced**
- 1 **cup shredded cooked chicken (4 oz.)**
- 2 **ears of corn, kernels cut off**
- 2 **oz. sunflower sprouts (1½ cups)**
- 1 **Hass avocado—peeled, pitted and sliced**
- 1½ **cups small basil leaves**
- 4 **small red lettuce leaves, torn**

1 In a small bowl, whisk the fish sauce with the lime juice, water, sugar and Thai chile.

2 Fill a large shallow bowl with hot water. Soak 1 rice paper wrapper at a time in the water for 30 seconds, until just pliable. Spread on a work surface. Top the wrapper with some of the beets, chicken, corn, sprouts, avocado, basil and lettuce. Tightly roll up the wrapper around the filling, tucking in the sides as you roll. Repeat with the remaining wrappers and fillings. Serve the rolls with the dipping sauce. —*Justin Chapple*

MAKE AHEAD

The summer rolls can be covered in moist paper towels and refrigerated in an airtight container for 3 hours. The dipping sauce can be refrigerated overnight.

"When the summer markets are full of great ingredients like corn, basil and sunflower sprouts, I like to make these fresh and colorful summer rolls. I add avocado for creaminess and chicken to make them more substantial when I'm taking them to a dinner." —JUSTIN CHAPPLE, CULINARY DIRECTOR

GOAT CHEESE, BACON AND OLIVE QUICK BREAD

MAKES **One 9-inch loaf**

TIME **Active 35 min; Total 1 hr 20 min plus cooling**

6 slices of thick-cut bacon, cut crosswise into ½-inch strips

1½ cups all-purpose flour

2 tsp. baking powder

1 to 2 tsp. cayenne

¼ tsp. kosher salt

4 large eggs, at room temperature

½ cup buttermilk

¼ cup extra-virgin olive oil

2 tsp. Dijon mustard

6 oz. fresh goat cheese, crumbled

1⅓ cups freshly grated Parmigiano-Reggiano cheese

½ cup pitted kalamata olives, halved lengthwise

2 scallions, thinly sliced

1 red serrano chile, seeded and minced

2 tsp. minced thyme leaves

1 Preheat the oven to 350°. Coat a 9-inch loaf pan with cooking spray; line the bottom with parchment paper. In a skillet, cook the bacon over moderate heat until crispy, 8 to 10 minutes. Drain on paper towels.

2 In a bowl, whisk flour with baking powder, cayenne and salt. In another bowl, whisk the eggs with buttermilk, olive oil and mustard. Make a well in the center of the dry ingredients and stir in the egg mixture until just combined. Fold in goat cheese, Parmigiano, olives, bacon, scallions, chile and thyme. Scrape batter into the prepared loaf pan and smooth the surface.

3 Bake the bread until golden on top and a toothpick inserted in the center comes out clean, 35 to 40 minutes. Let cool for 15 minutes, then run a knife around the loaf to loosen it from the pan. Invert onto a plate and let cool completely. Cut the loaf into thick slices and serve. —*David Lebovitz*

MAKE AHEAD

The bread can be wrapped well in plastic wrap and refrigerated for 1 week.

"Instead of sweet muffins, I like to bring these savory sausage and cheese muffins to a brunch. They're great with Bloody Marys or mimosas!"

—ANNE CAIN, BOOKS EDITOR

SAUSAGE-AND-CHEDDAR MUFFINS

MAKES **12 muffins**

TIME **Active 10 min;**
Total 40 min plus cooling

2 **cups all-purpose flour**

1 **Tbsp. baking powder**

¾ **tsp. kosher salt**

½ **tsp. baking soda**

4 **Tbsp. unsalted butter, melted**

1 **large egg, beaten**

1 **cup whole milk**

1 **cup shredded sharp cheddar cheese**

1 **cup chopped cooked breakfast sausage**

1 Preheat the oven to 375°. In a large bowl, whisk flour with baking powder, salt and baking soda. Stir in butter, egg, milk, cheese and sausage.

2 Spoon the batter into 12 greased muffin cups and bake for 25 to 30 minutes, until golden. Transfer to a rack to cool before serving. —*Kay Chun*

MAKE AHEAD

The muffins can be refrigerated overnight. Reheat in a 350° oven for about 10 minutes before serving.

WHITE CHOCOLATE-WALNUT MUFFINS ⓥ

MAKES **12 muffins**

TIME **Active 25 min; Total 50 min plus cooling**

1¼ **cups walnuts (4.75 oz.)**

1½ **cups all-purpose flour**

1¼ **tsp. kosher salt**

½ **tsp. baking powder**

¼ **tsp. baking soda**

1 **stick unsalted butter, softened**

⅔ **cup sugar plus more for sprinkling**

1 **large egg, at room temperature**

¾ **cup sour cream, at room temperature**

1 **tsp. pure vanilla extract**

6 **oz. Valrhona Ivoire white chocolate, chopped**

1 Preheat the oven to 350°. Line a 12-cup muffin pan with liners. Spread the walnuts on a baking sheet and toast for 7 minutes, until lightly browned. Let cool, then coarsely chop.

2 In a medium bowl, whisk the flour, salt, baking powder and baking soda. In a stand mixer fitted with the paddle, beat the butter with the ⅔ cup of sugar at medium speed until fluffy, about 2 minutes. Beat in the egg, then beat in the sour cream and vanilla. Scrape down the side of the bowl, then beat in the dry ingredients until just incorporated. At low speed, beat in three-fourths each of the chocolate and walnuts until mixed.

3 Spoon the batter into the prepared muffin cups, then scatter the remaining chocolate and walnuts on top, pressing them slightly into the batter. Sprinkle with sugar and bake for 25 minutes, until a toothpick inserted in the center comes out clean. Let the muffins cool slightly, then transfer to a rack to cool. —*Justin Chapple*

MEXICAN STREET CORN DROP BISCUITS ⓥ

MAKES **3 dozen**

TIME **Active 25 min; Total 1 hr 25 min**

2½ **cups all-purpose flour**

4 **tsp. baking powder**

½ **tsp. kosher salt**

1 **stick plus 2 Tbsp. cold unsalted butter, cubed**

2 **cups grated Cotija cheese (7 oz.)**

2 **cups corn kernels**

½ **cup chopped cilantro**

1 **tsp. finely grated lime zest**

1¼ **cups heavy cream**

1 Preheat the oven to 350°. Line 2 baking sheets with parchment paper. In a large bowl, whisk the flour with the baking powder and salt. Using your fingertips, blend in the cubed butter until pea-size pieces form.

2 Stir in the cheese, corn, cilantro, lime zest and heavy cream just until a soft dough forms. Spoon heaping 2-tablespoon mounds of dough onto the prepared sheets about 1 inch apart. Refrigerate for 30 minutes.

3 Bake the biscuits for 30 minutes, until golden. Transfer to a rack to cool slightly before serving. —*Kay Chun*

MAKE AHEAD

The biscuits can be stored in an airtight container at room temperature overnight and reheated before serving.

Mexican Street Corn
Drop Biscuits

MISO BANANA BREAD

(V)

MAKES One 10-by-5-inch loaf

TIME Active 30 min;
Total 2 hr plus cooling

5 medium overripe bananas
1¾ cups all-purpose flour
1 tsp. baking soda
½ tsp. baking powder
¼ tsp. kosher salt
1 stick unsalted butter, softened
1 cup sugar
¼ cup white miso
½ cup buttermilk
2 large eggs
Fresh butter, for serving

1 Preheat the oven to 350°. Butter and flour a 10-by-5-inch metal loaf pan. In a bowl, using a fork, mash 4 of the bananas until chunky. In another bowl, whisk the flour, baking soda, baking powder and salt.

2 Using a stand mixer fitted with the paddle, beat the softened butter, sugar and miso at medium speed until fluffy, about 5 minutes. At low speed, slowly add the buttermilk, then beat in the eggs 1 at a time until incorporated. Beat in the mashed bananas; the batter will look curdled. Add the dry ingredients and mix until just blended. Scrape into the prepared pan.

3 Slice the remaining banana lengthwise and arrange the halves on top of the batter side by side, cut side up. Bake for 1½ hours, or until a toothpick inserted in the center comes out clean. Let the bread cool on a rack for 30 minutes before turning out to cool completely. Serve with fresh butter.
—Jamie Bissonnette; Ken Oringer

MAKE AHEAD

The bread can be wrapped well and refrigerated overnight. Bring to room temperature before serving with fresh butter.

MULTILAYERED WALNUT BREAD

Ⓥ

MAKES   One 10-inch loaf

TIME   Active 30 min; Total 3 hr

- 3 cups plus 2 Tbsp. all-purpose flour
- 1 cup yogurt
- ½ cup canola oil
- 1 Tbsp. baking powder
- 1½ tsp. kosher salt
- ½ cup water
- 1 cup extra-virgin olive oil
- 2½ cups coarsely chopped walnuts (10 oz.)
- 1 large egg, beaten
-   Caraway seeds, for garnish

1 In a large bowl, combine the flour with the yogurt, canola oil, baking powder, salt and ½ cup of water. Mix with a wooden spoon until a soft dough forms. On a lightly floured work surface, knead the dough until smooth, about 5 minutes. Transfer the dough to a clean bowl, cover with a kitchen towel and let stand at room temperature for 1 hour.

2 Lightly grease a 10-inch round cake pan. Cut the dough into 4 equal pieces. Working with 1 piece at a time, on a lightly floured work surface and using a lightly floured rolling pin, roll out the dough to a 14-inch round. Transfer to a large rimmed baking sheet and brush the dough with ¼ cup of the olive oil. Scatter one-fourth of the walnuts on top in an even layer. Arrange another dough round on top and brush with ¼ cup of the oil; scatter one-fourth of the nuts on top. Repeat the layering with the remaining pieces of dough, olive oil and walnuts. Roll up tightly into a long log.

3 Transfer the log to the prepared cake pan, forming a big spiral. Press gently to flatten, then brush with the beaten egg and sprinkle with caraway seeds. Let stand for 20 minutes.

4 Preheat the oven to 350°. Bake the bread for 50 to 60 minutes, until golden and cooked through. Transfer to a rack to cool. Serve warm or at room temperature. —*Scott Conant*

MAKE AHEAD

The bread can be stored in an airtight container at room temperature for 3 days. Do not store in the refrigerator or it will get stale.

EXTRA-RICH BRIOCHE

Ⓥ

MAKES **One 10-by-5-inch loaf**

TIME **Active 1 hr;**
Total 5 hr 50 min
plus overnight chilling

One ¼-oz. packet active
dry yeast

⅓ cup plus 1 Tbsp. lukewarm
buttermilk (100°–105°)

3 cups bread flour

3 Tbsp. sugar

1 Tbsp. kosher salt

5 large eggs

2½ sticks unsalted butter, melted
and cooled

Canola oil, for greasing

1 In a small bowl, whisk the yeast with the buttermilk until it dissolves. Let stand for 10 minutes, until foamy.

2 In the bowl of a stand mixer fitted with the dough hook, mix the bread flour with the sugar and salt. With the machine at medium speed, add the yeast mixture, then add 4 of the eggs 1 at a time beating well after each addition. Drizzle in the butter and beat for 10 minutes; the dough will look slightly greasy. Transfer to an oiled bowl, cover with plastic wrap and refrigerate overnight. Let the dough stand at room temperature for 1 hour before proceeding.

3 Lightly oil a 10-by-5-inch loaf pan. On a work surface, roll out the dough to a 10-by-8-inch rectangle. With a long side facing you, fold the dough in thirds and fit seam side down in the prepared loaf pan. Cover with plastic wrap and let rise in a warm place until doubled in bulk, about 2½ hours.

4 Preheat the oven to 425° and set a rack in the center. In a small bowl, beat the remaining egg. Brush the top of the brioche with some of the egg wash and make a ¼-inch-deep slit down the center of the loaf. Bake for 20 minutes. Brush the top again with egg wash and bake for 20 minutes longer, until the top is deep golden and an instant-read thermometer inserted in the center of the loaf registers 182°. Transfer the brioche to a rack to cool for 30 minutes, then unmold and let cool completely. —*Iliana Regan*

MAKE AHEAD

The bread can be stored in an airtight container at room temperature for 3 days. Do not store in the refrigerator or it will get stale.

HALVAH-STUFFED CHALLAH

(v)

MAKES **2 loaves**

TIME **Active 1 hr; Total 3 hr 45 min plus cooling**

DOUGH

1½ cups warm water

1½ Tbsp. active dry yeast

½ cup plus 1 tsp. sugar

4 large eggs

⅔ cup canola oil, plus more for greasing

1 Tbsp. pure vanilla extract

8¼ cups all-purpose flour

2 tsp. kosher salt

2 tsp. ground cinnamon

⅛ tsp. ground cardamom

FILLING AND TOPPING

1 cup tahini

⅓ cup plus 1 Tbsp. honey

1½ tsp. pure vanilla extract

½ tsp. ground cinnamon

Pinch of kosher salt

3 Tbsp. water

1 large egg

1½ cups finely chopped halvah (6½ oz.)

Sesame seeds and turbinado sugar, for sprinkling

1 MAKE THE DOUGH In a small bowl, whisk the water with the yeast and 1 teaspoon of the sugar. Let stand for 10 minutes, until foamy.

2 In a medium bowl, whisk the eggs with the oil and vanilla. In the bowl of a stand mixer fitted with the dough hook, combine the flour, salt, cinnamon, cardamom and the remaining ½ cup of sugar. Mix to blend. Add the egg and yeast mixtures and knead until the dough comes together, scraping down the side and bottom of the bowl, about 3 minutes. Scrape the dough out onto a work surface and knead until smooth and slightly sticky, 8 to 10 minutes. Transfer the dough to an oiled large bowl and cover with plastic wrap. Let stand at room temperature until doubled in bulk, about 2 hours.

3 MEANWHILE, MAKE THE FILLING AND TOPPING In a medium bowl, stir the tahini with ⅓ cup of the honey, the vanilla, cinnamon, salt and 2 tablespoons of water until smooth. In a small bowl, beat the egg with the remaining 1 tablespoon of honey and 1 tablespoon of water.

4 Preheat the oven to 375° and line 2 baking sheets with parchment paper. Divide the dough into 2 equal pieces. Transfer 1 piece to a lightly floured work surface and keep the other piece covered with a damp kitchen towel. Divide the dough on the work surface into 3 equal pieces. Using a rolling pin, roll out 1 piece into a 14-by-6-inch rectangle. Spread ¼ cup of the tahini mixture on top, leaving a ½-inch border. Sprinkle ¼ cup of the halvah over the tahini in an even layer. With a long side facing you, tightly roll up the dough into a log, pressing the seam and ends together to seal in the filling. Repeat with the other 2 pieces of dough, ½ cup of the tahini mixture and ½ cup of the halvah. Arrange the 3 logs on one of the prepared sheets and braid them together. Brush with the egg wash and sprinkle with sesame seeds and turbinado sugar. Repeat with the second piece of dough and the remaining filling, egg wash and toppings. Bake the challahs for about 30 minutes on the middle and bottom racks of the oven, shifting and rotating halfway through, until deep golden. Transfer to racks to cool. —*Molly Yeh*

NOTE

Yeh recommends using an extra-smooth, pourable tahini (Whole Foods 365 brand is a good one), but if yours is cakey and thick, she advises mixing it with warm water until spreadable.

MAKE AHEAD

The stuffed challahs can be stored in an airtight container at room temperature overnight.

FIG-AND-ROSEMARY FOCACCIA
WITH PECORINO

(v)

MAKES **8 servings**

TIME **Active 25 min;
Total 4 hr 20 min**

¾ cup **extra-virgin olive oil
plus more for greasing**

1½ cups **warm water**

2½ tsp. **active dry yeast**

1½ tsp. **sugar**

3¾ cups **whole-wheat flour**

2 Tbsp. **chopped rosemary**

Fine sea salt

12 **plump dried Black Mission
figs (5 oz.)**

Boiling water

Freshly ground pepper

½ cup **freshly grated Pecorino
Romano cheese**

1 Grease the bottom of a large bowl with olive oil. Pour the warm water into the bowl of a stand mixer fitted with the dough hook. Evenly sprinkle the yeast and sugar over the water. Mix at low speed until combined, 30 seconds. Add the flour, rosemary, ½ cup of the olive oil and 4 teaspoons of salt and mix at medium speed until a dough forms, about 5 minutes; it will be a little sticky. Form the dough into a ball and transfer to the greased bowl. Cover tightly with plastic wrap and let stand at room temperature until it doubles in bulk, about 2 hours.

2 Punch the dough down in the bowl and form it into a loose ball. Cover with plastic wrap and let stand at room temperature for 1 hour.

3 Meanwhile, in a small, heatproof bowl, cover the figs with boiling water. Let stand until softened, 1 hour. Drain the figs and slice them ¼ inch thick.

4 Lightly grease a 9-by-13-inch rimmed baking sheet. Transfer the dough to the prepared pan and, using your fingertips, press it out to fill the pan. Cover with plastic wrap and let rise at room temperature for 30 minutes.

5 Preheat the oven to 375°. Arrange the fig slices all over the dough; gently press them in. Drizzle with 2 tablespoons of the olive oil and season with salt and pepper. Sprinkle the cheese over the top. Bake for 25 to 30 minutes, rotating the pan halfway through, until golden and firm. Let cool slightly on a rack. Drizzle with the remaining 2 tablespoons of olive oil and serve warm or at room temperature. —*Marco Canora*

MAKE AHEAD

The focaccia can be stored at room temperature overnight in an airtight container. Drizzle with the olive oil just before serving.

"Use store-bought pizza dough to save time when you make this addictive Persian flatbread. The trick is pulling and stretching the dough so it forms the classic oblong shape, then pressing deep ridges into it before brushing with yogurt and topping with the tasty mix of seeds and salt. It's easy to make and easy to take." —KAREN SHIMIZU, EXECUTIVE EDITOR

PERSIAN FLATBREAD

ⓥ

MAKES **8 servings**

TIME **Active 15 min; Total 40 min**

¼ **cup whole-milk yogurt**

¼ **cup water**

Two 1-lb. balls of pizza dough

Nigella seeds, sesame seeds and flaky sea salt (optional), for sprinkling

1 Preheat the oven to 450°. In a small bowl, whisk the whole-milk yogurt with ¼ cup of water.

2 On a large rimmed baking sheet, stretch and press 1 ball of the dough to a 14-by-5-inch oblong shape. Using your fingers, press 5 to 6 deep lengthwise channels into the dough (slight tearing is okay). Brush the surface with some of the yogurt mixture and sprinkle with nigella and sesame seeds; season with salt, if using. Repeat on another baking sheet with the other ball of dough.

3 Bake the flatbreads for 20 to 25 minutes, until browned; rotate halfway through. Serve at room temperature with an appetizer platter of fresh herbs, vegetables, nuts and feta cheese. —*Mahin Gilanpour Motamed*

BACON, ONION AND WALNUT KUGELHOPF

MAKES **10 servings**

TIME **Active 30; Total 4 hr 25 min**

- **4 slices of bacon, cut crosswise into ¼-inch strips**
- **1 small onion, finely chopped**
- **¾ cup lukewarm milk (100°–105°)**
- **¼ cup sugar**
- **1 tsp. active dry yeast**
- **1 large egg**
- **1 tsp. salt**
- **2⅔ cups all-purpose flour**
- **1½ sticks (6 oz.) unsalted butter, at room temperature— 11 Tbsp. cut into small pieces, 1 tablespoon melted, plus more for greasing**
- **⅔ cup coarsely chopped walnuts (about 3 oz.)**
- **17 whole almonds**

1 In a medium skillet, cook the bacon over moderate heat, stirring, until lightly browned, about 7 minutes. Using a slotted spoon, transfer the bacon to paper towels. Add the onion to the skillet and cook, stirring, until softened but not browned, about 5 minutes; using a slotted spoon, transfer to paper towels.

2 In a stand mixer fitted with the paddle, combine the milk, sugar and yeast and let stand for 5 minutes. Add the egg and salt and beat at medium speed until blended. Gradually add the flour and continue beating until the dough is elastic, about 4 minutes. Gradually add the 11 tablespoons of softened butter, beating until the dough comes cleanly off the side of the bowl, about 8 minutes. At low speed, beat in the bacon, onion and walnuts until evenly distributed throughout the dough. Cover the bowl with plastic wrap and let the dough rise at warm room temperature until doubled in bulk, 2 to 3 hours.

3 Generously butter a 9-inch kugelhopf mold or fluted tube pan and set the almonds in the indentations in the bottom. Punch down the dough, shape it into a ball and make a hole in the middle. Set the ring of dough in the mold, cover and let rise until the dough almost reaches the top of the mold, about 1 hour.

4 Preheat the oven to 375°. Bake the kugelhopf for about 40 minutes, or until golden brown. Transfer to a rack and let stand for 10 minutes, then unmold. Brush with the melted butter while still warm and serve at room temperature.
—*Frédérick Hermé; Pierre Hermé*

MAKE AHEAD

The unbuttered kugelhopf can be wrapped in foil and stored at room temperature for up to 1 day. Brush with the melted butter just before serving.

CARAWAY ROLLS WITH
GARLIC-PARSLEY BUTTER

Ⓥ

MAKES 16 rolls

TIME Active 45 min;
Total 3 hr 30 min

📷 PAGE 4

ROLLS

1½ cups lukewarm whole milk
(100°–105°)

2 tsp. active dry yeast

½ tsp. sugar

4 cups bread flour

1 Tbsp. caraway seeds

2 Tbsp. unsalted butter, at
room temperature plus more
for greasing

2 tsp. kosher salt

GARLIC-PARSLEY BUTTER

2 sticks unsalted butter

¼ cup minced garlic

1 cup chopped parsley

Flaky sea salt, for sprinkling

1 MAKE THE ROLLS In a stand mixer fitted with the dough hook, whisk the warm milk, yeast and sugar and let stand until foamy. With the machine at medium-low speed, beat in the flour, caraway seeds, 2 tablespoons of butter and the kosher salt. Knead the dough until smooth but a little tacky, 5 minutes. Transfer to a lightly oiled bowl, cover with plastic wrap and let stand in a warm place until doubled in bulk, 1 hour.

2 MEANWHILE, MAKE THE GARLIC-PARSLEY BUTTER In a small saucepan, melt the butter with the garlic. Scrape into a medium bowl and let cool, then stir in the parsley.

3 Butter a 12-inch cast-iron or ovenproof nonstick skillet. Divide the dough in half; keep 1 piece covered with a kitchen towel. Cut the other into 8 pieces; form each into a ball, then roll in the garlic-parsley butter. Arrange in concentric circles in the prepared skillet about ¼ inch apart. Repeat with the second piece of dough. Cover loosely with plastic and let stand in a warm place until doubled in bulk, 1 hour.

4 Preheat the oven to 350°. Brush the rolls with more of the garlic-parsley butter and bake for about 30 minutes, until golden. Brush with the remaining butter, sprinkle with sea salt and serve. —*Kay Chun*

MAKE AHEAD

You can make the rolls ahead and store at room temperature overnight in an airtight container before brushing with remaining butter. To serve, reheat and brush with butter.

PARKER HOUSE ROLLS

(ⓥ)

MAKES **36 rolls**

TIME **Active 35 min;
Total 2 hr 38 min**

**One ¼-oz. package active
dry yeast**

½ cup warm water

½ cup sugar

**2 sticks unsalted butter, melted
and cooled (1 cup)**

**2 cups whole milk, at room
temperature**

2 large eggs, lightly beaten

1 Tbsp. kosher salt

**7 ½ to 8 cups all-purpose flour
plus more for shaping**

Flaky sea salt, for sprinkling

1 MAKE THE DOUGH In a stand mixer fitted with the dough hook, mix the yeast with the water and 1 teaspoon of the sugar. Let stand until foamy, 10 minutes. Beat in the remaining sugar, ¾ cup of the butter and the milk, eggs and kosher salt. At low speed, stir in the 7½ cups of flour until the dough comes together; add more flour by the tablespoon, if necessary. Mix at medium speed until the dough forms a loose ball around the hook, 3 minutes. Brush a large bowl with some of the melted butter. Transfer the dough to the bowl and cover with plastic wrap. Let stand in a warm place until doubled in bulk, 1½ hours.

2 FORM THE ROLLS Preheat the oven to 375° and line 2 baking sheets with parchment paper. Scrape the dough out onto a lightly floured work surface and shape it into a 9-by-16-inch rectangle. Using a floured knife, cut the dough lengthwise into 3 strips, then cut each strip crosswise into 12 small strips. Working with 1 piece at a time, fold it unevenly so the top half slightly overlaps the bottom half. Tuck the overhang under and place the roll seam side down on a baking sheet. Repeat with remaining dough, forming 2 rows of 9 rolls on each baking sheet. Each roll should just touch its neighbors, but leave about 4 inches between the rows.

3 BAKE THE ROLLS Bake the rolls for about 18 minutes, until browned; rotate the baking sheets from top to bottom and front to back halfway through baking. Immediately brush the rolls with the remaining melted butter and sprinkle with sea salt. Transfer the rolls to a rack and let cool for 15 minutes before serving. To reheat, toast in a 350° oven for about 10 minutes.
—*Alexandra Guarnaschelli*

MAKE AHEAD

The fully formed unbaked rolls can be frozen for up to 1 month. Bake from frozen or thaw before baking.

SPELT GARLIC KNOTS

MAKES 16 knots

TIME Active 1 hr 45 min;
Total 5 hr 40 min

1¼ cups extra-virgin olive oil

2 tsp. active dry yeast

1¼ cups water

2 cups all-purpose flour
plus more for dusting

2 cups spelt flour, such as
Farmer Ground

1 Tbsp. kosher salt

2 sticks unsalted butter

20 garlic cloves (about 1 head),
coarsely chopped

Flaky sea salt and finely
chopped parsley, for sprinkling

1 In the bowl of a stand mixer fitted with the dough hook, mix ¼ cup of oil and yeast with 1¼ cups water. Let stand until foamy, about 5 minutes. Add flours; mix on low until dough comes together, about 5 minutes. The dough should be smooth but not sticky; add 1 tablespoon water if too dry. Let rest 15 minutes.

2 Add the salt and mix on medium-low speed until the dough is stiff and springs back when you touch it, 10 to 15 minutes. Shape into a ball and transfer to a large bowl. Cover the bowl with a damp kitchen towel and let stand in a warm place until the dough is doubled in bulk, about 1 hour.

3 Turn dough out onto a lightly floured work surface. Gently stretch into a square and fold each of the 4 sides into center. Flip dough seam side down and return to bowl. Cover with damp towel; let rise in a warm place until dough is doubled in bulk and springs back slowly after you touch it, about 1 hour.

4 Line 2 large rimmed baking sheets with parchment paper. Turn the dough out onto a lightly floured work surface and, using a large knife or a bench scraper, cut it into 16 equal portions. Gently roll each piece of dough into a ball and carefully transfer to the prepared baking sheets. Loosely cover with damp kitchen towels and let stand in a warm place for 30 minutes.

5 Invert 1 ball of dough onto an unfloured work surface, sticky side up. Using your pointer fingers, press outside edges of dough together to seal sticky side. Using your palm, flatten dough, then turn so longer side is facing you. Working from opposite side, fold dough over itself 3 or 4 times to form a tight log. Roll log into a 12-inch rope, then tie into a loose knot with 2 long tails. Transfer knot to baking sheet; repeat with remaining dough.

6 Carefully slide each baking sheet into a clean, unscented 13-gallon plastic kitchen bag and tie the bags closed; leave air in the bags to prevent the plastic from touching the dough. Let the knots rise in a warm place until the dough is puffed and springs back slowly after you touch it, about 1 hour.

7 In a medium saucepan, melt butter in remaining 1 cup olive oil. Add garlic and cook over low heat, stirring occasionally, until very soft and golden, about 45 minutes.

8 Preheat the oven to 425°. Gently brush knots with some of the garlic butter, leaving garlic pieces behind; sprinkle with salt. Bake knots for about 20 minutes, until puffed and browned. Drizzle with more garlic butter and sprinkle with parsley. Serve warm. —*Jake Novick-Finder*

MAKE AHEAD

Rolls can be stored at room temperature overnight in an airtight container. Reheat and drizzle with butter and parsley before serving.

sides

SAVORY KALE SALAD

MAKES **10 servings**

TIME **Active 30 min; Total 1 hr**

One 3½-lb. sugar pumpkin or butternut squash, peeled and cut into 1-inch pieces

½ **cup plus 1 tsp. extra-virgin olive oil**

1 **tsp. ground cumin**

Kosher salt

Freshly ground pepper

½ **cup pepitas**

1½ **cups whole-milk yogurt**

2 **Tbsp. fresh lemon juice**

1 **Tbsp. almond butter**

1 **Tbsp. minced chipotle chile in adobo sauce**

1 **small garlic clove, finely grated**

1 **tsp. sweet paprika**

15 **oz. baby kale**

1 **small red onion, very thinly sliced**

4 **oz. blue cheese, crumbled**

1 Preheat the oven to 425°. On a large rimmed baking sheet, toss the pumpkin with ½ cup of the oil and the cumin and season with salt and pepper. Bake for about 30 minutes, stirring halfway through, until tender and just browned in spots. Let cool. Leave the oven on.

2 On another baking sheet, toss the pepitas with the remaining 1 teaspoon olive oil. Toast for about 7 minutes, until puffed and lightly browned. Let cool.

3 Meanwhile, in a medium bowl, whisk the yogurt with the lemon juice, almond butter, chipotle, garlic and paprika. Season the dressing with salt and pepper.

4 In a large bowl, toss the kale with half the dressing and season with salt and pepper. Fold in the pumpkin and onion. Top with the pepitas and blue cheese and serve, passing the remaining dressing at the table. —*Amanda Mack*

MAKE AHEAD

When you're taking this salad to a potluck, season the salad with the salt and pepper, fold in the pumpkin, onion, pepitas and blue cheese but omit adding half of the dressing. Just before serving, toss with half of the dressing and serve the remaining dressing at the table.

OMA'S GREEN MOUNTAIN SALAD

MAKES 8 servings

TIME Active 40 min; Total 55 min

📷 PAGE 8

RAMP DRESSING

- 1 cup thinly sliced ramp bulbs or scallion bulbs plus ½ cup finely chopped ramp or scallion greens
- 1 small garlic clove, grated (use only if using scallions)
- 1 tsp. olive oil
- ¼ tsp. kosher salt
- 1 cup mayonnaise
- ¾ cup buttermilk
- 2 Tbsp. rice vinegar
- 1 tsp. finely grated lemon zest plus 2 Tbsp. fresh lemon juice
- 1 Tbsp. chopped dill
- ½ tsp. freshly ground pepper
- ½ tsp. kosher salt

SALAD

- 6 heads Little Gem lettuce
- 2 multicolor carrots, peeled and shaved with a peeler lengthwise
- 3 Tokyo (baby) turnips, sliced thin on a mandoline (about 1 cup)
- 1 heart of celery and leaves, sliced on a thin bias (about 1 cup)
- 6 French breakfast radishes, shaved thin lengthwise (about 1 cup)
- 1 cup cherry tomatoes, sliced in half
- 2 avocados, diced (about 2 cups)
- 1 sprig of dill, finely chopped
  Freshly ground pepper

1 MAKE THE DRESSING Heat the broiler to high. Line a rimmed baking sheet with foil and spread ramp or scallion bulbs and garlic, if using, in an even layer. Drizzle with olive oil and ¼ teaspoon salt. Broil until the ramps become charred around the edges, 8 to 10 minutes. Let cool.

2 In a medium bowl, whisk mayonnaise, buttermilk, rice vinegar, lemon zest and juice, chopped dill, pepper, and ½ teaspoon salt. Fold in ramp greens and charred ramps. Cover and chill until ready to serve.

3 MAKE THE SALAD In a large wooden salad bowl, arrange the Little Gem lettuce leaves. Top with the carrots, turnips, celery, radishes, tomatoes, avocados, and dill. Drizzle the vegetables with the ramp dressing and top with freshly ground pepper. —*Sarah Grueneberg*

MAKE AHEAD

You can make the dressing ahead and refrigerate up to 3 days.

"This stunning seasonal salad will add a touch of beauty and freshness to any potluck table. The charred ramps in the buttermilk dressing add another level of flavor." —MARY-FRANCES HECK, SENIOR FOOD EDITOR

BUTTERMILK-DRESSED SPRING GREENS (GF) (V)

MAKES 8 servings

TIME 30 min

- 1 cup buttermilk
- ½ cup cottage cheese (4% milk fat)
- 2 Tbsp. red wine vinegar
- 1 tsp. Dijon mustard
- 1 tsp. minced shallot
- 3 Tbsp. finely chopped tarragon
  Kosher salt
  Freshly ground pepper
- 1 medium head of red leaf lettuce, torn
- 2 heads of Boston lettuce, torn
- 1 cup smoked almonds (5 oz.), chopped

1 In a blender, puree the buttermilk with the cottage cheese, vinegar, Dijon and shallot until smooth. Scrape the dressing into a small bowl and stir in the tarragon; season with salt and pepper.

2 In a serving bowl, toss the lettuces with some of the dressing. Garnish with the almonds and serve, passing the remaining dressing at the table. —*Eli Dahlin*

MAKE AHEAD

The dressing can be refrigerated overnight. Toss salad with dressing just before serving.

WINTER GREENS SALAD
WITH BUTTERMILK DRESSING (GF) (V)

MAKES 8 to 10 servings

TIME 45 min

- 1 cup pecans, coarsely chopped
- ⅔ cup buttermilk
- 1 Tbsp. fresh lemon juice
- 1 Tbsp. finely chopped tarragon
- 1 Tbsp. finely chopped chives
- 1 tsp. finely grated garlic
- 1 cup extra-virgin olive oil
  Kosher salt
  Freshly ground pepper
- 8 oz. Belgian and curly endive, chopped (4 cups)
- 6 cups lightly packed arugula or spinach (4 oz.)
- 6 cups lightly packed baby kale (5 oz.)
- ½ cup thinly sliced scallions

1 Preheat the oven to 350°. Spread the pecans in a pie plate and toast for about 10 minutes, until golden. Let cool.

2 In a small bowl, whisk the buttermilk with the lemon juice, tarragon, chives and garlic. While whisking constantly, slowly drizzle in the olive oil and season with salt and pepper.

3 In a large bowl, combine the endive, arugula, kale and scallions with 1 cup of the dressing. Season with salt and pepper and toss to coat. Transfer the salad to a platter, top with the pecans and serve with the remaining dressing at the table. —*Melissa Clark*

MAKE AHEAD

The dressing can be refrigerated for 3 days. Toss salad with dressing just before serving.

Winter Greens Salad
with Buttermilk Dressing

SPINACH SALAD WITH
WALNUT VINAIGRETTE

(GF) (V)

MAKES **6 servings**

TIME **25 min**

1 **cup walnuts, finely chopped**

8 **oz. curly spinach (8 packed cups)**

4 **oz. white mushrooms, sliced**

1 **Hass avocado—peeled, seeded and sliced**

¼ **cup extra-virgin olive oil**

¼ **cup apple cider vinegar**

Kosher salt

Freshly ground pepper

1 In a small skillet, toast the walnuts over low heat, stirring, until golden, 6 to 8 minutes. Transfer to a large bowl and let cool.

2 Add the spinach, mushrooms, avocado, oil and vinegar. Season with salt and pepper, toss to coat and serve. —*Kay Chun*

MAKE AHEAD

If you're transporting the salad, go ahead and toss the walnuts, spinach, mushrooms, and avocado together in a serving bowl and cover with plastic wrap. Toss with the oil, vinegar, salt and pepper just before serving.

CHRISTMAS SALAD

Ⓥ

MAKES **10 to 12 servings**

TIME **45 min**

    Vegetable oil, for frying

24 small square or round wonton wrappers

    Kosher salt

¼ cup plus 2 Tbsp. soy sauce

¼ cup plus 2 Tbsp. extra-virgin olive oil

1 shallot, minced

½ tsp. finely grated lime zest plus ¼ cup fresh lime juice

1½ Tbsp. toasted sesame oil

2 medium garlic cloves, finely grated

    Large pinch of sugar

    Freshly ground pepper

    Three 4-oz. bunches of arugula (not baby), trimmed and very coarsely chopped

¾ lb. Belgian endives (4 small), halved lengthwise, cored and thickly sliced on the bias

2 small fennel bulbs, halved through the core and very thinly sliced crosswise

    Two 4-oz. bunches of watercress, thick stems discarded

1½ cups pomegranate seeds

1 cup thinly sliced scallions

1 In a large, deep skillet, heat ¼ inch of vegetable oil until shimmering. Add 2 or 3 wonton wrappers at a time to the hot oil and fry over moderately high heat, turning, until browned and crisp, 1 to 2 minutes per batch. Using tongs, transfer to paper towels to drain and season lightly with salt.

2 In a medium bowl, whisk the soy sauce with the olive oil, shallot, lime zest, lime juice, sesame oil, garlic and sugar. Season the dressing with salt and pepper.

3 In a large bowl, toss the arugula, endive, fennel, watercress, pomegranate seeds and scallions. Add the dressing and toss. Serve right away, with the crispy wontons. —*Natasha Phan*

MAKE AHEAD

The salad, dressing and crispy wontons can all be made earlier in the day and combined just before serving.

ESCAROLE AND GOLDEN BEET SALAD
WITH TOASTED HAZELNUTS

(GF) (V)

MAKES 12 servings

TIME 45 min

1 cup hazelnuts

1 medium shallot, minced

¼ cup Champagne vinegar

2 tsp. honey

2 tsp. Dijon mustard

⅓ cup extra-virgin olive oil

Kosher salt

Freshly ground pepper

Two 1¼-lb. heads of escarole, white and light green leaves only, torn

½ lb. small golden beets, peeled and very thinly sliced or julienned

¾ cup snipped chives

1 Preheat the oven to 375°. Spread the hazelnuts in a pie plate and bake for 10 to 12 minutes, until fragrant and lightly browned. Transfer the hazelnuts to a kitchen towel and rub them together in the towel to release the skins. Let the hazelnuts cool, then coarsely chop.

2 In a serving bowl, whisk the shallot with the vinegar, honey and mustard. Gradually whisk in the olive oil and season the dressing with salt and pepper. Add the escarole, beets, chives and toasted hazelnuts and toss well. Season with salt and pepper, toss again and serve. —*Justin Chapple*

MAKE AHEAD

When you're taking this salad to a potluck, toss the escarole, beets, chives and hazelnuts without the dressing, then add the dressing just before serving.

> "Escarole is one of the best greens to use in a salad for a potluck dinner. It's hardy and doesn't wilt when tossed with the dressing."
>
> —ALISON SPIEGEL, DEPUTY DIGITAL EDITOR

ESCAROLE SALAD
WITH TAHINI VINAIGRETTE

(GF) (V)

MAKES **6 to 8 servings**

TIME **30 min**

- **1 small garlic clove**
  Kosher salt
- **¼ cup tahini**
- **¼ cup apple cider vinegar**
- **¼ cup plus 2 Tbsp. extra-virgin olive oil**
  Freshly ground pepper
- **½ cup shelled pistachios**
  One 1-lb. head of escarole, dark green leaves reserved for another use, the rest torn into bite-size pieces
- **2 Bosc pears—halved, cored and thinly sliced lengthwise**
- **1 small bunch of cilantro, sprigs cut crosswise into 3-inch lengths**
- **6 Medjool dates, pitted and cut lengthwise into ¼-inch strips**
- **½ cup mint leaves**

1 Preheat the oven to 350°. Using the flat side of a chef's knife, crush the garlic to a paste with ½ teaspoon of kosher salt. In a small bowl, whisk the garlic paste with the tahini and vinegar, then gradually whisk in the olive oil. Season the tahini vinaigrette with salt and pepper.

2 Spread the pistachios in a pie plate and toast in the oven until lightly browned, about 10 minutes. Transfer to a work surface and let cool completely, then coarsely chop.

3 In a large bowl, toss the escarole and pears with the tahini vinaigrette. Add the cilantro, pistachios, dates and mint and season with salt and pepper. Toss the salad again and serve. —*Renee Erickson*

MAKE AHEAD

The tahini vinaigrette can be refrigerated for 3 days. Bring the dressing to room temperature and give it a stir before tossing with the salad.

ACORN SQUASH AND ESCAROLE SALAD

MAKES **10 servings**

TIME **Active 30 min; Total 1 hr 15 min**

 PAGE 50

- **1 cup raw hazelnuts**
- **1½ lbs. acorn squash—quartered lengthwise, seeded and cut crosswise into ¼-inch wedges (9 oz.)**
- **2 Tbsp. extra-virgin olive oil**
- **1 Tbsp. coriander seeds, crushed**
- **Kosher salt**
- **Freshly ground pepper**
- **¾ cup buttermilk**
- **¼ cup mayonnaise**
- **1 garlic clove, finely grated**
- **1 lb. escarole, white and light green parts only, leaves torn**
- **1 lb. arugula (not baby), stemmed and leaves torn**
- **1 cup pomegranate seeds**

1 Preheat the oven to 400°. Spread the hazelnuts on a large rimmed baking sheet. Bake for 8 to 10 minutes, until fragrant and lightly browned. Transfer the hazelnuts to a kitchen towel and rub together in the towel to release the skins. Let the hazelnuts cool, then coarsely chop. Leave the oven on.

2 On the large rimmed baking sheet, toss the squash with the olive oil and coriander and season with salt and pepper. Roast for about 20 minutes, turning once, until tender and browned in spots. Let cool.

3 Meanwhile, in a small bowl, whisk the buttermilk with the mayonnaise, garlic and 2 teaspoons of pepper. Season generously with salt.

4 On a large platter, toss half of the escarole with half of the arugula. Scatter half each of the squash, hazelnuts and pomegranate seeds on top. Repeat the layering one more time. Serve, passing the buttermilk drizzle at the table.
—*Justin Chapple*

MAKE AHEAD

The buttermilk drizzle can be refrigerated for up to 3 days. The layered salad can be covered with damp paper towels and refrigerated for up to 3 hours.

RADICCHIO SALAD WITH MANCHEGO VINAIGRETTE

GF · V

MAKES **8 to 10 servings**

TIME **Active 20 min;**
Total 1 hr 20 min

¼ cup balsamic vinegar

¼ cup sherry vinegar

1 red onion, chopped

3 heads of radicchio (2 lbs.)—
halved, cored and chopped
into 1-inch pieces

1 Tbsp. honey

¾ cup extra-virgin olive oil

6 oz. Manchego cheese, shredded
(1½ cups)

Kosher salt

Freshly ground pepper

1 In a large bowl, combine the balsamic vinegar, sherry vinegar and onion. Let stand at room temperature for 1 hour.

2 In another large bowl, cover the radicchio with ice water and let stand for 15 minutes. Drain and dry well.

3 Remove the onion from the vinegar; discard the onion. Whisk the honey and olive oil into the vinegar and add the radicchio and 1 cup of the Manchego. Season with salt and pepper and toss to coat evenly. Mound the radicchio on a serving platter, top with the remaining Manchego and serve. —*Food52*

MAKE AHEAD

The dressing can be refrigerated overnight. Toss the radicchio and dressing just before serving.

MUSTARD GREENS WITH APPLE CIDER-DIJON DRESSING

GF · V

MAKES **10 to 12 servings**

TIME **15 min**

📷 PAGE 7

¼ cup apple cider vinegar

½ cup canola oil

2 Tbsp. Dijon mustard

2 Tbsp. fresh lemon juice

12 oz. shredded mustard greens

2 apples, peeled and sliced

½ cup chopped dill

Kosher salt

Freshly ground pepper

1 In a large bowl, whisk vinegar with oil, mustard and lemon juice. Add shredded mustard greens, apples, and dill. Season with salt and pepper and toss well. Transfer to a platter and serve. —*Kay Chun*

MAKE AHEAD

The dressing can be refrigerated overnight. Toss with greens, apple and dill just before serving.

Radicchio Salad with
Manchego Vinaigrette

GRILLED ROMANESCO SALAD
WITH CHARRED-HERB DRESSING

MAKES 6 servings

TIME 40 min

- 3 cups loosely packed parsley sprigs
- 1 cup loosely packed basil sprigs
- ½ cup plus 2 Tbsp. extra-virgin olive oil
- Kosher salt
- Freshly ground pepper
- 2 cups 1½-inch Romanesco florets (10 oz.)
- 1 garlic clove, minced
- 2 tsp. finely grated lemon zest plus 3 Tbsp. fresh lemon juice
- One 7-oz. head of butter lettuce, leaves torn (4 cups)
- One 8-oz. bunch of curly kale, stemmed, cut into 2-inch pieces (4 cups)
- ½ cup cherry tomatoes, halved
- 1 medium, firm-ripe Hass avocado—peeled, pitted and cut into ¼-inch-thick wedges

1 Light a grill or preheat a grill pan. Tie the parsley and basil together with kitchen string to make a bouquet. Drizzle with 1 tablespoon of the olive oil and season with salt and pepper.

2 In a medium bowl, toss the Romanesco with 1 tablespoon of the olive oil and season with salt and pepper. Grill the Romanesco over moderately high heat, turning occasionally, until crisp-tender and charred in spots, 8 to 10 minutes; return to the bowl.

3 Grill the herb bouquet, turning often, until charred in spots, about 2 minutes. Transfer the bouquet to a work surface, discard the string and stems and chop the charred leaves.

4 In a large bowl, combine the chopped herbs with the garlic, lemon zest and lemon juice. Whisk in the remaining ½ cup of olive oil and season with salt and pepper. Add the Romanesco, lettuce, kale, tomatoes and avocado to the bowl and toss to coat; serve. —*Daniele Uditi*

MAKE AHEAD

Grill the herbs and Romanesco florets and make the vinaigrette ahead, then toss together just before serving.

BUTTER LETTUCE SALAD WITH FRESH CRANBERRY VINAIGRETTE

MAKES **12 servings**

TIME **30 min**

VINAIGRETTE

- ½ **cup fresh cranberries**
- 1 **Tbsp. sugar**
- 1 **tsp. grated lemon zest plus 2 Tbsp. fresh lemon juice**
- ¼ **cup extra-virgin olive oil**
  Kosher salt
  Freshly ground pepper

SALAD

- 2 **heads of butter lettuce**
- 2 **oz. goat cheese, crumbled (½ cup)**
- ¼ **cup sliced dried apricots**
- ¼ **cup dried cranberries**
- ½ **cup pecans, toasted and chopped**

1 MAKE THE VINAIGRETTE In a food processor, pulse the fresh cranberries and sugar until finely chopped. Transfer half of the cranberries to a bowl. Add the lemon zest and juice to the processor; pulse to combine. Slowly drizzle in the oil. Add the vinaigrette to the bowl; season with salt and pepper.

2 MAKE THE SALAD Arrange the lettuce, goat cheese, dried apricots, dried cranberries and pecans on a platter. Drizzle with the vinaigrette and serve. —*Carla Hall*

MAKE AHEAD

The vinaigrette can be refrigerated overnight. Drizzle over the salad just before serving.

"Cranberries are the star of this festive holiday salad. Toss dried cranberries in with the lettuce and use fresh berries for the vinaigrette."

—KELSEY YOUNGMAN, TEST KITCHEN MANAGER

WEDGE SALAD WITH SUNFLOWER TAHINI AND RANCH DRESSING

MAKES 8 to 10 servings

TIME Active 10 min;
Total 1 hr 10 min

DRESSING

½ cup Japanese Kewpie mayonnaise

⅓ cup buttermilk

⅓ cup sour cream

½ tsp. garlic powder

1½ tsp. finely chopped dill

1½ tsp. finely chopped thyme

1½ tsp. finely chopped marjoram

1½ Tbsp. minced shallot

1 Tbsp. rice wine vinegar

1 tsp. Asian fish sauce

Kosher salt

Freshly ground pepper

SUNFLOWER TAHINI

½ cup salted roasted sunflower seeds

¼ cup water

2 Tbsp. fresh lemon juice

2 Tbsp. grapeseed oil

Kosher salt

SALAD

1 large head of iceberg lettuce, quartered through the core and cut crosswise into 2-inch wedges

½ English cucumber, thinly sliced

3½ oz. enoki mushrooms, trimmed

Salted roasted sunflower seeds and chile oil, for garnish

1 MAKE THE DRESSING In a bowl, whisk together the mayonnaise, buttermilk, sour cream, garlic powder, dill, thyme, marjoram, shallot, vinegar and fish sauce; season with salt and pepper. Cover and refrigerate the dressing until well chilled, about 1 hour.

2 MAKE THE TAHINI In a blender, combine the sunflower seeds and ¼ cup of water and puree until nearly smooth. With the machine on, gradually add the lemon juice and grapeseed oil until the tahini is smooth. Scrape into a bowl and season with salt.

3 MAKE THE SALAD Arrange the iceberg wedges on a serving platter. Dollop ½ teaspoon of the tahini onto each wedge and top with a cucumber slice and a small amount of enoki; secure the toppings with toothpicks. Drizzle some of the ranch dressing on the wedges and garnish with sunflower seeds and chile oil. Serve right away with additional dressing and tahini.
—*Courtney McBroom*

MAKE AHEAD

The tahini and the dressing can be refrigerated overnight. Assemble the salad and drizzle with dressing just before serving.

FALL SALAD WITH SHERRY VINAIGRETTE

GF V

MAKES **10 to 12 servings**

TIME **30 min**

- ¾ **cup pecans**
- ½ **cup sherry vinegar**
- ¼ **cup Dijon mustard**
- 2 **Tbsp. honey**
- 1 **tsp. thyme leaves**
- 1½ **cups extra-virgin olive oil**
-     **Sea salt**
-     **Freshly ground pepper**
- 1 **head of red leaf lettuce, leaves torn**
- 2 **heads of Treviso or radicchio, cored and leaves torn**
- 1 **head of frisée (4 oz.), white and light green leaves only**
- 2 **Fuyu persimmons, cored and very thinly sliced crosswise on a mandoline**
- 1 **Pink Lady apple, cored and very thinly sliced on a mandoline**
- 1 **medium fennel bulb, cored and very thinly sliced on a mandoline**
-     **Nasturtium leaves, for garnish (optional)**

1 Preheat the oven to 375°. Spread the pecans in a pie plate and toast for about 7 minutes, until golden. Let cool.

2 In a medium bowl, whisk the vinegar with mustard, honey and thyme. Gradually whisk in olive oil and season dressing with sea salt and pepper.

3 In a very large serving bowl, toss the lettuce, Treviso and frisée. Scatter the persimmons, apple, fennel and pecans on top and garnish with nasturtium leaves, if using. Serve the salad, passing the dressing at the table.
—*Tyler Florence*

MAKE AHEAD

The nuts can be stored in an airtight container for up to 2 days. The dressing can be refrigerated overnight.

LEEKS VINAIGRETTE

MAKES 8 servings

TIME Active 20 min; Total 1 hr

- 8 baby leeks, white and light green parts only
- 12 medium leeks, white parts only
- ¼ cup blanched hazelnuts
- ¼ cup Champagne vinegar
- 2 Tbsp. minced shallots
- 2 Tbsp. fresh lime juice
- 2 Tbsp. honey
- ¼ cup canola oil
- 2 Tbsp. extra-virgin olive oil
-   Kosher salt
-   Freshly ground pepper
-   Chopped parsley, for garnish

1 Fill a large bowl with ice water. In a large saucepan of salted boiling water, blanch leeks until tender, about 12 minutes for baby leeks and 25 minutes for medium leeks. Drain, then transfer to ice bath to cool, 5 to 10 minutes. Drain well. Cut baby leeks crosswise into 3-inch pieces and halve medium leeks lengthwise; drain well on paper towels.

2 Meanwhile, preheat the oven to 400°. Spread the hazelnuts in a pie plate and toast for 5 minutes, until golden. Let cool, then coarsely chop.

3 In a medium bowl, combine vinegar, shallots, lime juice and honey. Slowly whisk in oils. Season vinaigrette with salt and pepper. Arrange leeks on plates and season with salt and pepper. Drizzle with three-quarters of vinaigrette; top with hazelnuts and parsley. Serve with remaining vinaigrette. —*Daniel Rose*

MAKE AHEAD

The vinaigrette can be refrigerated overnight. Drizzle vinaigrette over the leeks and top with hazelnuts and parsley just before serving.

GRILLED BREAD AND MARINATED TOMATO SALAD

MAKES 8 servings

TIME Active 30 min; Total 1 hr 30 min

- 1 garlic clove, smashed
-   Kosher salt
- 2 lbs. heirloom tomatoes, cut into 1-inch pieces
- 1 small red onion, thinly sliced
- ¼ cup red wine vinegar
- ¾ cup extra-virgin olive oil plus more for brushing
-   Freshly ground pepper
- 1 loaf country bread (12 oz.), sliced ½ inch thick
- 2 bunches arugula (6 oz. each), stems discarded
- 5 oz. ricotta salata, crumbled (1¼ cups)

1 On a cutting board, using the flat side of a chef's knife, mash garlic to a paste with a pinch of salt; transfer to a large bowl. Add tomatoes, onion, vinegar and ¾ cup olive oil and season with salt and pepper. Let mixture stand at room temperature, stirring a few times, for at least 1 hour or up to 2 hours.

2 Light a grill. Brush bread with olive oil and grill over high heat until toasted and lightly charred in spots, 1 minute per side. Let cool slightly, then cut into ½-inch cubes.

3 Add bread and arugula to tomatoes along with ricotta salata and toss to combine.—*Ethan Stowell*

MAKE AHEAD

Marinate the tomatoes ahead of time so all you have to do is grill the bread and assemble the salad to serve.

> "This brussels sprouts version of a Caesar salad is ideal for a party because it can be prepared ahead, doesn't wilt or get soggy, and makes great leftovers."
> —ANNE CAIN, BOOKS EDITOR

CAESAR BRUSSELS SALAD (GF) (V)

MAKES 10 servings

TIME Active 25 min;
Total 1 hr 25 min

DRESSING

- 2 large egg yolks
- 2 Tbsp. fresh lemon juice
- 5 oil-packed anchovy fillets, drained
- 3 Tbsp. chopped parsley leaves plus more leaves for garnish
- 2 Tbsp. chopped chives
- 1 tsp. Dijon mustard
- 1 tsp. white wine vinegar
- ¼ cup extra-virgin olive oil
- ¼ cup grapeseed oil

BRUSSELS SPROUTS

- 2 lbs. brussels sprouts
- ¼ cup extra-virgin olive oil
- 3 Tbsp. white wine vinegar
- 1 garlic clove, finely grated
  Kosher salt
  Freshly ground pepper
- ½ cup freshly grated Parmigiano-Reggiano

1 MAKE THE DRESSING In a food processor, pulse the egg yolks, lemon juice, anchovies, chopped parsley, chives, mustard and vinegar until smooth. With the machine on, drizzle in both oils until smooth. Transfer to a bowl, cover with plastic and refrigerate. Wipe out the processor.

2 MAKE THE BRUSSELS SPROUTS Thinly slice 2 cups of the smallest brussels sprouts and transfer to a large bowl. In a food processor fitted with the slicing blade, shred the remaining brussels sprouts; transfer to the bowl. Toss with the olive oil, vinegar and garlic and season with salt and pepper. Cover and let stand for 1 hour. Toss in the Caesar dressing and cheese. Garnish with parsley and serve. —*Julia Sherman*

MAKE AHEAD

The dressing and the brussels sprouts can be made ahead and refrigerated. Toss with dressing and cheese just before serving.

Grilled Baby Potato Salad

BUTTER BEAN SALAD
WITH LIME AND MINT

MAKES 8 servings

TIME Active 45 min;
Total 2 hr 45 min

6 cups fresh butter beans or
three 10-oz. boxes frozen baby
lima beans

½ cup extra-virgin olive oil

¼ cup plus 2 Tbsp. fresh lime juice

¼ cup plus 2 Tbsp. buttermilk

Kosher salt

Freshly ground pepper

1 cup chopped mint

1 Bring a large saucepan of salted water to a boil. Add the butter beans and cook until they are tender, 8 to 10 minutes. Drain and rinse the beans under cold running water. Drain well and pat the beans dry.

2 In a large bowl, whisk the olive oil with the lime juice and buttermilk; season the dressing with salt and pepper. Add the beans, cover and refrigerate for 2 hours. Fold in the mint before serving. —*Matt and Ted Lee*

MAKE AHEAD

The butter bean salad can be refrigerated for up to 2 days. Add the chopped mint just before serving.

GRILLED BABY POTATO SALAD

MAKES 8 servings

TIME Active 30 min; Total 1 hr

3 lbs. baby potatoes

Kosher salt

1 small red onion, sliced

½ cup Champagne vinegar

¼ cup extra-virgin olive oil plus
more for brushing

1 cup lightly packed parsley,
chopped

Freshly ground pepper

2 cups kettle-cooked salt-and-
vinegar chips, coarsely crushed

1 In a large saucepan, cover the potatoes with water and bring to a boil. Add a generous pinch of salt and cook over moderately high heat until tender, about 20 minutes. Drain and spread on a baking sheet to cool, then cut in half.

2 Meanwhile, in a large bowl, mix the red onion with the Champagne vinegar and let stand for 10 minutes.

3 Light a grill and oil the grate. Grill the potatoes cut side down over moderately high heat until lightly charred, about 5 minutes. Transfer to the bowl with the onions. Add the ¼ cup of olive oil and mix well. Let cool completely. Stir in the parsley and season with salt and pepper. Top with the chips; serve. —*Justin Chapple*

MAKE AHEAD

The potato salad can be refrigerated overnight. Top with the chips just before serving.

ROASTED CAULIFLOWER SALAD

MAKES **8 servings**

TIME **Active 30 min; Total 1 hr**

- 1 **large head of cauliflower (2½ lbs.), quartered lengthwise and cored**
- ½ **cup plus 2 Tbsp. extra-virgin olive oil**
- 8 **thyme sprigs**
- 3 **garlic cloves, crushed**
  Kosher salt
- ½ **tsp. finely grated lemon zest plus 4 Tbsp. fresh lemon juice**
- 1 **Tbsp. white wine vinegar**
- ¼ **cup capers**
  Freshly ground pepper
- 1 **bunch of red or green kale (8 oz.), stemmed and cut into ¾-inch-wide ribbons**
- 3 **cups baby arugula**
- 6 **radishes, trimmed and cut into ½-inch wedges**
- ½ **cup dried tart cherries, coarsely chopped**
- ¼ **cup roasted pepitas (hulled pumpkin seeds)**

1 Preheat the oven to 400°. Cut three-quarters of the cauliflower into 2-inch florets. Thinly slice the remaining cauliflower and reserve.

2 On a rimmed baking sheet, combine the cauliflower florets with 2 tablespoons of the olive oil, the thyme and garlic; season with salt and toss to coat. Spread the cauliflower in an even layer and roast for 25 to 30 minutes, stirring halfway through, until golden and tender. Discard the thyme and garlic. Sprinkle the cauliflower with the lemon zest and 1 tablespoon of the lemon juice, season with salt and toss to coat.

3 Meanwhile, in a medium bowl, whisk the remaining ½ cup of olive oil and 3 tablespoons of lemon juice with the vinegar and capers until emulsified. Season with salt and pepper.

4 In a large bowl, combine the kale with ¼ cup of the dressing and mix, gently massaging the kale to tenderize it. Add the arugula and another 2 tablespoons of the dressing and mix well.

5 Arrange the roasted cauliflower on a platter and top with the radishes, cherries, greens and the reserved raw cauliflower. Spoon on the remaining dressing, scatter the pepitas on top and serve. —*Jessica Largey*

MAKE AHEAD

The dressing can be refrigerated for up to 2 days.

CELERY ROOT, APPLE AND FENNEL SLAW

MAKES   **8 servings**

TIME   **45 min**

- 1 **lb. celery root, peeled and julienned, preferably on a mandoline**
- ½ **cup sugar**
- 1 **tsp. kosher salt plus more for seasoning**
- ¼ **cup extra-virgin olive oil**
- 2 **Tbsp. apple cider vinegar**
- 1 **Tbsp. Dijon mustard**
- 1 **Tbsp. drained capers, chopped**
- 1 **Tbsp. drained prepared horseradish**
- 2 **Braeburn or Lady apples, cored and julienned, preferably on a mandoline**
- 5 **celery ribs, thinly sliced plus ½ cup lightly packed celery leaves**
- 1 **small fennel bulb—halved, cored and julienned, preferably on a mandoline**
- ½ **cup lightly packed parsley leaves**
- 2 **Tbsp. finely chopped oregano**
  Freshly ground pepper

1 In a large bowl, toss the celery root with the sugar and 1 teaspoon of salt; let stand for 15 minutes. Drain the celery root well in a colander and squeeze out some of the excess liquid. Wipe out the bowl.

2 In the same bowl, whisk the olive oil with the vinegar, Dijon, capers and horseradish. Add the celery root, apples, celery ribs and leaves, fennel, parsley and oregano; toss well. Season with salt and pepper and toss again. Serve right away. —*Colby Garrelts; Megan Garrelts*

MAKE AHEAD

If you're taking this slaw to a potluck dinner, go ahead and combine the celery root, apples, celery ribs, celery leaves, fennel and herbs, but wait until just before serving to toss with the vinaigrette.

> "With crisp romaine and rich, salty nuggets of cheese and salami, this hearty salad adds a "wow" factor to a pizza buffet dinner." —ANNE CAIN, BOOKS EDITOR

ANTIPASTO CHOPPED SALAD

(GF)

MAKES **8 servings**

TIME **20 min**

- 3 Tbsp. extra-virgin olive oil
- 1 Tbsp. white wine vinegar
- 1 Tbsp. chopped parsley
- 1½ tsp. fresh lemon juice
- ½ garlic clove, minced
- ½ tsp. dried basil
- ⅛ tsp. crushed red pepper
- Pinch of dried oregano
- Kosher salt
- Freshly ground black pepper
- One 15-oz. can chickpeas, drained
- 1 heart of romaine (8 oz.), sliced
- ½ small head of radicchio, sliced
- 1 small English cucumber, chopped
- 4½ oz. soppressata, diced
- 4 oz. provolone cheese, diced
- 4 oz. black olives, pitted and chopped
- ½ small red onion, thinly sliced
- ¼ cup chopped peperoncini peppers
- ¼ cup packed celery leaves

1 In a large bowl, whisk the olive oil with the vinegar, parsley, lemon juice, garlic, basil, crushed red pepper, and oregano. Season with salt and black pepper. Add the chickpeas, romaine, radicchio, cucumber, soppressata, provolone, black olives, onion, peperoncini, and celery leaves; toss to coat.
—*Brooks Reitz*

MAKE AHEAD

You can make the vinaigrette and assemble the salad ingredients the night before, then toss together in a large bowl just before serving.

RADISH AND AVOCADO SALAD

MAKES **8 servings**

TIME **15 min**

20 **radishes, thinly sliced**

 1 **small red onion, thinly sliced (1 cup)**

 1 **jalapeño, thinly sliced**

¼ **cup fresh lime juice**

 1 **Tbsp. extra-virgin olive oil plus more for drizzling**

   Flaky sea salt

 3 **ripe Hass avocados—peeled, pitted and sliced**

 1 **cup cilantro leaves**

½ **cup basil leaves**

1 In a medium bowl, combine the radishes with the onion, jalapeño, lime juice and the 1 tablespoon of olive oil and toss to coat. Season with salt. Arrange the avocados on a platter, drizzle with olive oil and season with salt. Spoon the radish salad on top, top with the cilantro and basil and serve as soon as possible. —*Lorena Herrera*

MAKE AHEAD

The ingredients can all be prepped up to 4 hours ahead. Toss the radish mixture with the lime juice and olive oil and then assemble the salad just before serving or the radishes will get soggy.

"Bright from the lime juice and buttery from the avocado, this salad offers nice balance on a menu that includes spicy, smoky, braised or slow-roasted meats and vegetables." —JORDANA ROTHMAN, RESTAURANT EDITOR

Fresh Cherries with Spring Onions and Cilantro

LEMONY ZUCCHINI-FREGOLA SALAD

(V)

MAKES 8 servings

TIME 40 min

3 large zucchini (2½ lbs.), cut in half lengthwise and sliced crosswise into ½-inch half-moons

½ cup extra-virgin olive oil

Kosher salt

Freshly ground black pepper

1 lb. uncooked fregola

1 cup unsalted roasted shelled pistachios, coarsely chopped

¾ cup packed torn basil leaves

½ tsp. finely grated lemon zest plus ¼ cup fresh lemon juice

1 tsp. crushed red pepper

1 Preheat the oven to 450°. Position racks in the top and bottom thirds of the oven. In a large bowl, toss the zucchini with ¼ cup of the olive oil and season with salt and black pepper. Divide the zucchini between 2 rimmed baking sheets and spread in even layers. Roast until tender, about 30 minutes, rotating the baking sheets halfway through. Let cool.

2 Meanwhile, bring a large pot of salted water to a boil. Add the fregola and cook, stirring occasionally, until the fregola is al dente, about 10 minutes. Drain and transfer to a large bowl. Let cool.

3 Add the zucchini, the remaining ¼ cup olive oil, pistachios, basil, lemon zest and juice, and crushed red pepper to the fregola. Season with salt and black pepper and toss to coat. Serve. —*Brooks Reitz*

MAKE AHEAD

The salad can be made ahead and stored in the refrigerator overnight.

FRESH CHERRIES WITH SPRING ONIONS AND CILANTRO

(GF) (V)

MAKES 8 servings

TIME 40 min

3¼ lbs. fresh cherries, pitted and halved (about 8 cups)

3 spring onions, thinly sliced

1 cup coarsely chopped cilantro plus leaves for garnish

1 Tbsp. white wine vinegar plus more for seasoning

1 Tbsp. Asian fish sauce plus more for seasoning

1 In a large bowl, toss cherries, spring onions, cilantro, vinegar and fish sauce. Season with more vinegar and fish sauce, if desired. Transfer to a platter, garnish with cilantro and serve. —*Zakary Pelaccio*

MAKE AHEAD

To make this salad ahead, combine the cherries, onions, and cilantro, then toss with vinegar and fish sauce just before serving.

> "What's not to love about this make-ahead grain salad? You can serve it at room temperature, plus there's an olive in every bite!"
>
> —KELSEY YOUNGMAN, TEST KITCHEN MANAGER

FARRO AND GREEN OLIVE SALAD
WITH WALNUTS AND RAISINS

MAKES **6 to 8 servings**

TIME **40 min**

1¼ cups farro (½ lb.)

4 cups water

Fine sea salt

1 cup walnuts (3½ oz.)

2½ cups pitted green olives, preferably Castelvetrano, chopped (11 oz.)

4 scallions, white and light green parts only, finely chopped

⅓ cup snipped chives

2 Tbsp. golden raisins

½ tsp. crushed red pepper

¼ cup extra-virgin olive oil

3 Tbsp. fresh lemon juice

1 Tbsp. honey

Shaved Pecorino cheese, for serving

1 Preheat the oven to 375°. In a medium saucepan, combine the farro with 4 cups of water and ½ teaspoon of salt. Bring to a boil and simmer, partially covered, until the farro is tender, about 20 minutes. Drain the farro and spread it on a baking sheet to cool.

2 Meanwhile, place the walnuts in a pie plate and toast for 5 to 7 minutes, until lightly golden and fragrant. Let cool, then coarsely chop.

3 In a large bowl, combine the farro, walnuts, olives, scallions, chives, raisins, crushed red pepper, olive oil, lemon juice and honey and season with salt. Toss well. Transfer the salad to a platter, garnish with the cheese and serve. —*Heidi Swanson*

MAKE AHEAD

The salad can be refrigerated overnight. Bring the salad to room temperature before serving.

WHEAT BERRY AND SQUASH SALAD

(v)

MAKES 10 to 12 servings

TIME Active 45 min;
Total 1 hr 10 min

3 cups wheat berries

One 2-lb. kabocha squash—
halved, seeded, peeled and cut
into 1½-inch pieces

One 1½-lb. acorn squash—
scrubbed, halved, seeded
and cut into 1½-inch pieces

12 oz. parsnips (2 large), peeled
and cut into 1-inch pieces

¾ cup extra-virgin olive oil

Kosher salt

Freshly ground pepper

1 shallot, minced

3 Tbsp. fresh lemon juice

3 Tbsp. red wine vinegar

8 oz. Tuscan kale, thinly sliced
crosswise

½ cup pomegranate seeds

½ cup dried sour cherries

1 persimmon, halved and thinly
sliced (optional)

4 oz. feta cheese, crumbled

½ cup lightly packed mint leaves

1 In a large saucepan of salted boiling water, cook the wheat berries until tender, about 45 minutes. Drain well, then spread on a baking sheet to cool completely.

2 Meanwhile, preheat the oven to 425°. In a large bowl, toss the kabocha, acorn squash and parsnips with ¼ cup of the olive oil and season with salt and pepper. Spread on 2 large rimmed baking sheets and roast for about 25 minutes, until tender but not falling apart. Let cool completely.

3 In a large bowl, whisk the shallot with the lemon juice, vinegar and the remaining ½ cup of olive oil. Season with salt and pepper. Add the wheat berries, squash, parsnips, kale, pomegranate seeds, cherries and persimmon (if using) and toss well. Season with salt and pepper and toss again. Scatter the feta and mint on top. Serve. —*Ellen Bennett*

MAKE AHEAD

The salad can be made up to 2 hours ahead and kept at room temperature. Add the feta and mint just before serving.

WILD RICE SALAD WITH BEETS, GRAPES AND PECANS

MAKES 8 to 10 servings
TIME Active 30 min; Total 1 hr

- 2 cups wild rice (12 oz.), rinsed and drained
- Kosher salt
- 12 baby golden beets
- ¼ cup extra-virgin olive oil plus more for rubbing
- Freshly ground pepper
- 1½ cups pecans
- ¼ cup plus 1 Tbsp. apple cider vinegar
- 1 small shallot, minced
- 2 cups seedless green grapes (10 oz.), halved
- 5 oz. arugula (not baby), thick stems discarded, leaves chopped

1 Preheat the oven to 400°. In a large saucepan, cover the rice with at least 3 inches of water and bring to a boil. Add a generous pinch of salt and simmer over moderate heat until the rice is tender, about 45 minutes. Drain well, then spread on a large baking sheet to cool; stir occasionally.

2 Meanwhile, rub the beets with olive oil and season with salt and pepper. Roast for about 30 minutes, until just tender. Let cool, then rub off the skins and cut into ½-inch wedges.

3 Spread the pecans in a pie plate. Bake for about 10 minutes, until fragrant and browned. Let cool, then coarsely chop.

4 In a large serving bowl, whisk the vinegar with the shallot and let stand for 5 minutes. Whisk in the ¼ cup of olive oil. Add the rice, beets and grapes and toss well. Season with salt and pepper; toss again. Fold in the arugula and pecans and serve. —*Justin Chapple*

MAKE AHEAD

The rice salad can be refrigerated overnight. Bring to room temperature and fold in the arugula and toasted pecans before serving.

> "For one of my favorite make-ahead salads, I simply dress up no-cook bulgur with a bounty of fresh herbs, a lemony dressing and crunchy roasted sunflower seeds. It actually gets better as it sits."
>
> —JUSTIN CHAPPLE, CULINARY DIRECTOR

BULGUR AND HERB SALAD
WITH SUNFLOWER SEEDS

ⓥ

MAKES 6 servings

TIME 35 min

- 1 cup medium bulgur
- 2 cups boiling water
  Kosher salt
  One 2-oz. bunch of parsley
  One 2-oz. bunch of cilantro
  One 1-oz. bunch of chives
  One 1-oz. bunch of dill
- ½ cup salted toasted sunflower seeds
- ¼ cup fresh lemon juice
- 3 Tbsp. extra-virgin olive oil
  Freshly ground pepper

1 In a large heatproof bowl, cover the bulgur with the boiling water. Add a generous pinch of salt, cover with plastic wrap and let stand until the bulgur is tender and the water is absorbed, about 20 minutes. Fluff with a fork.

2 Hold the herb bunches together in one hand. Using scissors, snip the herbs over the bulgur until you reach the thick stems (you should have about 1½ cups each of parsley and cilantro and ¾ cup each of chives and dill); discard the stems. Add the sunflower seeds, lemon juice and olive oil to the bulgur and toss very well. Season with salt and pepper and toss again. Serve the salad at room temperature. —*Justin Chapple*

MAKE AHEAD

The bulgur salad can be made early in the day. The prepared bulgur can be refrigerated for up to 3 days.

ITALIAN RICE SALAD WITH SOPPRESSATA AND CACIOCAVALLO

(GF)

MAKES **6 servings**

TIME **30 min**

1½ cups arborio rice (10 oz.)

1½ cups fresh or thawed frozen peas

3 Tbsp. white wine vinegar plus more for drizzling (optional)

2 cups loosely packed shaved caciocavallo or aged provolone cheese (5 oz.)

4 oz. thinly sliced soppressata, sliced into ½-inch strips

1 cup pitted green olives, such as Cerignola or Castelvetrano, halved

1 medium fennel bulb—halved lengthwise, cored and very thinly sliced on a mandoline plus ⅓ cup small fronds for garnish

4 scallions, white and light green parts only, thinly sliced

⅓ cup parsley leaves

⅓ cup extra-virgin olive oil

Kosher salt

Freshly ground pepper

1 In a medium saucepan of salted boiling water, cook the rice over moderate heat until al dente, about 15 minutes. Just before draining, add the peas and cook for 1 minute. Drain the rice and peas well and spread in an even layer on a large rimmed baking sheet. Drizzle the 3 tablespoons of vinegar over the rice and peas and let cool slightly, about 15 minutes.

2 In a large bowl, toss the rice and peas with the cheese, soppressata, olives, sliced fennel, scallions and parsley. Drizzle with the olive oil and more vinegar, if desired. Season with salt and pepper and toss to combine. Garnish with the fennel fronds and serve. —*Chris Behr*

MAKE AHEAD

The salad can be refrigerated overnight. Toss with more olive oil and vinegar before serving if needed.

WARM BARLEY AND CARAMELIZED MUSHROOM SALAD

MAKES **8 to 10 servings**

TIME **Active 20 min;
Total 1 hr 10 min**

¼ cup olive oil plus 2 Tbsp.
2 lbs. mixed mushrooms
5 cups cooked hulled barley
2 tsp. chopped fresh sage
¼ cup fresh lemon juice
¼ cup olive oil
  Kosher salt
  Freshly ground pepper

1 In a large skillet, heat 2 tablespoons olive oil. Add ¾ pound of mixed mushrooms and cook over high heat, stirring, until golden, about 5 minutes. Transfer to a bowl. Repeat twice to cook all of the mushrooms, adding more oil as necessary.

2 Stir in cooked barley, sage, lemon juice and ¼ cup olive oil; season with salt and pepper. Serve warm or at room temperature. —*Kay Chun*

NOTE

To get 5 cups of cooked hulled barley, use 1⅔ cups uncooked barley and 5 cups of water. In a medium saucepan, cover the barley with water and bring to a boil. Cover and cook over low heat until just tender, about 45 minutes.

MAKE AHEAD

The salad can be refrigerated overnight. Bring the salad to room temperature before serving.

GREEN BEAN CASSEROLE WITH GOAT CHEESE, ALMONDS AND SMOKED PAPRIKA

(v)

MAKES **8 to 10 servings**

TIME **Active 25 min; Total 55 min**

4 Tbsp. unsalted butter plus more for greasing

2½ lbs. green beans

¼ cup all-purpose flour

3 cups milk

1 garlic clove, finely grated

5 oz. fresh goat cheese

Kosher salt

Freshly ground pepper

½ tsp. pimentón de la Vera (smoked Spanish paprika)

¾ cup almonds, coarsely chopped

1 Preheat the oven to 350° and butter a shallow 9-by-13-inch ceramic baking dish. In a large pot of boiling salted water, blanch the green beans until crisp-tender, about 4 minutes. Drain and cool under running water. Pat dry and thinly slice on the diagonal. Pat dry again.

2 In a medium saucepan, melt the 4 tablespoons of butter. Add the flour and whisk over moderate heat until lightly browned, about 4 minutes. Gradually whisk in the milk and garlic and bring to a boil. Reduce the heat to moderately low and simmer, whisking constantly, until thick, about 5 minutes. Remove from the heat and stir in the goat cheese. Season the sauce with salt, pepper and ¼ teaspoon of the pimentón.

3 In a large bowl, toss green beans with the sauce. Spread mixture into the prepared casserole and sprinkle almonds and remaining ¼ teaspoon of pimentón over the top. Bake for 20 to 25 minutes, until bubbling and the almonds are lightly browned. Let the casserole stand for 10 minutes before serving. —*Justin Chapple*

MAKE AHEAD

The casserole can be assembled and refrigerated, then baked just before serving.

GREEN BEANS WITH ROASTED ALMOND CRUMBLE

Ⓥ

MAKES 12 servings

TIME 45 min

- 2 cups (3 oz.) crustless white bread (½-inch pieces)
- ¼ cup extra-virgin olive oil
- Kosher salt
- Freshly ground pepper
- ½ cup finely chopped salted roasted almonds
- 2 lbs. green beans, trimmed
- ¼ tsp. finely grated orange zest plus 1 Tbsp. fresh orange juice
- 2 Tbsp. chopped tarragon
- 2 Tbsp. chopped basil

1 Preheat the oven to 450°. On a baking sheet, toss the bread with 1 tablespoon of oil; season with salt and pepper. Bake for 8 minutes, until golden. Cool, then finely chop. Transfer to a bowl; stir in the almonds.

2 Meanwhile, on a rimmed baking sheet, toss the green beans with the remaining 3 tablespoons of oil and season with salt and pepper. Roast for 20 minutes, stirring occasionally, until lightly browned. Add the orange zest, orange juice, tarragon and basil and toss. Transfer the beans to a platter, top with the almond crumble and serve. —*Carla Hall*

MAKE AHEAD

You can prepare the green beans ahead, then reheat and top with the almond crumble just before serving.

"I like to dress up roasted green beans with citrus zest, fresh herbs and a crunchy almond topping."

—ANNE CAIN, BOOKS EDITOR

LIMA BEAN AND SWEET PEPPER GRATIN

MAKES **8 servings**

TIME **Active 30 min;**
Total 1 hr 35 min

- **2 Tbsp. unsalted butter plus more for greasing**
- **1 shallot, minced**
- **3 cups frozen baby lima beans**
- **1 cup chicken stock**
- **1 bay leaf**
- **1 cup water**
  Kosher salt
- **1 Tbsp. extra-virgin olive oil**
- **1 large sweet onion, cut into 1-inch dice**
- **¼ lb. thick-cut bacon, cut into ½-inch pieces**
- **4 garlic cloves, minced**
- **2 roasted red peppers, cut into 1-inch pieces**
- **1 Tbsp. chopped parsley**
- **1 tsp. chopped thyme**
- **1 cup freshly grated Parmigiano-Reggiano cheese**
  Freshly ground pepper
- **½ cup torn basil leaves**
- **1 cup fresh breadcrumbs, made from country-style bread**

1 Butter a 9-by-13-inch baking dish. In a medium saucepan, melt 1 tablespoon of the butter. Add the shallot and cook over moderate heat until softened. Add the lima beans, stock, bay leaf, 1 cup of water and a large pinch of salt and bring to a boil. Cover and simmer over low heat until the beans are tender, 30 minutes; drain, reserving 1 cup of the cooking liquid. Discard the bay leaf.

2 Preheat the oven to 375°. In a large, deep skillet, heat the oil. Add the onion and bacon and cook over moderately high heat, stirring occasionally, until the onion is lightly caramelized, 10 minutes. Stir in the garlic, roasted peppers, parsley, thyme and lima beans; remove the skillet from the heat. Stir in the reserved 1 cup of cooking liquid and half of the cheese and season with salt and pepper.

3 Transfer the lima beans to the prepared baking dish. Sprinkle on the basil, followed by the remaining cheese and the breadcrumbs. Dot with the remaining 1 tablespoon of butter and bake in the upper third of the oven for 25 minutes, until golden brown. Let stand for 10 minutes before serving.
—*Hugh Acheson*

MAKE AHEAD

The gratin can be made ahead and refrigerated. Reheat before serving.

> "Simple roasted brussels sprouts are always a crowd-pleaser on a holiday table, but they're even better when you spice them up with cumin and coriander."
> —WINSLOW TAFT, CREATIVE DIRECTOR

ROASTED BRUSSELS SPROUTS
WITH CUMIN AND CORIANDER

(GF) (V)

MAKES 8 servings

TIME 45 min

- 1½ tsp. coriander seeds
- 1½ tsp. cumin seeds
- 2 lbs. brussels sprouts, trimmed and halved
- ¼ cup extra-virgin olive oil
- Kosher salt
- Freshly ground pepper
- Finely grated lemon zest, for garnish

1 Preheat the oven to 450°. In a mortar, lightly crush the coriander and cumin seeds until coarsely ground.

2 On a large rimmed baking sheet, toss the brussels sprouts with the olive oil and season with salt and pepper. Arrange them in a single layer. Roast for 8 minutes, then add the crushed coriander and cumin and toss to coat the sprouts evenly. Roast for 10 to 15 minutes longer, until golden and crisp in spots. Transfer the sprouts to a serving platter, garnish with lemon zest and serve. —*Melissa Clark*

MAKE AHEAD

The brussels sprouts can be made 3 hours ahead. Serve the dish warm or at room temperature.

RATATOUILLE TART

ⓥ

MAKES 6 servings

TIME Active 50 min; Total 4 hr

CRUST

- **1 stick plus 2 Tbsp. unsalted butter, at room temperature**
- **2 Tbsp. whole milk**
- **1 Tbsp. sugar**
- **1 large egg yolk**
- **1¼ cups all-purpose flour**

RATATOUILLE

- **½ cup extra-virgin olive oil**
- **1 small onion, cut into ½-inch dice**
- **1 large Japanese eggplant, quartered lengthwise and sliced ⅓ inch thick**
- **Kosher salt**
- **Freshly ground pepper**
- **2 small red peppers, cut into ¾-inch dice**
- **1 zucchini, quartered lengthwise and sliced ⅓ inch thick**
- **One 8-oz. can crushed tomatoes**
- **2 Tbsp. chopped oregano**
- **1 tsp. red wine vinegar**

1 MAKE THE CRUST In a bowl, beat butter with milk, sugar and egg yolk until smooth. Add flour and beat at low speed until the dough starts to come together. Pat dough into a disk and wrap in plastic. Refrigerate for 1 hour.

2 On a lightly floured surface, using a lightly floured rolling pin, roll out the dough to a 12-inch round. Ease it into a fluted 9-inch tart pan with a removable bottom; trim the overhang. Refrigerate until firm, 1 hour.

3 Preheat oven to 375°. Line the dough with parchment paper and fill with pie weights. Bake for about 30 minutes, until set. Remove weights and parchment paper and bake until golden, 8 to 10 minutes longer. Transfer tart shell to a rack and let cool to room temperature, about 1 hour.

4 MEANWHILE, MAKE THE RATATOUILLE In a large saucepan, heat 2 tablespoons of the olive oil. Add the onion and cook over moderate heat until softened. Add the eggplant and 3 tablespoons of the olive oil, season with salt and pepper and cook, stirring occasionally, until starting to soften, about 3 minutes. Add the red peppers, zucchini and the remaining 3 tablespoons of olive oil and cook until softened, 7 minutes. Stir in the tomatoes and oregano and cook until the vegetables are tender and the sauce is thick, about 20 minutes. Stir in the vinegar. Season with salt and pepper and let cool. Spoon the ratatouille into the tart shell and serve. —*Koren Grieveson*

MAKE AHEAD

The ratatouille can be refrigerated for 2 days. Bring to room temperature, and spoon into tart shell before serving.

> "Because this cheesy corn pudding recipe uses frozen corn instead of fresh, it's an easy option for a savory side dish at your Thanksgiving meal."
>
> —JUSTIN CHAPPLE, CULINARY DIRECTOR

FALL CORN PUDDING WITH WHITE CHEDDAR AND THYME

(GF) (V)

MAKES 8 to 10 servings

TIME Active 20 min; Total 1 hr 15 min

- 4 Tbsp. unsalted butter plus more for greasing
- 1 onion, finely chopped
- 2 tsp. minced thyme
- 4 cups frozen corn kernels (about 20 oz.), thawed
- ½ cup stone-ground cornmeal
  Kosher salt
  Freshly ground pepper
- 5 large eggs
- 3 cups half-and-half
- 1 cup shredded sharp white cheddar cheese

1 Preheat the oven to 350°. Butter a 9-by-13-inch shallow ceramic baking dish. In a large skillet, melt the 4 tablespoons of butter. Add the onion and thyme and cook over moderate heat until the onion is softened, about 8 minutes. Remove from the heat. Add the corn and cornmeal and toss to combine. Season with salt and pepper and let cool.

2 In a large bowl, whisk the eggs with the half-and-half. In a blender or food processor, combine 1 cup of the custard with 1 cup of the corn mixture and puree until smooth. Whisk the puree into the custard. Then stir in the corn mixture, cheese, 2 teaspoons of salt and ½ teaspoon of pepper until mixture is well blended.

3 Spread mixture in prepared baking dish and bake for about 40 minutes, until the pudding is slightly puffed and just starting to brown. Let stand for 10 minutes before serving. —*Justin Chapple*

MAKE AHEAD

The pudding can be prepared through Step 2 and refrigerated overnight. Bring to room temperature before proceeding.

GRILLED EGGPLANT INVOLTINI

(GF)

MAKES   **10 to 12 servings**

TIME   **Active 1 hr; Total 2 hr 20 min**

- 6 **lbs. tomatoes**
- **Extra-virgin olive oil**
- 1 **small yellow onion, finely chopped**
- **Kosher salt**
- 1 **basil sprig plus ½ cup chopped basil leaves**
- **Freshly ground pepper**
- 1½ **cups water**
- 1 **cup long-grain white rice, rinsed and drained**
- **Three 1¼-lb. Italian eggplants, sliced lengthwise ¼ inch thick (about 36 slices)**
- 2 **cups shredded fresh mozzarella cheese (8 oz.)**
- 1½ **cups freshly grated Parmigiano-Reggiano cheese plus more for sprinkling**

1 Bring a large saucepan of water to a boil. Using a paring knife, core the tomatoes and mark an X on the bottom of each one. Add half of the tomatoes to the saucepan at a time and blanch until they begin to soften and the skins are wrinkled, 3 to 5 minutes. Transfer the hot tomatoes to a work surface and let cool slightly, then peel and coarsely chop. Working in 2 batches, puree the tomatoes in a food processor; you should have about 9½ cups of puree.

2 In the saucepan, heat 2 tablespoons of oil. Add onion and a generous pinch of salt and cook over moderate heat, stirring occasionally, until onion is softened and beginning to brown, 8 minutes. Add tomato puree and basil sprig and bring to a boil. Simmer over moderately high heat, stirring frequently, until tomato sauce is thickened and reduced to 5½ cups, 45 minutes. Discard basil and season with salt and pepper. Let cool slightly.

3 Meanwhile, in a medium saucepan, bring 1½ cups of water to a boil. Add the rice and a generous pinch of salt and stir once. Cover and simmer over low heat until the rice is tender and the water is absorbed, about 20 minutes. Remove from the heat and let steam, covered, for 20 minutes. Fluff the rice with a fork and let cool.

4 Light a grill or preheat a grill pan. Brush the eggplant slices with oil and grill over moderately high heat, turning once, until tender and lightly charred, about 4 minutes per batch. Transfer the eggplant to a work surface and season with salt and pepper.

5 Preheat the oven to 350°. In a large bowl, combine the rice with 2 cups of the tomato sauce. Fold in the mozzarella, chopped basil and 1 cup of the Parmesan. Season the filling with salt and pepper.

6 Spread ¾ cup of the tomato sauce in the bottom of each of two 9-by-13-inch baking dishes. Dollop 2 tablespoons of the rice filling near one end of each eggplant slice and roll into a tight cylinder; arrange in the prepared baking dishes. Spoon 1 cup of the tomato sauce over the involtini in each baking dish and top with the remaining ½ cup of Parmesan. Bake the involtini until the filling is hot and the sauce is just bubbling, 15 to 20 minutes. Let stand for 5 minutes before serving. —*Giuseppe Angelini*

MAKE AHEAD

The tomato sauce can be refrigerated for up to 3 days; the grilled eggplant can be refrigerated overnight.

CHEESY ZUCCHINI CASSEROLE

(V)

MAKES **8 servings**

TIME **Active 15 min; Total 40 min**

- 2 Tbsp. unsalted butter, plus more for greasing
- 1 Tbsp. vegetable oil
- 3 medium zucchini (about 2 lbs.), cut into 1-inch dice
- 1 medium onion, very finely chopped

  Kosher salt

  Freshly ground pepper
- 1½ cups finely crushed saltine crackers
- 7½ oz. farmer cheese (1 cup)
- 2 large eggs, beaten
- 2 Tbsp. unsalted butter, melted

1 Preheat the oven to 350°. Grease a 9-by-13-inch baking dish. In a 12-inch ovenproof skillet, melt 2 tablespoons of the butter in the vegetable oil. Add the chopped zucchini and onion, season with salt and pepper and cook over moderate heat, stirring occasionally, until the vegetables are softened, about 10 minutes. Remove the zucchini and onion from the heat and let cool slightly. Transfer to a large bowl.

2 In a medium bowl, stir the cracker crumbs with the farmer cheese. Stir half of the mixture into the zucchini and season generously with salt and pepper. Stir in the beaten eggs. Transfer mixture to the prepared baking dish. Spread the remaining cracker crumb and farmer cheese mixture on top of the zucchini. Drizzle the casserole with the 2 tablespoons of melted butter. Bake for about 25 minutes, until lightly browned and crisp on top. Let stand for 5 minutes, then serve warm. —*Jeremy Jackson*

MAKE AHEAD

The casserole can be prepared earlier in the day and reheated in a 350° oven.

SQUASH GRATIN

(V)

MAKES **6 servings**

TIME **Active 10 min; Total 40 min**

- 2 Tbsp. extra-virgin olive oil plus more for greasing
- 4 medium summer squash (zucchini and/or yellow squash), sliced lengthwise ⅛ inch thick
- 3 garlic cloves, sliced

  Kosher salt

  Freshly ground pepper
- 1 cup panko
- 1 cup shredded Gruyère cheese (3 oz.)

1 Preheat the oven to 450°. Grease a 2-quart baking dish. Add the squash, 2 tablespoons of oil and the garlic, season with salt and pepper and toss. Arrange the squash in the dish and bake for 20 minutes, until tender.

2 Sprinkle with the panko and cheese and bake the squash for 10 minutes longer, until golden and crisp on top. —*Kay Chun*

CURRIED SQUASH GALETTE

(v)

MAKES	**6 to 8 servings**
TIME	**Active 40 min;**
	Total 2 hr 25 min

DOUGH

- **1¼ cups all-purpose flour**
- **Kosher salt**
- **Freshly ground pepper**
- **1 stick unsalted butter, frozen**
- **Ice water**

FILLING

- **1 lb. butternut squash—peeled, seeded and cut into ¼-inch-thick slices**
- **1 lb. kabocha squash—peeled, seeded and cut into ¼-inch-thick slices**
- **1 red onion, cut through the core into ½-inch wedges**
- **¼ cup extra-virgin olive oil**
- **2 tsp. Madras curry powder**
- **½ cup sour cream**
- **½ cup shredded Manchego cheese, plus more for serving**

1 MAKE THE DOUGH In a large bowl, whisk the flour with ¾ teaspoon each of salt and pepper. Working over the bowl, grate the frozen butter on the large holes of a box grater. Gently toss the grated butter in the flour. Stir in ⅓ cup of ice water until the dough is evenly moistened. Scrape out onto a work surface, gather up any crumbs and knead gently just until the dough comes together. Pat into a disk, wrap in plastic and refrigerate until chilled, about 1 hour.

2 MEANWHILE, MAKE THE FILLING Preheat oven to 425°. On a large rimmed baking sheet, toss butternut and kabocha squash and onion with olive oil and curry powder. Season generously with salt and pepper. Roast for 15 to 20 minutes, until squash is tender but not falling apart. Let cool.

3 Increase the oven temperature to 450°. On a lightly floured work surface, roll out the dough to a 14-inch round. Carefully transfer to a parchment paper-lined baking sheet. Spread the sour cream over the dough, leaving a 1½-inch border. Sprinkle ¼ cup of the cheese on top. Arrange the squash and onion over the sour cream and sprinkle the remaining ¼ cup of cheese on top. Fold the pastry edge up and over the vegetables to create a 1½-inch border.

4 Bake the squash galette for 30 to 35 minutes, until the crust is browned; let cool slightly. Sprinkle with shredded cheese, cut into wedges and serve warm. —*Justin Chapple*

MAKE AHEAD

If you are taking this galette to a potluck dinner, bake and let cool. Reheat and sprinkle with shredded cheese just before serving.

BUTTERNUT SQUASH AND KALE STRATA
WITH MULTIGRAIN BREAD

MAKES 8 to 10 servings

TIME Active 1 hr; Total 3 hr

2½ Tbsp. unsalted butter plus more for greasing

2 lbs. butternut squash—peeled, seeded and cut into ½-inch dice

¼ cup plus 1 Tbsp. extra-virgin olive oil

Kosher salt

Freshly ground black pepper

2 medium onions, thinly sliced plus ½ small onion, finely chopped

¾ lb. kale, ribs discarded and leaves chopped

2 garlic cloves, minced

Pinch of crushed red pepper

2 tsp. finely chopped thyme

¼ cup all-purpose flour

2½ cups milk

1 cup heavy cream

½ cup crème fraîche

1 tsp. sugar

8 large eggs

One ¾-lb. multigrain baguette, cut into 1-inch pieces

⅓ cup freshly grated Parmigiano-Reggiano cheese

1 Preheat the oven to 425° and butter a 9-by-13-inch baking dish. On a rimmed baking sheet, toss the squash with 2 tablespoons of the olive oil and season with salt and black pepper. Bake for about 25 minutes, tossing once, until the squash is just tender.

2 Meanwhile, in a large skillet, heat 2 tablespoons of the oil. Add the sliced onions, season with salt and cook over moderately low heat, stirring occasionally, until golden, about 25 minutes. Scrape the onions into a bowl.

3 In the same skillet, heat the remaining 1 tablespoon of olive oil until shimmering. Add the kale, garlic, crushed red pepper and 1 teaspoon of the thyme and season with salt. Cook over moderately high heat, tossing, until the kale is wilted and just tender, about 5 minutes. Scrape the kale into the bowl with the cooked onions.

4 In a medium saucepan, melt 2½ tablespoons of butter. Add chopped onion and remaining 1 teaspoon of thyme and cook over moderately low heat, stirring, until softened, 5 minutes. Add flour and cook over moderate heat, whisking constantly, until a light golden paste forms, 3 minutes. Whisk in 1 cup of the milk and cook, whisking, until very thick and no floury taste remains, 8 to 10 minutes. Remove from the heat and whisk in the cream, crème fraîche, sugar, 2 teaspoons of salt, ½ teaspoon of pepper and the remaining 1½ cups of milk. Let the béchamel cool.

5 Beat the eggs into the cooled béchamel in the saucepan. Pour into a bowl, add the bread and the vegetables and mix well. Pour the strata mixture into the prepared baking dish and let stand for 30 minutes, pressing down the bread occasionally.

6 Preheat oven to 325°. Bake the strata for 55 minutes to 1 hour, until almost set. Increase the oven temperature to 475°. Sprinkle Parmigiano on strata and bake for about 10 minutes more, until top is lightly browned. Let strata stand for 15 minutes before serving. —*Zoe Nathan*

MAKE AHEAD

The recipe can be prepared through Step 5 and refrigerated overnight.

OMBRÉ POTATO AND ROOT VEGETABLE GRATIN

GF

MAKES **12 servings**

TIME **Active 45 min; Total 3 hr**

Unsalted butter, for greasing

2 **cups heavy cream**

3 **garlic cloves, minced**

1 **small shallot, minced**

½ **tsp. freshly grated nutmeg**

1½ **tsp. kosher salt**

½ **tsp. freshly ground pepper**

1¾ **cups freshly grated Parmigiano-Reggiano cheese (5 oz.)**

1 **lb. red beets, peeled and sliced on a mandoline 1/16 inch thick**

1 **lb. sweet potatoes or garnet yams, peeled and sliced on a mandoline 1/16 inch thick**

1 **lb. Yukon Gold potatoes, peeled and sliced on a mandoline 1/16 inch thick**

1 **lb. turnips, peeled and sliced on a mandoline 1/16 inch thick**

 Preheat the oven to 375°. Lightly butter a 9-by-13-inch baking dish. In a medium bowl, whisk the cream with the garlic, shallot, nutmeg, salt and pepper. Stir in 1 cup of the grated cheese.

 In a large bowl, gently toss the beets with one-fourth of the cream mixture. Arrange the beets in the baking dish in an even layer, overlapping them slightly. Scrape any remaining cream from the bowl over the beets. Repeat this process with the sweet potatoes, Yukon Golds and turnips, using one-fourth of the cream mixture for each vegetable. Press a sheet of parchment paper on top of the turnips, then cover the dish tightly with foil.

3 Bake the gratin for about 1 hour and 30 minutes, until the vegetables are tender. Uncover and top with the remaining ¾ cup of cheese. Bake for about 15 minutes longer, until golden on top. Transfer the gratin to a rack and let cool for at least 15 minutes before serving. —*Carla Hall*

MAKE AHEAD

The gratin can be refrigerated overnight. Reheat gently before serving.

"Layer thin slices of beets, sweet potatoes, turnips and Yukon Golds for a hearty gratin that will be appreciated by the folks at your Thanksgiving table who don't eat meat." —KAREN SHIMIZU, EXECUTIVE EDITOR

> "When you take this savory tomato tart to a potluck dinner, leave it whole until it's time to serve. Transport and serve the tart on a large wooden cutting board."
>
> —KELSEY YOUNGMAN, TEST KITCHEN MANAGER

GIANT SUMMER TOMATO TART ⓥ

MAKES **8 to 10 servings**

TIME **Active 15 min;
Total 1 hr 10 min**

- 6 **Tbsp. extra-virgin olive oil,
  plus more for drizzling**
- 8 **sheets of phyllo dough, thawed**
- ½ **cup fine dry breadcrumbs**
- 8 **oz. cream cheese**
- ¼ **cup mayonnaise**
- 1½ **lbs. mixed heirloom tomatoes,
  thinly sliced**
-    **Flaky sea salt**
-    **Freshly ground pepper**
-    **Basil leaves, for garnish**

1 Preheat the oven to 375°. Brush a large rimmed baking sheet with 2 teaspoons of the olive oil. Lay 1 sheet of the phyllo dough on the baking sheet; keep the rest covered with damp paper towels. Brush the phyllo with 2 teaspoons of olive oil and sprinkle all over with 1 tablespoon of the breadcrumbs. Repeat the layering with the remaining phyllo, olive oil and breadcrumbs.

2 Bake the crust for about 25 minutes, until golden and crisp; rotate the baking sheet halfway through cooking. Let cool completely.

3 In a food processor, pulse the cream cheese with the mayonnaise until smooth. Spread the cream cheese mixture in the center of the tart, leaving a ½-inch border all around. Arrange the tomato slices on top and sprinkle with flaky sea salt and pepper. Drizzle lightly with olive oil and garnish with basil leaves. Cut into squares and serve. —*Laura Rege*

MAKE AHEAD

This tart can be assembled 1 to 2 hours ahead and stored at room temperature until serving time.

SEARED FENNEL AND TOMATOES
WITH MUSTARD VINAIGRETTE

(GF) (V)

MAKES 8 servings

TIME 30 min

- 2 Tbsp. Dijon mustard
- 2 Tbsp. red wine vinegar
- ½ cup plus 6 Tbsp. extra-virgin olive oil
- Kosher salt
- Freshly ground pepper
- 4 large plum tomatoes (1 lb.), halved lengthwise
- 3 fennel bulbs (1 lb.)—trimmed and sliced ½ inch thick lengthwise through the core, small fronds reserved for garnish
- Tarragon leaves, for garnish

1 In a small bowl, whisk the mustard with the vinegar. While whisking constantly, drizzle in ½ cup of the olive oil until emulsified. Season with salt and pepper.

2 Heat a griddle or large cast-iron skillet. Brush the tomatoes and fennel all over with the remaining 6 tablespoons of olive oil and season with salt and pepper. Working in batches, cook the tomatoes cut side down until lightly charred, about 3 minutes. Transfer to a platter charred side up. Working in batches, cook the fennel, turning once, until just tender and lightly charred, about 6 minutes. Transfer to the platter with the tomatoes. Drizzle the vegetables with the vinaigrette and garnish with the reserved fennel fronds and tarragon. Serve warm or at room temperature. —*José Catrimán*

HERB-SCENTED MASHED POTATOES

MAKES   **10 servings**

TIME   **Active 30 min; Total 1 hr**

📷 PAGE 51

1¼ **cups heavy cream**

1¼ **cups whole milk**

  2 **sticks unsalted butter plus melted butter for brushing**

    Two 4-inch rosemary sprigs

  2 **sage sprigs**

  2 **garlic cloves, crushed**

  5 **lbs. baking potatoes, peeled and cut into 2-inch pieces**

    Kosher salt

    Freshly ground pepper

1 In a medium saucepan, combine cream, milk and 2 sticks of butter with rosemary, sage and garlic and bring just to a simmer. Remove from heat and let steep for 15 minutes, then discard rosemary, sage and garlic.

2 Meanwhile, in a large pot, cover potatoes with water and bring to a boil. Add a generous pinch of salt and simmer over moderate heat until tender, about 20 minutes. Drain well, then pass potatoes through a ricer into the pot. Fold in cream mixture and season generously with salt and pepper.

3 Light broiler and position the rack 8 inches from the heat. Scrape potatoes into a 12-inch round ovenproof pan or baking dish (2 inches deep) and, using a spoon, decoratively swirl the top. Gently brush with melted butter. Broil for about 8 minutes, until the top is browned in spots. Serve hot. —*Justin Chapple*

MAKE AHEAD

The mashed potatoes can be prepared through Step 2 and refrigerated overnight. Reheat gently before scraping into the baking dish and broiling.

> "It's easy to make plain mashed potatoes more luxurious when you add Fontina cheese, Parmigiano-Reggiano, butter and crème fraîche! This recipe is great for potlucks because you can assemble the night before and bake just before serving."
>
> —ANNE CAIN, BOOKS EDITOR

MASHED POTATO CASSEROLE
WITH SAGE AND FONTINA

MAKES   **8 to 10 servings**

TIME   **Active 20 min; Total 1 hr**

  6 **Tbsp. unsalted butter, at room temperature, plus more for greasing**

  3 **lbs. baking potatoes, peeled and cut into 2-inch pieces**

  ½ **cup crème fraîche (4 oz.)**

  2 **Tbsp. chopped parsley**

  1 **Tbsp. chopped sage plus 12 sage leaves**

  8 **oz. imported Fontina cheese, shredded**

  Kosher salt

  Freshly ground pepper

  ⅓ **cup plain dry breadcrumbs**

  ⅓ **cup freshly grated Parmigiano-Reggiano cheese**

  Olive oil, for frying

1 Preheat the oven to 400°. Lightly grease a 2-quart shallow baking dish. In a large saucepan, combine the potatoes with enough water to cover by 2 inches. Bring to a boil and cook until fork-tender, 15 to 20 minutes. Drain well and transfer to a large bowl. Mash the potatoes with 4 tablespoons of the butter, the crème fraîche, parsley and chopped sage. Fold in the Fontina and season with salt and pepper. Spread the potato mixture in the prepared dish in an even layer.

2 In a small bowl, using your fingers, blend the remaining 2 tablespoons of butter with the breadcrumbs and Parmigiano until coarse crumbs form. Top the potatoes with the breadcrumb mixture. Bake for about 30 minutes, until golden and crisp on top.

3 Meanwhile, in a small skillet, heat ¼ inch of olive oil over low heat. Add the sage leaves and cook, stirring occasionally, until crisp, about 3 minutes. Transfer the sage to paper towels to drain. Scatter the fried sage over the casserole and serve. —*Melissa Clark*

MAKE AHEAD

The assembled unbaked casserole can be refrigerated overnight, then baked just before serving.

BUTTERY PUMPKIN MASHED POTATOES (GF) (V)

MAKES **10 to 12 servings**

TIME **Active 25 min; Total 50 min**

4 lbs. Yukon Gold potatoes, peeled and cut into 1-inch cubes

1½ sticks butter

2 cups milk

1½ cups pumpkin puree

Kosher salt

Freshly ground pepper

1 In a large saucepan, boil the potatoes in salted water until tender, 20 minutes. Drain well and set aside.

2 In a medium saucepan, combine butter and milk and cook over medium heat until butter melts. Add pumpkin puree and stir well. Remove from heat.

3 Press the potatoes through a ricer into a bowl and mix in the pumpkin mixture. Season with salt and pepper. —*Justin Chapple*

AUNT ELSIE'S TEXAS POTATOES

MAKES **10 to 12 servings**

TIME **Active 30 min; Total 1 hr 30 min**

2½ sticks unsalted butter— 1½ sticks cubed, 1 stick melted

1 large onion, finely chopped

Kosher salt

¼ cup plus 2 Tbsp. all-purpose flour

2½ cups chicken stock or low-sodium broth

2½ cups cornflakes

1 cup plain dry breadcrumbs

Freshly ground pepper

4 lbs. baking potatoes—peeled, shredded and squeezed dry

16 oz. sour cream

1 Preheat the oven to 350°. In a large skillet, melt the 1½ sticks of cubed butter. Add the onion and a generous pinch of salt and cook over moderate heat, stirring occasionally, until softened, about 7 minutes. Whisk in the flour and cook, whisking constantly, until bubbling, about 2 minutes. Gradually whisk in the stock and bring to a boil over moderately high heat, then simmer over moderately low heat until the sauce is thickened and no floury taste remains, 8 to 10 minutes.

2 In a medium bowl, toss the cornflakes with the breadcrumbs and the 1 stick of melted butter. Season with salt and pepper.

3 In a large bowl, combine the sauce with the potatoes, sour cream, 2 teaspoons of salt and 1 teaspoon of pepper and mix well. Scrape into a 9-by-13-inch baking dish and bake for about 20 minutes, until bubbling. Sprinkle the cornflake mixture evenly over the potatoes and bake for 20 to 25 minutes longer, until the topping is browned and crisp. Let stand for 10 minutes before serving. —*Eric Stonestreet; Elsie Ball*

MAKE AHEAD

The casserole can be baked earlier in the day and kept at room temperature. Reheat to serve.

> "Luscious, creamy potatoes are a worthy side dish to bring to a holiday meal that features beef tenderloin or prime rib roast and, of course, bottles of Cabernet Sauvignon." —KAREN SHIMIZU, EXECUTIVE EDITOR

POTATO GRATIN   (GF) (V)

MAKES **8 servings**

TIME **Active 20 min; Total 2 hr 15 min**

Butter, for greasing

3 **lbs. russet potatoes, peeled and sliced crosswise ¼ inch thick**

5 **cups heavy cream**

Kosher salt

Freshly ground white pepper

1 Preheat the oven to 250° and butter a 9-by-13-inch baking dish. In a large pot, combine the potatoes and cream and season with salt and pepper. Bring to a boil, then press a round of parchment or wax paper on the potatoes. Simmer over moderately low heat until the potatoes are tender, 15 to 20 minutes.

2 Using a slotted spoon, transfer the potatoes to the baking dish in layers. Season the potatoes with salt and pepper as you go. Return the pot with the cream to high heat and boil, stirring constantly, until the cream is reduced to 2½ cups, 6 to 7 minutes. Pour the cream over the potatoes while shaking the baking dish.

3 Bake the gratin for 1½ hours, or until golden on top. Blot any excess fat and let stand 15 minutes before cutting. —*Tom Colicchio*

MAKE AHEAD

The gratin can be prepared through Step 2 and refrigerated overnight.

PARSNIP MASH WITH FRIED BRUSSELS SPROUT LEAVES

MAKES 6 to 8 servings

TIME Active 30 min; Total 40 min

- 2 lbs. parsnips, peeled and cut into ½-inch pieces
- 4 cups whole milk
- 1 stick unsalted butter
- 1 cup heavy cream
  - Kosher salt
  - Freshly ground black pepper
- 1 lb. brussels sprouts, leaves removed, cores reserved for another use
- 1 Tbsp. extra-virgin olive oil
  - Flaky sea salt and crushed red pepper, for serving

1 In a medium saucepan, combine the parsnips and milk. Bring to a boil over moderately high heat, then simmer over moderately low heat until the parsnips are tender, about 30 minutes. Drain the parsnips.

2 Set a food mill over the saucepan and pass the parsnips through it. Alternatively, mash the parsnips with a masher. Add the butter and cream and cook over low heat, stirring, until the butter is melted and fully combined. Season the mash with salt and black pepper.

3 Meanwhile, preheat the oven to 375°. On a rimmed baking sheet, toss the brussels sprout leaves with the olive oil. Roast for about 15 minutes, stirring a few times, until golden and crisp.

4 Spoon the parsnip puree into a serving bowl and top with the brussels sprout leaves. Sprinkle with flaky sea salt and crushed red pepper and serve.
—*Jocelyn Guest*

MAKE AHEAD

The parsnip puree can be refrigerated overnight. Reheat over low heat and add additional heavy cream to thin out if necessary.

WINTER GALETTE

MAKES   6 to 8 servings

TIME   Active 1 hr;
        Total 2 hr 30 min
        plus cooling

DOUGH

- ¾ cup all-purpose flour plus more for dusting
- ¾ cup whole-wheat flour
- ½ tsp. kosher salt
- 1 stick unsalted butter, cubed and chilled
- ¼ cup sour cream
- 2 Tbsp. ice water
- 1 Tbsp. fresh lemon juice

FILLING

- 2 Tbsp. extra-virgin olive oil
- 1 large shallot, thinly sliced
  Kosher salt
- 1 cup whole-milk ricotta
- 1½ tsp. finely grated lemon zest plus 1 tsp. fresh lemon juice
- 1 large garlic clove, finely grated
- 1 tsp. thyme leaves plus more for sprinkling
- 1 tsp. minced oregano plus leaves for sprinkling
- ½ tsp. minced rosemary plus leaves for sprinkling
  Freshly ground pepper
- ½ lb. acorn squash—peeled, seeded and shaved into ribbons
- ½ lb. celery root, peeled and shaved into ribbons
- 1 small baking potato, peeled and shaved into ribbons
- 1 large egg beaten with 1 Tbsp. water
- ¼ cup freshly grated Parmigiano-Reggiano cheese
- 2 tsp. honey, warmed

1 MAKE THE DOUGH In a food processor, combine both flours with the salt and pulse to mix. Add the butter and pulse until pea-size pieces form. Add the sour cream, ice water and lemon juice and pulse until the dough starts to come together. Transfer to a lightly floured work surface and pat into a disk. Wrap in plastic and refrigerate until chilled, about 1 hour.

2 MAKE THE FILLING Preheat the oven to 400°. Line a baking sheet with parchment paper. In a small skillet, heat 1 tablespoon of the olive oil. Add the shallot, season with salt and cook over moderately low heat, stirring, until softened, about 5 minutes. Let cool.

3 In a small bowl, mix the ricotta with the lemon zest, garlic, 1 teaspoon of thyme and the minced oregano and rosemary. Season with salt and pepper. In a large bowl, toss the squash with the celery root, potato and remaining 1 tablespoon of olive oil. Season with salt and pepper.

4 On a lightly floured work surface, roll out the dough to a 13-inch round. Transfer to the prepared baking sheet. Spread the ricotta on the dough, leaving a 1-inch border. Pile the squash mixture on the ricotta and fold 1½ inches of the dough edge over the vegetables. Sprinkle with thyme, oregano and rosemary leaves. Brush the dough edge with the beaten egg.

5 Bake the galette for 15 minutes, until starting to brown. Sprinkle the Parmigiano over the filling and bake for 15 to 20 minutes, until the vegetables are tender and the crust is golden.

6 In a small bowl, mix the honey with the lemon juice. Drizzle the lemon honey over the galette. Serve warm or at room temperature. —*Gail Simmons*

MAKE AHEAD

The galette can be baked up to 3 hours ahead and rewarmed before serving.

ROOT VEGETABLE HOT DISH
WITH PARSNIP PUREE

(V)

MAKES   8 to 10 servings

TIME   Active 1 hr 45 min;
       Total 3 hr

SORGHUM

- 2 Tbsp. grapeseed or canola oil
- 1 small onion, finely chopped
- 2 garlic cloves, minced
  Kosher salt
- 2 cups pearled sorghum (13 oz.), rinsed
- 4 cups chicken stock or low-sodium chicken or vegetable broth
  Freshly ground pepper

ROOT VEGETABLES

- ¾ lb. rutabaga, peeled and cut into ½-inch dice
- ¾ lb. carrots, peeled and cut into ½-inch dice
- ¾ lb. celery root, peeled and cut into ½-inch dice
- ¾ lb. turnips, peeled and cut into ½-inch dice
- ¼ cup extra-virgin olive oil
  Kosher salt
  Freshly ground pepper

PARSNIP PUREE

- 2 Tbsp. unsalted butter
- 1 small onion, finely chopped
- 1 lb. parsnips, peeled and cut into 1-inch pieces
- 3 cups chicken stock or low-sodium chicken or vegetable broth
  Kosher salt

CRISPY SHALLOTS

- Grapeseed or canola oil, for frying
- 3 large shallots, thinly sliced into rings
- 1 Tbsp. all-purpose flour
  Kosher salt
  Snipped chives, for serving

1 COOK THE SORGHUM Preheat the oven to 400°. In a large saucepan, heat the oil. Add the onion, garlic and a generous pinch of salt and cook over moderate heat, stirring occasionally, until the onion begins to soften, 3 to 5 minutes. Add the sorghum and stock and bring to a boil over high heat. Reduce the heat to low, cover and simmer, stirring occasionally, until the sorghum is tender and the stock is absorbed, about 1 hour. Season the sorghum with salt and pepper.

2 MEANWHILE, COOK THE ROOT VEGETABLES In a very large bowl, toss rutabaga, carrots, celery root and turnips with the olive oil and season generously with salt and pepper. Spread the vegetables in an even layer on 2 large rimmed baking sheets. Roast until tender and lightly browned, 30 to 35 minutes; stir the vegetables halfway through roasting.

3 MAKE THE PARSNIP PUREE In a medium saucepan, melt the butter. Add the onion and cook over moderate heat, stirring occasionally, until just softened, about 5 minutes. Add the parsnips, stock and a generous pinch of salt and bring to a boil. Simmer over moderately high heat until the parsnips are tender and the stock is slightly reduced, about 20 minutes. Let cool slightly, then transfer the parsnips and their cooking liquid to a food processor and puree until smooth. Season with salt.

4 Fold the cooked sorghum into the parsnip puree and spread evenly in a 9-by-13-inch or 4-quart baking dish that's at least 2 inches deep. Scatter the roasted vegetables evenly over the puree. Cover with foil and bake for about 25 minutes, until bubbling.

5 MEANWHILE, MAKE THE CRISPY SHALLOTS In a large saucepan, heat ½ inch of oil until shimmering. In a bowl, toss the sliced shallots with the flour. Working in batches, fry the shallots over moderately high heat, stirring, until lightly browned and crisp. Using a slotted spoon, transfer the fried shallots to a paper towel-lined plate to drain; season with salt. Garnish the casserole with the crispy shallots and chives and serve. —*Gavin Kaysen*

MAKE AHEAD

The casserole can be prepared through Step 4 and refrigerated overnight. Bring to room temperature and reheat gently before topping with the shallots and chives.

ROASTED KABOCHA WITH MAPLE SYRUP AND GINGER

MAKES   **8 to 10 servings**

TIME   **45 min**

- **3 lbs. kabocha squash—peeled, seeded and cut into 1-inch-thick wedges**
- **3 Tbsp. pure maple syrup**
- **3 Tbsp. extra-virgin olive oil**
- **1 Tbsp. finely grated peeled fresh ginger**
- **6 thyme sprigs plus thyme leaves for garnish**
- **Kosher salt**

1 Preheat the oven to 450°. On a rimmed baking sheet, toss the squash wedges with the maple syrup, olive oil, ginger, thyme sprigs and salt. Arrange the squash in a single layer and roast for 15 minutes. Flip and roast for 15 minutes longer, until golden and tender. Transfer the squash to a serving platter and garnish with thyme leaves. —*Melissa Clark*

MAKE AHEAD

The squash can be made up to 6 hours ahead. Reheat gently before serving

RICE AND PEAS

MAKES   **8 servings**

TIME   **Active 25 min; Total 2 hr plus overnight soaking**

BEANS

- **2 cups dried kidney beans, soaked overnight and drained**
- **⅓ cup unsweetened coconut milk**
- **¼ cup unsweetened coconut cream**
- **14 thyme sprigs**
- **½ medium onion, finely chopped**
- **6 scallions, thinly sliced**
- **1½ tsp. kosher salt**
- **¼ tsp. ground allspice**

RICE

- **2 cups parboiled white rice**
- **1 cup unsweetened coconut milk**
- **½ cup finely chopped onion**
- **3 scallions, thinly sliced**
- **2 garlic cloves, minced**
- **2¼ tsp. kosher salt**
- **3¾ cups water**

1 PREPARE THE BEANS In a large enameled cast-iron casserole, combine the soaked and drained beans with the coconut milk, coconut cream, thyme sprigs, onion, scallions, salt and allspice. Add enough water to cover the beans by 2 inches and bring to a boil. Cover, reduce the heat to low and simmer the beans until tender, about 1 hour. Drain the beans; discard the thyme sprigs.

2 PREPARE THE RICE In a medium pot, combine the parboiled rice with the coconut milk, onion, scallions, garlic, salt and 3¾ cups of water. Bring to a boil. Reduce the heat to moderately low, cover and simmer for 10 minutes.

3 Stir 4 cups of the drained beans into the rice. (Save the remaining 2 cups for another use.) Cover and cook for 10 minutes, then uncover and cook for 5 minutes longer. Fluff the rice and peas with a fork and serve. —*Adam Schop*

NOTE

The name for this typical Jamaican side dish is a bit of a misnomer, as the peas in the title are, in fact, kidney beans.

MAKE AHEAD

The rice and peas can be refrigerated for up to 3 days. Reheat before serving.

TURKISH TABBOULEH

MAKES 8 servings

TIME Active 30 min;
Total 4 hr 30 min

2 cups (12 oz.) medium grade
  bulgur

¼ cup extra-virgin olive oil

3 Tbsp. tomato paste

2 Tbsp. fresh lemon juice

1 Tbsp. harissa

  Kosher salt

2 cups boiling water

2 tomatoes, cut into ¼-inch dice

⅓ cup finely chopped red onion

½ hothouse cucumber, cut into
  ¼-inch dice

1 yellow bell pepper, seeded
  and cut into ¼-inch dice

1 cup chopped parsley

½ cup thinly sliced scallions

½ cup chopped mint

1 In a large bowl, combine the bulgur, olive oil, tomato paste, lemon juice and harissa and season with salt. Mix well, then stir in the boiling water. Add the tomatoes, onion, cucumber, bell pepper, parsley and scallions and mix well. Cover and refrigerate until the bulgur is tender, about 4 hours.

2 Season the tabbouleh with salt and stir in the mint. Transfer to a platter or spoon into bowls and serve. —*Sasha Martin*

MAKE AHEAD

The tabbouleh can be prepared ahead and refrigerated overnight.

"When you want to bring something healthy but exciting to a potluck, this grain salad, which gets a hit of heat from the harissa, is an excellent choice. Better yet, you can make it the night before."

—ALISON SPIEGEL, DEPUTY DIGITAL DIRECTOR

QUINOA WITH SPINACH AND ROASTED ALMONDS

MAKES	**6 servings**
TIME	**Active 15 min; Total 40 min**

1⅓ cups quinoa, rinsed and drained

8 oz. curly spinach (8 packed cups), stemmed and finely chopped (4 cups)

3 radishes, thinly sliced

6 Tbsp. extra-virgin olive oil

2 Tbsp. fresh lemon juice

Salt

Freshly ground pepper

½ cup chopped roasted almonds

1 In a medium saucepan of boiling water, cook the quinoa until tender, about 10 minutes. Drain and return the quinoa to the pan. Cover and let stand for 10 minutes; fluff with a fork.

2 In a large bowl, toss the quinoa with the spinach, radishes, olive oil and lemon juice. Season with salt and pepper and toss again. Garnish with the almonds and serve. —*Kay Chun*

MAKE AHEAD

This dish can be kept at room temperature for up to 3 hours.

RED QUINOA TABBOULEH

MAKES	**8 servings**
TIME	**Active 30 min; Total 1 hr 45 min**

2 cups red quinoa, rinsed and drained

One ½-inch piece of ginger

1 tsp. ras el hanout (see Note)

Kosher salt

3 cups water

½ cup extra-virgin olive oil

1 tsp. honey

½ tsp. finely grated lemon zest plus 3 Tbsp. fresh lemon juice

Freshly ground pepper

1 red apple, such as Fuji, cored and finely chopped

1 English cucumber, peeled and finely chopped

1 red bell pepper—stemmed, seeded and finely chopped

1 cup grape or cherry tomatoes, halved plus more for garnish

½ cup chopped mint leaves

Lemon wedges, for serving

1 In a medium saucepan, combine the quinoa with the ginger, ras el hanout, ½ teaspoon of salt and 3 cups of water and bring to a boil. Cover and simmer over low heat until the water is absorbed and the quinoa is tender, about 15 minutes. Fluff with a fork and let cool slightly; discard the ginger. Cover and refrigerate for 1 hour.

2 In a large bowl, whisk the olive oil with the honey and the lemon zest and juice. Season with salt and pepper. Add the quinoa, apple, cucumber, bell pepper, 1 cup of tomatoes and the mint leaves. Season with salt and pepper. Garnish with more halved tomatoes and serve with lemon wedges. —*José Catrimán*

NOTE

Ras el hanout, a North African spice mix, is available at specialty food stores and from kalustyans.com.

Quinoa with Spinach and
Roasted Almonds

FARRO WITH VINEGAR-GLAZED SWEET POTATO AND APPLES

MAKES **6 servings**

TIME **1 hr**

- ¼ cup plus 3 Tbsp. extra-virgin olive oil
- 1 small fennel bulb, finely chopped
- 1 small onion, finely chopped
- 5 garlic cloves, minced
- Kosher salt
- 4 cups chicken stock or low-sodium broth
- 2 cups farro
- ¾ lb. sweet potato (1 large), scrubbed and cut into 1½-inch pieces
- Freshly ground pepper
- ¼ cup sherry vinegar
- 2 Granny Smith apples—peeled, cored and cut into 1½-inch pieces
- ¾ cup dried cherries, soaked in warm water for 10 minutes and drained
- 1 cup roasted cashews, coarsely chopped
- ¾ cup coarsely chopped parsley
- Shaved pecorino cheese, for serving

 1 Heat ¼ cup of the olive oil in a large saucepan. Add the fennel, onion, garlic and a generous pinch of salt. Cook over moderate heat, stirring occasionally, until the fennel is softened, about 8 minutes. Add the stock and farro and bring to a boil over high heat. Reduce the heat to moderate and simmer, stirring occasionally, until the farro is tender and the stock is absorbed, 25 to 30 minutes.

 2 Meanwhile, preheat the oven to 425°. On a large rimmed baking sheet, toss sweet potato with remaining 3 tablespoons of olive oil and season with salt and pepper. Drizzle with sherry vinegar and roast for about 15 minutes, until just starting to soften. Add the apples and toss to coat. Roast for about 20 minutes longer, until the sweet potato and apples are tender but not falling apart. Let cool slightly.

3 In a large bowl, toss the farro mixture with the dried cherries, cashews, parsley and the roasted sweet potato and apples. Season with salt and pepper. Transfer to plates, top with shaved pecorino cheese and serve.
—*Michael Scelfo*

MAKE AHEAD

The farro salad can be refrigerated overnight. Stir in the cashews and parsley just before serving at room temperature.

CACIO E PEPE PASTA PIE

MAKES **8 servings**

TIME **Active 30 min;**
Total 1 hr 30 min

- 1 **lb. spaghetti**
- 1½ **cups milk**
- ¾ **cup grated Parmigiano-Reggiano**
  cheese
- 3 **large eggs, lightly beaten**
- 2½ **tsp. freshly ground pepper**
- 2 **tsp. kosher salt**
- 6 **oz. Fontina cheese, shredded**
  (2 cups)
- 6 **oz. sharp white cheddar cheese,**
  shredded (2 cups)
  Butter, for greasing

1 Preheat the oven to 425°. In a pot of salted boiling water, cook the spaghetti until al dente. Drain well.

2 In a bowl, mix the pasta, milk, Parmigiano, eggs, pepper, salt and 1½ cups each of the Fontina and cheddar. Scrape into a buttered 9-inch springform pan, then sprinkle the remaining ½ cup each of Fontina and cheddar on top. Bake for 35 to 40 minutes, until the cheese is melted and bubbling.

3 Turn on the broiler. Broil the pie 8 inches from the heat for 2 to 3 minutes, until browned on top. Transfer to a rack and let cool for 15 minutes. Remove the ring, cut the pie into wedges and serve. —*Justin Chapple*

"If I'm taking this pasta pie to a dinner, I take it in the springform pan, then remove it when I arrive and cut it into wedges. It's a sturdy pie and travels well."

—JUSTIN CHAPPLE, CULINARY DIRECTOR

PIZZOCCHERI GRATIN

MAKES **8 servings**

TIME **Active 45 min;**
Total 1 hr 20 min

- 1 stick unsalted butter
- 2 Tbsp. chopped sage
- 1 tsp. poppy seeds
- ½ tsp. caraway seeds
- One ½-lb. baking potato, peeled and cut into ½-inch pieces
- 1 lb. fresh lasagna sheets, cut into 6-by-1½-inch strips, or fresh pappardelle
- 1 small head of Napa cabbage, thinly sliced (6 packed cups)
- Kosher salt
- Freshly ground pepper
- 5 oz. Fontina cheese, shredded (1⅔ cups)
- ½ cup freshly grated Parmigiano-Reggiano cheese
- ½ cup dry breadcrumbs
- 2 Tbsp. chopped flat-leaf parsley

1 Preheat the oven to 350°. In a small skillet, melt 6 tablespoons of the butter with the sage, poppy seeds and caraway seeds and cook over moderate heat, stirring, until nutty and fragrant, about 5 minutes. Transfer to a bowl.

2 Meanwhile, bring a large pot of salted water to a boil. Add the potato and cook until tender, about 5 minutes. Using a slotted spoon, transfer the potato to a bowl. Add the pasta to the pot and cook, stirring, until al dente, about 2 minutes. Using a slotted spoon, transfer pasta to a colander. Add cabbage to pot and cook until just wilted, about 3 minutes. Drain cabbage and shake out the excess water. Pour off the water and return cabbage to the pot, along with the pasta and potato. Add the browned butter, season with salt and pepper and toss well. Stir in 1 cup of the Fontina and half of the Parmigiano and transfer the mixture to a 9-by-13-inch baking dish.

3 In the small skillet, melt the remaining 2 tablespoons of butter. Add the breadcrumbs and parsley and cook over moderate heat, stirring, until golden and toasted, 3 minutes. Stir in the remaining Fontina and Parmigiano and sprinkle over the pasta. Bake for 35 minutes, or until golden brown on top. Serve warm. —*Jonathan Sawyer*

MAKE AHEAD

The unbaked gratin can be refrigerated overnight. Bring to room temperature before baking.

GLUTEN-FREE PENNE WITH CURRY-ROASTED CAULIFLOWER AND RAISINS

(GF) (V)

MAKES 4 to 6 servings

TIME Active 40 min; Total 1 hr

One 2½-lb. head of cauliflower, cored and cut into 1-inch florets

2 Tbsp. Madras curry powder

2 Tbsp. garam masala

¼ cup plus 3 Tbsp. extra-virgin olive oil

Kosher salt

⅓ cup sliced almonds

1 cup golden raisins, ½ cup soaked in hot water for 15 minutes and drained

3 Tbsp. fresh lemon juice

½ lb. gluten-free penne

1 leek, halved lengthwise and thinly sliced crosswise

1 large garlic clove, thinly sliced

½ cup chopped parsley leaves, plus more for garnish

Yogurt, for topping

1 Preheat the oven to 450°. On a large rimmed baking sheet, toss the cauliflower with the curry powder, garam masala and ¼ cup of the olive oil. Season with salt and toss again. Roast the cauliflower for about 12 minutes, until tender.

2 Meanwhile, spread the almonds in a pie plate and toast for about 5 minutes, until they are golden. In a mini food processor, puree the soaked raisins with the lemon juice, 1 tablespoon of the olive oil and a pinch of salt until smooth.

3 In a large saucepan of salted boiling water, cook the pasta until al dente. Drain well, reserving ¾ cup of the cooking water.

4 Wipe out the saucepan and heat the remaining 2 tablespoons of olive oil in it. Add the leek and garlic and cook over moderate heat, stirring occasionally, until softened and lightly browned, 5 to 7 minutes. Stir in the raisin puree, then add the cauliflower, pasta and the reserved cooking water and cook over moderate heat, tossing, until the pasta is coated in the sauce. Remove from the heat and stir in the ½ cup of parsley and the remaining ½ cup of golden raisins. Transfer to a large bowl and serve with the toasted almonds, chopped parsley and yogurt. —*Franklin Becker*

PASTA BUNDT LOAF

MAKES **8 servings**

TIME **Active 25 min;**
Total 1 hr 15 min

Unsalted butter, for greasing

1 lb. spaghetti

6 oz. Fontina cheese, shredded
(2 cups)

6 oz. sharp white cheddar cheese,
shredded (2 cups)

1½ cups whole milk

¾ cup grated Parmigiano-Reggiano
cheese

3 large eggs, lightly beaten

2½ tsp. freshly ground pepper

2 tsp. kosher salt

1 Preheat the oven to 425°. Generously butter a 10-inch Bundt pan. In a pot of salted boiling water, cook the spaghetti until al dente. Drain well.

2 In a large bowl, mix pasta with the cheeses, milk, Parmigiano, eggs, pepper and salt. Scrape into the prepared pan and bake until cheese is melted and bubbling, 35 to 40 minutes.

3 Transfer the pan to a rack and let cool for 15 minutes. Invert the loaf onto a platter, cut into wedges and serve. —*Justin Chapple*

SPICY PEANUT NOODLES

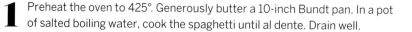

MAKES **6 servings**

TIME **20 min**

1 lb. spaghetti

¾ cup smooth peanut butter

½ cup unseasoned rice vinegar

3 Tbsp. plus 1 tsp. sugar

6 Tbsp. soy sauce

¼ cup water

1 Tbsp. toasted sesame oil

2 tsp. crushed red pepper

One 2-inch piece of fresh ginger,
peeled and coarsely chopped

1 large garlic clove

3 celery ribs, thinly sliced

½ cup coarsely chopped cilantro
leaves and tender stems

Lime wedges, for serving

1 In a pot of salted boiling water, cook spaghetti until tender. Drain and rinse under cold water until cooled. Drain well.

2 In a blender, puree peanut butter with 6 tablespoons vinegar, 3 tablespoons sugar, soy sauce, water, sesame oil, crushed red pepper, ginger and garlic. Transfer ½ cup peanut dressing to a bowl and toss with noodles.

3 In another bowl, toss celery with cilantro and remaining 2 tablespoons vinegar and 1 teaspoon sugar. Transfer noodles to serving bowl and drizzle with remaining peanut dressing. Top with celery and serve with lime wedges.
—*Joanne Chang*

MAKE AHEAD

The peanut dressing can be refrigerated for 2 days. You can make the noodles ahead and serve chilled or at room temperature.

> "The key to the mushroom topping in this recipe is a splash of balsamic vinegar, which adds both tang and subtle sweetness. Serve the pasta with a Sicilian red such as Nero D'Avola." —RAY ISLE, EXECUTIVE WINE EDITOR

SPAGHETTINI WITH WARM BACON-MUSHROOM VINAIGRETTE

MAKES 6 servings

TIME 1 hr

- ¼ cup extra-virgin olive oil
- 1 lb. sliced bacon, cut crosswise into ½-inch strips
- 1 large onion, finely chopped
- 8 oz. mixed mushrooms, such as cremini and stemmed shiitake, thinly sliced
- 2 tsp. finely grated garlic
  Kosher salt
  Freshly ground pepper
- ¼ cup balsamic vinegar
- 1 lb. spaghettini
- ½ cup freshly grated Parmigiano-Reggiano cheese plus more for garnish
- ½ cup thinly sliced basil plus basil leaves for garnish
  White truffle oil, for drizzling (optional)

1 Bring a large pot of water to a boil. In a large nonstick skillet, heat the olive oil. Add the bacon and cook over moderate heat, stirring occasionally, until golden brown and the fat is rendered, about 8 minutes. Add the onion and cook, stirring occasionally, until softened, about 3 minutes. Add the mushrooms and garlic, season with salt and pepper and cook until the vegetables are tender, about 5 minutes. Stir in the balsamic vinegar.

2 Add salt to the boiling water. Add the pasta and cook until al dente. Drain, reserving 1 cup of the pasta water. Return the pasta and water to the pot. Add the bacon-mushroom vinaigrette and the ½ cup each of grated cheese and sliced basil and toss over moderate heat until the pasta is evenly coated. Season with salt and pepper. Transfer to plates and garnish with additional cheese and basil leaves. Drizzle with truffle oil, if desired, and serve.
—Tim Cushman

DAD'S BUCATINI PIE

MAKES **6 servings**

TIME **1 hr**

- 1 lb. bucatini, broken in half
- 4 Tbsp. unsalted butter, melted and cooled, plus more for greasing
- 6 large eggs, beaten
- 1½ cups freshly grated Parmigiano-Reggiano cheese (4 oz.)
- ¾ cup heavy cream
- ⅓ cup chopped parsley
- ¼ cup extra-virgin olive oil
- 1 Tbsp. minced garlic
- 1 Tbsp. freshly ground pepper
- 2 tsp. kosher salt
- Warm marinara sauce, for serving

1 Preheat the oven to 375°. Lightly grease a 10-inch cast-iron skillet. In a large pot of salted boiling water, cook the bucatini until al dente. Drain and run under cold water to stop the cooking. Drain well.

2 In a large bowl, whisk together the butter, eggs, cheese, cream, parsley, olive oil, garlic, pepper and salt. Add the pasta and toss to coat thoroughly. Scrape into the prepared skillet and bake for about 30 minutes, until just set. Remove from the oven.

3 Preheat the broiler. Broil the bucatini pie 6 inches from the heat until golden, about 5 minutes. Transfer to a rack and let cool for 10 minutes before cutting into wedges. Serve with warm marinara sauce. —*Vinny Dotolo*

MAKE AHEAD

The pie can be kept at room temperature for 4 to 6 hours before serving.

"Rather than transferring this cheesy pasta pie to a rack to cool, I like to serve it directly from the cast-iron skillet. You can serve it at room temperature, so it's great for a potluck table." –KAREN SHIMIZU, EXECUTIVE EDITOR

MAC AND CHEESE WITH WHOLE-WHEAT PASTA AND SMOKED CHEDDAR

Ⓥ

MAKES **8 servings**

TIME **Active 25 min;**
Total 1 hr 15 min

1 lb. whole-wheat penne rigate

6½ Tbsp. unsalted butter

¼ cup plus 1½ tsp. all-purpose
flour

4½ cups whole milk

8 oz. smoked cheddar cheese,
coarsely grated (3 cups)

8 oz. sharp cheddar cheese,
coarsely grated (3 cups)

Pinch of cayenne

Kosher salt

Freshly ground pepper

1 cup panko

1 Preheat the oven to 375°. Bring a large pot of salted water to a boil. Add the pasta and cook until al dente. Drain and return the pasta to the pot.

2 Meanwhile, in a large saucepan, melt 4½ tablespoons of the butter. Whisk in the flour and cook over moderate heat, whisking constantly, until smooth, about 1 minute. Add the milk and whisk over high heat until the mixture comes to a boil. Reduce the heat to moderate and simmer, whisking, until thickened, about 2 minutes.

3 Remove saucepan from the heat and stir in the cheeses until smooth. Season the cheese sauce with cayenne, salt and pepper. Fold the pasta into the cheese sauce and scrape the mixture into a large glass or ceramic baking dish.

4 In a medium heatproof bowl, melt the remaining 2 tablespoons of butter in the microwave. Stir in the panko and season with salt and pepper. Sprinkle the panko over pasta. Bake for about 40 minutes, until the top is golden and the sauce is bubbly. —*Melissa Rubel Jacobson*

"Mac and cheese is always popular at potlucks, and you can turn it into a one-dish meal by adding fresh broccoli. It's a good option for the guests who don't eat meat." —CAITLIN MURPHREE MILLER, MANAGING EDITOR

BROCCOLI MAC 'N' CHEESE

(V)

MAKES **6 to 8 servings**

TIME **Active 25 min; Total 50 min**

1 **lb. rigatoni pasta**

1½ **lbs. broccoli, stems peeled and cut into pieces**

Kosher salt

3 **Tbsp. unsalted butter**

2 **Tbsp. all-purpose flour**

3 **cups whole milk**

2½ **cups grated cheddar cheese**

Freshly ground pepper

1 **cup coarse breadcrumbs**

1 Preheat the oven to 475℉. Cook the pasta in a large pot of boiling salted water until al dente. Add the broccoli to the pasta cooking water after the pasta has cooked 6 minutes. When the pasta is al dente and the broccoli is crisp-tender, drain the pasta and broccoli.

2 In a medium saucepan, melt 2 tablespoons butter over medium-high heat until hot. Stir in flour and cook, stirring, 2 minutes. Whisk in milk in a steady stream and bring to a boil, whisking. Boil milk sauce until slightly thickened, about 5 minutes. Stir in cheddar, 1 teaspoon salt and ½ teaspoon pepper. Toss the cooked pasta and broccoli in the cheese sauce and place in a 9-by-13-inch baking dish.

3 In a small, heavy skillet, melt remaining 1 tablespoon butter over low heat, then toss breadcrumbs in butter. Sprinkle breadcrumbs over the gratin.

4 Bake the gratin until the breadcrumbs are golden and the cheese sauce is bubbling around the edges of the dish, about 25 minutes. Let cool slightly, then serve. —*Ian Knauer*

CRUSTY BAKED SHELLS AND CAULIFLOWER

MAKES **6 to 8 servings**

TIME **Active about 1 hr; Total about 1 hr 30 min**

Kosher salt

¾ lb. medium shells, such as Barilla

Good olive oil

2½ lbs. cauliflower, cut into small florets (1 large head)

3 Tbsp. roughly chopped sage leaves

2 Tbsp. capers, drained

1 Tbsp. minced garlic (3 cloves)

½ tsp. grated lemon zest

¼ tsp. crushed red pepper

Freshly ground black pepper

2 cups freshly grated Italian Fontina Val d'Aosta cheese, lightly packed (10 oz. with rind)

1 cup (8 oz.) fresh ricotta

½ cup panko

6 Tbsp. freshly grated Italian pecorino cheese

2 Tbsp. minced parsley leaves

1 Preheat the oven to 400°. Fill a large pot with water, add 2 tablespoons of salt and bring to a boil. Add the pasta and cook until al dente, according to the instructions on the package. (Since it will be baked later, don't overcook.) Drain and pour into a large bowl.

2 Meanwhile, heat 3 tablespoons of olive oil in a large sauté pan over medium-high heat, add half of the cauliflower in one layer and sauté for 5 to 6 minutes, tossing occasionally, until the florets are lightly browned and tender. Pour the cauliflower, including the small bits, into the bowl with the pasta. Add 3 more tablespoons of olive oil to the sauté pan, add the remaining cauliflower, cook until browned and tender and add to the bowl.

3 Add the sage, capers, garlic, lemon zest, crushed red pepper, 2 teaspoons salt and 1 teaspoon black pepper to the bowl and stir carefully. Stir in the Fontina. Transfer half of the mixture to a 9-by-13-inch baking dish. Spoon rounded tablespoons of ricotta on the pasta and spoon the remaining pasta mixture on top. Combine the panko, pecorino, parsley and 1 tablespoon of olive oil in a small bowl and sprinkle it evenly on top. Bake for 25 to 30 minutes, until browned and crusty on top. Serve warm. —Ina Garten

MAKE AHEAD

You can assemble the dish, cover and refrigerate overnight. Bake the casserole before serving.

PROSCIUTTO BREAD STUFFING
WITH SAUSAGE

MAKES   **12 servings**

TIME   **Active 20 min;**
   Total 1 hr 55 min

Butter, for greasing

Two 1-lb. loaves of prosciutto bread, cut into ¾-inch dice

¼ **cup extra-virgin olive oil**

¾ **lb. sweet Italian sausages, casings removed**

4 **oz. sliced lean pancetta, finely chopped**

1 **lb. leeks, white and tender green parts, sliced crosswise ¼ inch thick**

1 **celery rib, finely chopped, plus 1 Tbsp. finely chopped celery leaves**

¼ **cup finely chopped flat-leaf parsley**

½ **cup freshly grated Parmesan cheese**

3 **cups chicken stock or canned low-sodium broth**

Kosher salt

Freshly ground pepper

2 **Tbsp. unsalted butter, melted**

1 Preheat the oven to 325°. Lightly butter a 9-by-13-inch glass baking dish. Spread the bread on 2 large rimmed baking sheets and bake for 30 minutes, stirring twice, until crisp and golden.

2 Meanwhile, in a large, deep skillet, heat 2 tablespoons of the olive oil until shimmering. Add the sausage and cook over moderately high heat, breaking it up as you stir, until cooked through, about 10 minutes. Using a slotted spoon, transfer the sausage to a large bowl and let cool.

3 Add the remaining 2 tablespoons of olive oil to the skillet and heat until shimmering. Add the pancetta and cook over moderately high heat, stirring occasionally, until softened, about 5 minutes. Add the leeks and chopped celery rib and cook, stirring frequently, until the leeks are softened and golden, 8 to 9 minutes. Spoon off as much fat from the pan as possible. Add the leeks to the sausage meat along with the parsley and celery leaves and let cool.

4 Add the toasted prosciutto bread and all but 2 tablespoons of the Parmesan to the bowl and toss very well. Mix in the stock, season with salt and pepper and spoon the stuffing into the baking dish. Brush with the melted butter. Sprinkle the remaining 2 tablespoons of Parmesan cheese over the top and cover with foil.

5 Preheat the oven to 375°. Bake the stuffing for 45 minutes, or until heated through and lightly browned on the bottom. Remove the foil and bake for about 20 minutes longer, until the top is golden and crisp. Serve warm.
—*Grace Parisi*

MAKE AHEAD

The recipe can be prepared through Step 4 and refrigerated for up to 2 days. Bring to room temperature before baking.

SOURDOUGH STUFFING WITH SAUSAGE, RED ONION AND KALE

MAKES 10 servings

TIME Active 1 hr;
Total 2 hr 35 min

 PAGE 50

- ½ stick unsalted butter, cubed, plus more for greasing
- 1 lb. sweet Italian sausage, casings removed and meat crumbled
- 2 medium red onions, cut into 1-inch wedges through the core
- ¼ cup extra-virgin olive oil
- Kosher salt
- Freshly ground black pepper
- 1 lb. curly kale, leaves torn
- 4 large eggs
- 2½ cups chicken stock or low-sodium broth
- 1¼ lbs. sourdough bread, torn into 2-inch pieces
- ½ cup chopped parsley
- 1 Tbsp. thyme leaves
- 1 tsp. crushed red pepper

1 Preheat the oven to 375°. Butter a 9-by-13-inch baking dish. On a large rimmed baking sheet, toss sausage, onions and oil and season with salt and black pepper. Roast for about 20 minutes, until browned and softened. Scatter kale on top of sausage and onions and roast for about 5 minutes, until just wilted. Transfer one-fourth of the mixture to a plate and reserve. Let cool slightly.

2 In a large bowl, beat eggs with the chicken stock. Add bread, ½ stick of butter, parsley, thyme, crushed red pepper, 1½ teaspoons of salt and 1 teaspoon of black pepper; mix well. Fold in three-fourths of sausage-kale mixture, then scrape into prepared baking dish. Decoratively scatter reserved sausage-kale mixture on top, gently pressing it into the stuffing. Cover the baking dish tightly with foil.

3 Bake stuffing for 30 minutes, until hot. Uncover and bake 30 minutes longer, until lightly browned. Let stand for 10 minutes before serving.
—*Justin Chapple*

MAKE AHEAD

The stuffing can be prepared the day before and baked just before serving.

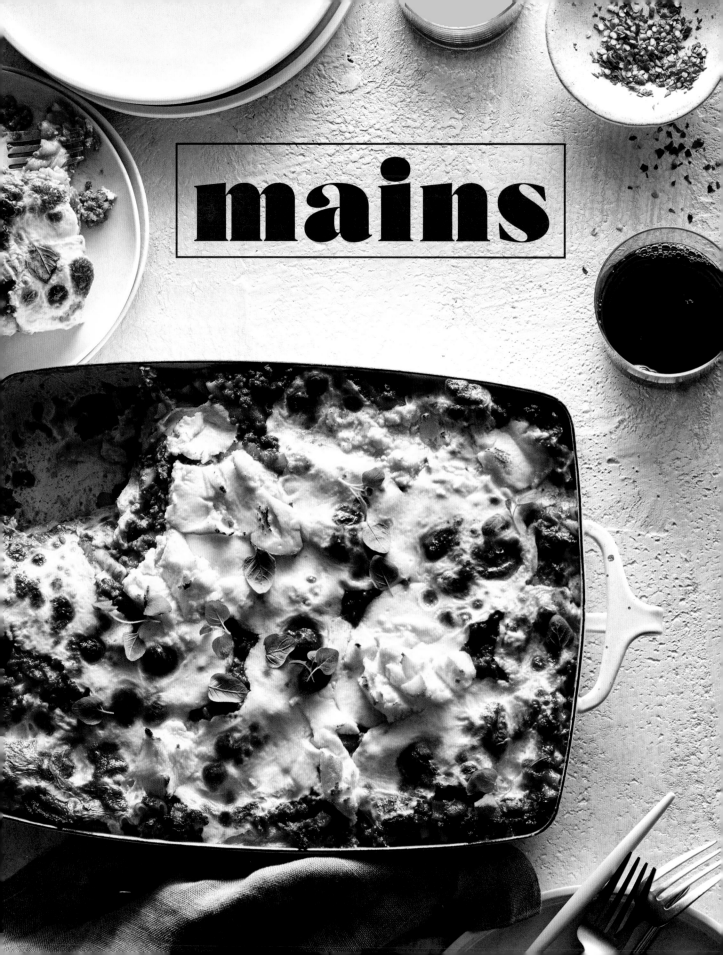

mains

RICOTTA AND SCALLION EGG PIE

(v)

MAKES **8 to 10 servings**

TIME **Active 40 min;
Total 3 hr 55 min**

PIECRUST

1¾	**cups all-purpose flour plus more for dusting**
½	**tsp. kosher salt**
1½	**sticks unsalted butter, cubed and chilled**
6	**oz. cream cheese, cubed and chilled**
2	**Tbsp. ice water**

FILLING

10	**scallions, trimmed**
1	**Tbsp. extra-virgin olive oil**
½	**tsp. thyme leaves**
	Kosher salt
	Freshly ground pepper
6	**large eggs**
1¼	**cups heavy cream**
1	**cup whole milk**
1	**cup loosely packed baby spinach leaves**
1	**cup grated Gruyère cheese**
1	**cup ricotta cheese**

1 MAKE THE PIECRUST In a large bowl, whisk the 1¾ cups of flour with the salt. Using a pastry blender or your fingers, cut the butter and cream cheese into the flour until pea-size. Add the ice water and gently knead just until the dough comes together. Press into a disk, wrap in plastic and refrigerate until firm, at least 30 minutes.

2 On a lightly floured surface, roll out the dough to a 14-inch round. Ease into a 10-inch cast-iron skillet and trim the overhang to ½ inch. Fold the edge of the dough in over itself and, if desired, crimp it. Wrap in plastic and refrigerate for at least 30 minutes.

3 Preheat the oven to 350°. Line the piecrust with parchment paper and fill with pie weights or dried beans. Blind bake for about 1 hour, until the crust is set and lightly browned. Remove the weights and parchment paper, transfer the skillet to a wire rack and let cool completely. Leave the oven on.

4 MAKE THE FILLING On a rimmed baking sheet, toss the scallions with the olive oil and thyme. Season with salt and pepper. Roast for 10 minutes, until tender. Let cool. Reserve 3 whole scallions. Coarsely chop the remaining scallions.

5 Reduce the oven temperature to 325°. In a large bowl, whisk the eggs with the cream, milk and 2 teaspoons of salt. Stir in the chopped scallions, the spinach, Gruyère and ricotta. Pour the custard into the piecrust and arrange the reserved whole scallions on top. Bake for 45 to 55 minutes, rotating halfway through, until the filling is puffed and lightly browned. Transfer to a rack and let cool for at least 20 minutes. Serve the pie warm or at room temperature.
—Roxana Jullapat

MAKE AHEAD

You can make the pie ahead and let it sit at room temperature for up to 2 hours.

DEEP-DISH SPINACH-AND-FETA QUICHE ⓥ

MAKES One 9-inch quiche

TIME Active 1 hr; Total 3 hr

One 14.1-oz. package refrigerated double piecrust dough

5 jalapeños, stemmed and seeded

8 garlic cloves—4 cloves crushed, 4 cloves minced

1 cup parsley leaves

1 cup cilantro leaves

1 tsp. ground cumin

½ tsp. ground coriander

¼ tsp. cayenne

½ cup extra-virgin olive oil

Kosher salt

Freshly ground black pepper

1 Tbsp. unsalted butter

1 large onion, finely chopped

10 large eggs

2¾ cups heavy cream

10 oz. thawed frozen chopped spinach, squeezed dry

1½ cups crumbled feta cheese

1 Preheat the oven to 450°. On a lightly floured work surface, stack the 2 rounds of pie dough and roll together into a 16-inch round. Ease the round into a 9-inch springform pan, pressing into the bottom and up the side. Trim the dough, leaving ¼ inch of overhang. Tuck the dough under itself and crimp the edge decoratively. Line the dough with parchment paper and fill with pie weights or dried beans. Bake for about 15 minutes, until lightly golden. Transfer to a rack to cool. Reduce the oven temperature to 375°. Remove the paper and weights.

2 Meanwhile, in a food processor, pulse the jalapeños and crushed garlic until finely chopped. Add the parsley, cilantro, cumin, coriander, cayenne and olive oil, season with salt and pepper and pulse the zhoug until blended.

3 In a large nonstick skillet, melt the butter. Add the onion, season with salt and black pepper and cook over moderate heat, stirring occasionally, until softened, about 8 minutes. Add the minced garlic and cook for 2 minutes. Scrape the mixture into a large bowl and cool to room temperature.

4 Add the eggs and heavy cream to the onion and beat until combined, then mix in the spinach, feta, ¾ teaspoon salt, ⅛ teaspoon pepper and ¼ cup of the zhoug. (Refrigerate or freeze the remaining zhoug.) Pour the filling into the quiche shell and bake for about 1 hour and 10 minutes, until the center is set. Tent the crust with foil if the edge starts to get too dark. Transfer the quiche to a rack to cool for about 30 minutes before serving with extra zhoug, if desired. —*Molly Yeh*

MAKE AHEAD

The zhoug can be refrigerated for 3 days or frozen for up to 3 months. The quiche can be refrigerated for up to 2 days; reheat before serving.

"For this spring-greens pizza, I bake a store-bought pizza dough until it's warm and crisp, then spread it with hummus and top it with a mix of lemony greens and herbs. I like to toss the greens with the lemon juice and top the pizza just before serving."

—JUSTIN CHAPPLE, CULINARY DIRECTOR

HUMMUS AND SALAD PIZZA ⓥ

MAKES   **One 12-inch pizza**

TIME   **Active 30 min; Total 45 min**

📷 PAGE 147

- 1 **lb. pizza dough**
  Extra-virgin olive oil, for brushing and drizzling
- 1 **cup mesclun greens**
- 1 **cup parsley leaves**
- 1 **cup mint leaves**
- 1 **cup snipped pea shoots, sunflower sprouts or purslane**
- 2 **Tbsp. fresh lemon juice**
- 1 **cup prepared hummus, at room temperature**
  Flaky sea salt
  Freshly ground pepper
  Shredded ricotta salata, for serving

1 Preheat the oven to 450° for at least 30 minutes. On a large rimmed baking sheet, stretch and pull dough to a 14-inch-long oval and brush with olive oil. Bake for about 15 minutes, until crust is puffed and browned.

2 In a bowl, toss mesclun with parsley, mint, pea shoots and lemon juice. Spread hummus on hot crust. Pile the salad on pizza and season with flaky sea salt and pepper. Drizzle with olive oil and top with shredded ricotta salata. Cut into wedges to serve. —*Justin Chapple*

MAKE AHEAD

If you are taking this pizza to a potluck dinner, make the crust and top with hummus. Prepare the salad, but wait until you arrive to top the pizza with the salad and the cheese.

ROMAN PIZZA

(V)

MAKES   **One pizza**

TIME   **Active 30 min;**
                Total 2 hr 45 min

¾ **cup warm water (100°–110°)**

1½ **tsp. active dry yeast**

¼ **tsp. sugar**

1¾ **cups plus 2 Tbsp. bread flour
plus more for dusting**

7 **Tbsp. extra-virgin olive oil**

¾ **tsp. kosher salt**

1 **small garlic clove, finely grated**

**One 14.5-oz. can crushed
tomatoes**

Kosher salt

Freshly ground pepper

8 **oz. stracciatella cheese**

Torn basil leaves, for garnish

1 In a large bowl, stir together warm water with yeast and sugar and let stand until foamy, about 5 minutes.

2 Stir ¾ cup flour and 3 tablespoons olive oil into yeast mixture. Let stand until small bubbles appear, about 20 minutes.

3 Brush a large bowl with 1 tablespoon olive oil. Stir remaining 1 cup and 2 tablespoons flour and ¾ teaspoon salt into dough. On a lightly floured work surface, knead the dough until it comes together in a uniform ball. Transfer to prepared bowl, cover with plastic wrap, and let stand until the dough has doubled in size, about 1 hour and 15 minutes.

4 Meanwhile, in a medium saucepan, heat 1 tablespoon olive oil. Add garlic and cook over moderate heat, stirring, until garlic begins to turn light golden, about 30 seconds. Stir in crushed tomatoes and bring to a simmer. Remove from heat, season with salt and pepper, and let cool.

5 Brush a 13-by-18-inch rimmed baking sheet with 1 tablespoon olive oil and press dough into pan. Using fingers, dimple the dough all over and drizzle with the remaining 1 tablespoon olive oil. Let dough rise until puffed, about 30 minutes.

6 Preheat the oven to 450°. Spread 6 tablespoons sauce over dough, leaving a ½-inch border; reserve remaining sauce for another use. Tear stracciatella into pieces and scatter over pizza. Bake until crust is golden and the cheese is lightly browned, about 25 minutes. Scatter basil leaves over pizza and serve.
—*Brooks Reitz*

MAKE AHEAD

If you're taking this pizza to a potluck, bake it before you leave, then cover and keep warm. Top with the basil leaves just before serving.

SUMMER MARGHERITA PIZZAS

Ⓥ

MAKES **Two 12-inch pizzas**

TIME **Active 30 min;**
      Total 6 hr 30 min

PIZZA DOUGH

- **1 cup lukewarm water (100°–105°)**
- **½ tsp. active dry yeast**
- **2¾ cups type 0 flour**
- **1¼ tsp. kosher salt**
- **1 Tbsp. extra-virgin olive oil**

PIZZA

- **1 Tbsp. extra-virgin olive oil plus more for greasing and brushing**
- **2 large tomatoes, sliced**
- **1 small garlic clove, minced**
- **Kosher salt**
- **Freshly ground pepper**
- **1½ lbs. fresh mozzarella, torn**
- **Torn basil, for garnish**

1 MAKE THE PIZZA DOUGH In a large bowl, whisk lukewarm water with the yeast and let stand until foamy, 5 minutes. Stir in the flour, kosher salt and the olive oil until a dough forms. Scrape onto a work surface and knead until smooth, about 5 minutes. Transfer to a large greased bowl, cover with plastic and let stand in a warm place for 1 hour. Cut the dough in half and form into 2 balls. Transfer the balls to 2 large greased bowls, cover with plastic wrap and let stand in a warm place until doubled in bulk, about 5 hours. Punch down the dough before using.

2 Light a grill and oil the grate. Spread tomato slices on a platter and top with 1 tablespoon olive oil and garlic. Season generously with salt and pepper.

3 MAKE THE PIZZAS On a lightly oiled large baking sheet, stretch 1 ball of pizza dough to a 12-inch oval or round and brush with olive oil. Grill the dough over moderate heat until lightly charred on the bottom, 2 to 3 minutes. Flip the crust and scatter half of the mozzarella on top. Close the grill and cook until the cheese is melted and the crust is firm, 3 to 5 minutes. Transfer to a large board and top with half of the tomatoes. Sprinkle with salt and pepper. Garnish with torn basil.

4 Repeat with the remaining dough, mozzarella, tomatoes, seasoning and basil. Cut the pizzas into wedges and serve. —*Daniele Uditi*

NOTE

"Tipo 0" (or type 0) is the Italian designation for finely ground, high-protein flour; all-purpose flour can be substituted.

MAKE AHEAD

You can make the pizzas ahead and refrigerate until ready to serve. Reheat before serving and top with the basil.

WILD MUSHROOM SHEPHERD'S PIE
WITH POTATO-CHESTNUT TOPPING

ⓥ

MAKES 8 to 10 servings

TIME Active 1 hr 30 min;
Total 4 hr 45 min

SAUCE

- 3 lbs. white mushrooms, chopped
- 1 lb. leeks, white and light green parts only, chopped
- 1 carrot, chopped
- 3 garlic cloves, crushed
- 2 bay leaves
- 1½ Tbsp. kosher salt
- 1 Tbsp. thyme leaves
- 1 Tbsp. black peppercorns
- ½ tsp. hot curry powder
- 2 cups heavy cream
- 1 qt. water
- 6 Tbsp. unsalted butter
- 6 Tbsp. all-purpose flour

FILLING

- 6 Tbsp. unsalted butter
- 1 large shallot, finely chopped
- 2 garlic cloves, minced
- 8 oz. rutabaga, peeled and diced
- 8 oz. turnips, peeled and diced
- ¼ lb. sunchokes, peeled and diced
- 1 small carrot, diced
- 1 small parsnip, peeled and diced
  Kosher salt and pepper
- 1 lb. shiitake mushrooms, stemmed and caps quartered
- 2 lbs. mixed cremini, oyster, maitake and portobello mushrooms, chopped
- 1⅓ cups mixed chopped parsley, chives and thyme

TOPPING

- 2 lbs. Yukon Gold potatoes, peeled and cut into large chunks
  One 5-oz. package roasted chestnuts
- 1 small parsnip, peeled and cut into 1-inch pieces
- 1 qt. heavy cream
- ½ tsp. freshly grated nutmeg
- 4 large egg yolks

1 MAKE THE SAUCE In a food processor, pulse mushrooms in 4 batches until finely chopped; transfer to a 12-quart pot. Add leeks and next 7 ingredients to food processor and pulse until finely chopped; transfer to pot. Add cream and 1 quart water; bring to a boil over high heat, then simmer over moderate heat, stirring occasionally, for 1 hour.

2 Strain stock through a fine sieve set over a large heatproof bowl, pressing on the solids; discard solids. Return stock to pot and boil over moderately high heat until reduced to 3 cups, about 10 minutes. Pour stock into bowl.

3 Wipe out pot and melt the butter in it. Whisk in flour and cook over moderate heat, whisking often, until browned, about 7 minutes. Gradually whisk in stock until smooth and bring to a boil. Simmer over low heat, whisking often, until thickened and no floury taste remains, about 15 minutes. Scrape into bowl.

4 MAKE THE FILLING Wipe out the pot and melt the butter in it. Add the shallot and garlic and cook over moderately high heat, stirring, until softened, about 2 minutes. Add the rutabaga, turnips, sunchokes, carrot, parsnip and a generous pinch of salt. Cook, stirring occasionally, until just softened, about 7 minutes. Add all of the mushrooms and cook, stirring occasionally, until tender and their liquid evaporates, 10 to 12 minutes. Add the sauce and cook over moderately low heat, stirring often, until the vegetables are coated in a creamy sauce, 10 to 15 minutes. Remove the pot from the heat and stir in 1 cup herbs. Season with salt and pepper. Spread the filling in a 9-by-13-inch gratin dish.

5 MAKE THE TOPPING In a large saucepan, cover potatoes, chestnuts and parsnip with cream and 1 quart of water; bring to a boil over high heat. Stir in nutmeg and 1 tablespoon salt and simmer over moderate heat, stirring occasionally, until vegetables are tender, about 30 minutes.

6 Drain vegetables in a colander set over a heatproof bowl. Transfer half of vegetables to a food processor, add ¾ cup cooking liquid and puree until smooth. Scrape into a large bowl. Repeat with remaining vegetables and ¾ cup cooking liquid. Let puree cool slightly, then stir in egg yolks, ⅓ cup chopped herbs and salt. Spread topping over filling and swirl decoratively.

7 Preheat the oven to 375°. Bake about 40 minutes, until filling bubbles. Turn on broiler and broil 8 to 10 inches from heat for 2 to 3 minutes, until top is lightly browned. Let stand for 20 minutes. —*Grant Achatz*

MAKE AHEAD

The pie can be prepared through Step 6 and refrigerated overnight. Let stand at room temperature for at least 45 minutes before baking.

RYE AND CRÈME FRAÎCHE STRATA
WITH SMOKED SALMON

MAKES	6 to 8 servings
TIME	Active 25 min; Total 2 hr 25 min

8 oz. crème fraîche

6 large eggs, at room temperature

2½ cups half-and-half

2 tsp. kosher salt

1 tsp. freshly ground pepper

1 lb. rustic rye bread with crust,
cut into 1-inch pieces

4 scallions, thinly sliced

¼ cup drained capers plus more
for garnish

Thinly sliced smoked salmon
and sliced red onion, for serving

1 In a large bowl, whisk the crème fraîche with the eggs, half-and-half, salt and pepper. Add the bread, scallions and the ¼ cup of capers and mix well. Scrape into a 9-by-13-inch baking dish, cover with plastic wrap and let soak for 1 hour.

2 Preheat the oven to 375°. Bake strata for 45 to 50 minutes, until puffed and top is golden. Let stand for 10 minutes. Scatter some salmon on top and garnish with red onion and capers. Serve, passing more salmon at the table.
—*Justin Chapple*

MAKE AHEAD

The unbaked strata can be covered and refrigerated overnight. Bring to room temperature before baking.

"This custardy rye bread pudding with capers is a fun riff on a bagel with cream cheese and lox. You can make it ahead, and it's a guaranteed crowd-pleaser at any brunch." —JUSTIN CHAPPLE, CULINARY DIRECTOR

JALAPEÑO-PICKLED SHRIMP AND VEGETABLES

(GF)

MAKES	6 servings
TIME	Active 30 min; Total 4 hr 30 min

PICKLE

- 3 cups water
- 1 cup red wine vinegar
- ½ cup diced carrot
- ½ cup diced trimmed shiitake mushrooms
- ½ cup diced turnip
- 1 jalapeño, thinly sliced crosswise
- 2 Tbsp. sugar
- 1 Tbsp. kosher salt
- 1 Tbsp. dried oregano
- 1 tsp. ground fennel
- 1 tsp. crushed red pepper
- 1 tsp. freshly ground black pepper

SHRIMP

- 8 cups water
- 1 lemon, halved
- 5 bay leaves
- 1 Tbsp. kosher salt
- 2 tsp. cayenne
- 1 lb. shell-on large shrimp

1 MAKE THE PICKLE In a medium saucepan, combine water, vinegar, carrots, mushrooms, turnip, jalapeño, sugar, salt, oregano, fennel, red pepper and black pepper and bring just to a boil, stirring to dissolve the sugar and salt. Transfer the pickling mixture to a large bowl and let cool completely.

2 MEANWHILE, PREPARE THE SHRIMP Wipe out the saucepan. Add water, lemon, bay leaves, salt and cayenne and bring to a boil for 2 minutes. Add the shrimp and cook over moderately high heat until just white throughout, 2 to 3 minutes. Drain and transfer the shrimp to an ice bath to cool. Add the shrimp to the pickle, cover and refrigerate for 4 to 5 hours. Drain and peel the shrimp and serve with the pickled vegetables. —*Donald Link*

MAKE AHEAD

The drained pickled shrimp can be refrigerated for up to 3 days.

"Trust us: You'll want to double the recipe. Pickle the shrimp, chill it, and then watch it magically disappear when served on a buffet." —HUNTER LEWIS, EDITOR IN CHIEF

EMPANADA GALLEGA
WITH TUNA

MAKES **8 to 10 servings**

TIME **Active 50 min;
Total 3 hr 30 min**

**⅓ cup extra-virgin olive oil,
plus more for greasing**

**1 large white onion, quartered
lengthwise and very thinly
sliced crosswise**

**2 medium green bell peppers—
stemmed, seeded and very
thinly sliced into strips**

**2 large garlic cloves, very thinly
sliced**

Kosher salt

**Large pinch of saffron, finely
ground in a mortar**

¼ cup boiling water

**2 medium tomatoes, halved
crosswise**

**2 roasted red bell peppers,
drained well and very thinly
sliced**

1 tsp. sweet paprika

**Two 6-oz. jars oil-packed tuna,
preferably ventresca (from the
belly), drained well and flaked**

**½ cup pitted green Spanish
olives, sliced**

**½ cup finely chopped flat-leaf
parsley**

1 Tbsp. fresh lemon juice

Freshly ground pepper

**Two 13-oz. cans pizza crust,
such as Pillsbury**

**1 large egg beaten with 1 Tbsp.
water**

1 In a large skillet, heat ⅓ cup of olive oil until shimmering. Add the onion and cook over moderate heat, stirring occasionally, until just starting to soften, about 5 minutes. Add the green bell peppers, garlic and a generous pinch of salt. Cover and cook over moderately low heat, stirring occasionally, until very soft, about 25 minutes; add a bit of water if the pan is too dry.

2 Meanwhile, in a small heatproof bowl, mix the saffron with the boiling water until dissolved. Let stand until cooled, about 10 minutes. Grate the tomato halves on the large holes of a box grater set in a bowl until only the skins remain; discard the skins.

3 Add the roasted red peppers, grated tomatoes, brewed saffron and the paprika to the skillet and cook over moderate heat, stirring occasionally, until the mixture is very thick, about 10 minutes. Scrape the mixture into a colander and let drain for 10 minutes.

4 In a large bowl, combine the pepper mixture with the tuna, olives, parsley and lemon juice and season with salt and pepper. Let the filling cool completely, about 45 minutes.

5 Preheat the oven to 425°. Grease a large rimmed baking sheet. Unroll 1 of the pizza crusts on the prepared baking sheet. Spoon the cooled filling evenly on the dough, leaving a 1-inch border. Unroll the remaining pizza crust and lay it on top of the filling; crimp the edges to seal. Brush the empanada with the egg wash and, using a paring knife, cut a few slits in the top. Bake empanada for 13 to 15 minutes, until puffed and browned. Slide onto a rack to cool completely, about 1 hour. Cut into squares and serve. —*Anya von Bremzen*

MAKE AHEAD

The tuna empanada can be kept at room temperature for a few hours before serving.

TANDOORI CHICKEN WINGS
WITH YOGURT SAUCE

(GF)

MAKES   **6 servings**

TIME   **Active 45 min;
Total 6 hr 45 min**

WINGS

- ½ **cup Greek yogurt**
- 2 **Tbsp. minced peeled fresh ginger**
- 6 **garlic cloves, minced**
- 3 **Tbsp. garam masala**
- 1 **tsp. finely grated lemon zest plus 2 Tbsp. fresh lemon juice**
- 1 **Tbsp. hot paprika**
- 2 **Tbsp. vegetable oil plus more for brushing**
- 2½ **tsp. kosher salt**
- 1 **tsp. turmeric**
- 18 **whole chicken wings**
- **Cilantro sprigs and thinly sliced white onion, for garnish**
- **Lemon wedges, for serving**

YOGURT SAUCE

- 1 **cup Greek yogurt**
- ¼ **cup cream cheese, softened**
- ½ **cup finely chopped mint**
- 3 **Tbsp. fresh lemon juice**
- 2 **garlic cloves, minced**
- 1 **tsp. ground cumin**
- **Kosher salt**
- **Freshly ground pepper**

1 MARINATE THE WINGS In a large bowl, whisk together yogurt, ginger, garlic, garam masala, lemon zest and juice, paprika, oil, salt and tumeric. Add the chicken wings and toss to coat. Cover wings and refrigerate for at least 6 hours or overnight.

2 MEANWHILE, MAKE THE YOGURT SAUCE In a medium bowl, whisk together yogurt, cream cheese, mint, juice, garlic and cumin and season with salt and pepper.

3 Set up a grill for direct and indirect cooking, then light the grill and oil the grate. Remove the wings from the marinade, scraping off all but a thin layer. Grill over moderately high heat, turning, until the wings are lightly charred all over, about 8 minutes. Move to indirect heat, cover and cook at 425° until an instant-read thermometer inserted in the thickest part of a wing registers 165°, about 15 minutes.

4 Transfer the wings to a platter and garnish with cilantro sprigs and thinly sliced white onion. Serve with the yogurt sauce and lemon wedges. —*Ben Ford*

MAKE AHEAD

The yogurt sauce can be refrigerated for up to 3 days. You can grill the wings ahead and reheat before serving.

Left to right: Tandoori Chicken Wings with Yogurt Sauce; Hill Country Smoked Chicken Wings with Texas Ranch Dressing, p. 164

HILL COUNTRY SMOKED CHICKEN WINGS
WITH TEXAS RANCH DRESSING (GF)

MAKES **6 servings**

TIME **Active 1 hr;
Total 3 hr 40 min**

📷 PAGE 163

WINGS

¼ cup unrefined cane sugar,
    such as turbinado

¼ cup packed dark brown sugar

2 Tbsp. kosher salt

1½ Tbsp. chili powder

1½ tsp. chipotle chile powder

1 tsp. ground cumin

1 tsp. cayenne

1 tsp. smoked paprika

1 tsp. onion powder

1 tsp. garlic powder

1 tsp. mustard powder

18 whole chicken wings

2 cups hardwood chips, such as
    hickory or applewood, soaked in
    water for 1 hour and drained

DRESSING

⅔ cup mayonnaise

⅓ cup buttermilk

1 Tbsp. packed torn basil leaves

1 Tbsp. packed parsley leaves

1 tsp. finely chopped thyme

1 tsp. sugar

¼ tsp. apple cider vinegar

1 pickled jalapeño with seeds,
    minced

2 small garlic cloves, minced

2 tsp. minced onion

    Kosher salt

    Freshly ground pepper

1 SMOKE THE WINGS In a food processor, combine sugars, salt, chili powder, chipotle chile powder, cumin, cayenne, paprika, onion powder, garlic powder, and mustard powder and pulse until well blended. In a large bowl, toss the wings with the spice rub until well coated. Refrigerate for 2 hours or overnight.

2 Set up a grill for indirect cooking, then heat to 425° and oil the grate. Wrap the wood chips in a double layer of heavy-duty foil and poke holes in the top. Place the packet directly on the flames of the grill. When the chips are smoking, add chicken wings to the grill, cover and smoke the wings, turning occasionally, until an instant-read thermometer inserted in the thickest part of a wing registers 165°, about 40 minutes.

3 MEANWHILE, MAKE THE DRESSING In a food processor, combine mayonnaise, buttermilk, basil, parsley, thyme, sugar and vinegar and puree until nearly smooth. Add the jalapeño, garlic and onion and pulse to mix; it will still be slightly chunky. Scrape into a bowl and season the dressing with salt and pepper.

4 Transfer the smoked chicken wings to a serving platter and serve the wings with the ranch dressing. —*Ben Ford*

MAKE AHEAD

The spice rub can be refrigerated in an airtight container for up to 2 weeks, and the ranch dressing can be refrigerated for up to 3 days. You can smoke the wings ahead and reheat before serving.

CLASSIC BBQ CHICKEN DRUMSTICKS

(GF)

MAKES   6 servings

TIME   Active 30 min;
         Total 2 hr 10 min

BARBECUE SAUCE

- ½ lb. plum tomatoes
- 1 medium onion, thinly sliced
- 6 large garlic cloves, crushed
- ¼ cup vegetable oil
  Kosher salt
  Freshly ground pepper
- 1 cup ketchup
- ¾ cup apple cider vinegar
- ½ cup packed light brown sugar
- 2 Tbsp. unsulfured molasses
- 1½ Tbsp. Worcestershire sauce
- 1 Tbsp. chili powder
- 1 Tbsp. paprika
- ¼ tsp. ground coriander
- ¼ tsp. ground cumin
- ½ cup water

CHICKEN

- 1 Tbsp. kosher salt
- 1 Tbsp. packed light brown sugar
- 2 garlic cloves, minced
- 1½ tsp. sweet paprika
- 1 tsp. freshly ground black pepper
- 1 tsp. ground coriander
- ½ tsp. cayenne
- 12 chicken drumsticks (3 lbs.)
  Bread-and-butter pickles,
  for serving

1 MAKE THE SAUCE Preheat the oven to 350°. On a large rimmed baking sheet, toss the tomatoes, onion and 6 garlic cloves with the oil and season with salt and pepper. Roast for about 40 minutes, until the tomatoes and onion are tender and browned in spots.

2 In a saucepan, bring the roasted tomato mixture, ketchup, vinegar, brown sugar, molasses, Worcestershire sauce, chili powder, paprika, coriander and cumin to a boil over moderately high heat. Cook over low heat, stirring often, until thick, about 30 minutes.

3 Scrape the mixture into a blender, add ½ cup of water and puree until smooth. Season the barbecue sauce with salt and pepper.

4 PREPARE THE CHICKEN In a small bowl, whisk together salt, brown sugar, 2 minced garlic cloves, paprika, black pepper, 1 teaspoon coriander and cayenne. Rub the chicken all over with the spice mix.

5 Set up a grill for direct and indirect cooking, then light the grill and oil the grate. Grill the chicken over moderately high heat, turning occasionally, until lightly charred all over, 8 to 10 minutes.

6 Move the chicken to indirect heat. Brush all over with the barbecue sauce. Cover and cook at 425°, basting and turning occasionally, until an instant-read thermometer inserted in the thickest part registers 165°, about 20 minutes. —Ben Ford

MAKE AHEAD

You can grill the drumsticks ahead and reheat just before serving, basting with barbecue sauce as needed.

> "This is one of my favorite ways to prepare chicken thighs. Instead of just roasting them, you crisp the skin, then braise in a briny mix of marinated artichokes, olives, sherry, garlic, lemon and thyme."
> —MARY-FRANCES HECK, SENIOR FOOD EDITOR

BRAISED CHICKEN THIGHS
WITH MARINATED ARTICHOKES

(GF)

MAKES	4 to 6 servings
TIME	Active 30 min; Total 1 hr 45 min

- 8 skin-on, bone-in chicken thighs (3¾ lbs.)
  Sea salt
  Freshly ground pepper
- 1 Tbsp. extra-virgin olive oil
- 15 oz. marinated artichoke hearts plus ¼ cup brine from the jar
- 1 cup Castelvetrano olives
- 1 head of garlic, halved crosswise
- 1 lemon, thinly sliced
- 6 thyme sprigs
- 1 cup chicken stock or low-sodium broth
- ½ cup semidry sherry, such as amontillado
- 1 Tbsp. Asian fish sauce

1 Preheat the oven to 375°. Season the chicken all over with salt and pepper. In a large cast-iron skillet or black steel pan, heat the oil. Add half of the chicken skin side down and top the pieces (not the pan) with a pot lid; cook over moderate heat until browned and crisp, 5 to 7 minutes. Transfer skin side up to a large baking dish. Repeat with the remaining chicken. Scatter the artichoke hearts, olives, garlic, lemon slices and thyme in the baking dish.

2 Pour off the fat from the skillet. Add the artichoke brine, stock, sherry and fish sauce; bring to a boil. Stir in 1 teaspoon of salt, then pour the mixture around the chicken. Cover tightly with foil and braise in the oven for 1 hour, until the chicken is very tender.

3 Uncover and increase the oven temperature to 400°. Roast the chicken for 15 minutes longer, until the skin is crisp. Discard the thyme. Transfer to plates and serve. —*Naomi Pomeroy*

COLD FRIED CHICKEN

MAKES 6 to 8 servings

TIME Active 1 hr;
Total 2 hr 15 min plus
overnight brining

📷 PAGE 2

CHICKEN

- **2 Tbsp. kosher salt**
- **2 Tbsp. pimentón de la Vera**
- **1 Tbsp. granulated garlic**
- **1 Tbsp. coarsely ground black pepper**
- **One 4-lb. chicken, cut into 8 pieces**
- **1 qt. buttermilk**

COATING

- **2 Tbsp. coriander seeds**
- **2 Tbsp. cumin seeds**
- **1 Tbsp. caraway seeds**
- **1 Tbsp. dried oregano**
- **1 Tbsp. black peppercorns**
- **1 tsp. crushed red pepper**
- **2 Tbsp. pimentón de la Vera**
- **1 Tbsp. granulated garlic**
- **1 Tbsp. kosher salt**
- **4 cups all-purpose flour**
- **1 cup rice flour**
- **2 Tbsp. cornstarch**
- **Canola oil, for frying**

1 MAKE THE CHICKEN In a bowl, combine the salt, pimentón, garlic and pepper. Add the chicken and rub all over with the spices. Add the buttermilk and turn to coat. Cover with plastic wrap and refrigerate overnight.

2 MAKE THE COATING In a small skillet, toast the coriander, cumin, caraway, oregano, peppercorns and red pepper over low heat, stirring, until very fragrant, about 3 minutes. Transfer to a spice grinder, let cool slightly, then finely grind. Transfer to a bowl and whisk in the pimentón, garlic, salt and all-purpose flour. Transfer half of the flour mixture to another bowl and whisk in the rice flour and cornstarch.

3 Drain the chicken, reserving the buttermilk. Coat the chicken in the seasoned all-purpose flour, shaking off any excess. Set on a rack and refrigerate for 1 hour. Let stand at room temperature for 15 minutes.

4 In a large enameled cast-iron casserole, heat 3 inches of oil to 325°. Dip the chicken in the reserved buttermilk, then dredge in the rice flour mixture. Fry in 2 batches, turning, until the dark meat registers 155° on an instant-read thermometer and the breast meat registers 150°, about 15 minutes for the dark meat and 20 minutes for the breast. Transfer to a rack and let cool, then refrigerate until cold. —*Justin Yu*

MEXICAN CHICKEN CASSEROLE

(GF)

MAKES **6 to 8 servings**

TIME **Active 25 min; Total 1 hr 10 min**

- 2 **lbs. boneless, skinless chicken thighs, cut into pieces**
- **Kosher salt**
- **Freshly ground pepper**
- 3 **Tbsp. extra-virgin olive oil**
- 1 **large onion, chopped**
- 4 **garlic cloves, minced**
- 2 **tsp. ground cumin**
- 1 **Tbsp. dried oregano, crumbled**
- 2 **Tbsp. chopped chipotles in adobo**
- 1 **(32-oz.) can whole tomatoes in juice**
- 2 **cups shredded Mexican cheese blend**
- **Fresh cilantro, for garnish**

1 Preheat the oven to 375°F. Season the chicken with 1 teaspoon salt and ¾ teaspoon pepper.

2 In a large heavy pot, heat the oil over medium-high heat until hot. Brown the chicken, in batches if necessary, turning occasionally with tongs, about 6 minutes per batch. Transfer chicken to a plate. Add onion and garlic to pot and cook, stirring occasionally, until golden brown, about 8 minutes. Stir in the cumin and oregano and cook, stirring, until fragrant, about 1 minute. Stir in the chipotles in adobo, tomatoes and the reserved chicken with any accumulated juices. Simmer until slightly thickened and the chicken is cooked, about 25 minutes.

3 Season with salt and pepper to taste, then transfer to a 3-quart baking dish. Top the filling with the cheese and bake until the filling is bubbling and the cheese is melted, about 20 minutes. Serve garnished with cilantro.
—*Ian Knauer*

MAKE AHEAD

The baked casserole can be refrigerated overnight and reheated before serving.

CHICKEN AND WILD RICE CASSEROLE

MAKES **8 to 10 servings**

TIME **Active 1 hr 45 min;
Total 2 hr 30 min**

WILD RICE

- ½ lb. wild rice (1½ cups)
- 1 medium carrot, finely chopped
- 1 small onion, finely chopped
- 1 celery rib, finely chopped
- 1 bay leaf
- 1 thyme sprig
   Kosher salt
   Freshly ground pepper

SWISS CHARD

- 3 Tbsp. grapeseed or canola oil
- 1 large shallot, minced
- 2 large garlic cloves, minced
- 3 lbs. Swiss chard, stems discarded and leaves coarsely chopped

MUSHROOM SAUCE

- ¼ cup grapeseed or canola oil
- 1½ lbs. cremini mushrooms, sliced
- 2 Tbsp. unsalted butter
- ½ small onion, finely chopped
- 1 small celery rib, finely chopped
- 2 garlic cloves, minced
- 3 thyme sprigs
- 1½ tsp. minced rosemary
   Kosher salt
   Freshly ground pepper
- ¼ cup all-purpose flour
- 4 cups chicken stock or low-sodium broth
- ½ cup heavy cream
- 2 lbs. thinly sliced chicken scaloppine, pounded ¼ inch thick
- 1½ cups panko
- 3 Tbsp. unsalted butter, melted
   Parsley leaves, for garnish

1 MAKE THE WILD RICE In a large saucepan, combine all of the ingredients with a generous pinch each of salt and pepper. Cover with water and bring to a boil over high heat. Simmer over moderate heat until the rice is tender, about 1 hour. Drain well. Discard bay leaf and thyme sprig.

2 MEANWHILE, COOK THE SWISS CHARD Set a rack over a large rimmed baking sheet. In a pot, heat the oil. Add the shallot and garlic and cook over moderately high heat, stirring, until softened, 1 to 2 minutes. Add the Swiss chard in large handfuls, letting each batch wilt slightly before adding more. Cook, stirring occasionally, until all of the chard is wilted, 8 to 10 minutes. Spread the chard out on the rack to drain and let cool completely. Squeeze out any excess water.

3 MAKE THE MUSHROOM SAUCE In a large, deep skillet, heat 2 tablespoons of the oil until shimmering. Add half of the mushrooms and cook over moderately high heat, undisturbed, until browned on the bottom, 5 minutes. Cook, stirring, until the mushrooms are tender and browned all over, 5 minutes longer; transfer to a plate. Repeat with the remaining oil and mushrooms.

4 Wipe out the skillet and melt the 2 tablespoons of butter in it. Add the onion, celery, garlic, thyme, rosemary and a generous pinch each of salt and pepper. Cook over moderate heat, stirring occasionally, until the vegetables are just starting to brown, about 8 minutes. Stir in the mushrooms. Sprinkle the flour over the vegetables and cook, stirring, until incorporated, about 2 minutes. Gradually whisk in the stock and bring to a boil, stirring frequently. Reduce the heat to moderate and simmer, stirring occasionally, until the sauce is thickened and no floury taste remains, about 7 minutes. Stir in the cream and season the sauce with salt and pepper.

5 Preheat the oven to 375°. Arrange half of the chicken in the bottom of a 9-by-13-inch or 4-quart baking dish that's at least 2 inches deep. Scatter half of the Swiss chard over the chicken, followed by half of the wild rice and half of the mushroom cream sauce. Repeat the layering once more with the remaining chicken, greens, rice and sauce.

6 In a medium bowl, toss the panko with the 3 tablespoons of melted butter and sprinkle evenly over the casserole. Cover with foil and bake for about 35 minutes, until bubbling. Uncover the casserole and turn on the broiler. Broil 6 inches from the heat until the panko is lightly browned, about 3 minutes. Let stand for 10 minutes. Garnish with parsley and serve. —*Gavin Kaysen*

MAKE AHEAD

The baked casserole can be cooled and refrigerated overnight. Reheat gently and crisp the panko under the broiler before serving.

CHICKEN AND SPAGHETTI CASSEROLE

MAKES **6 to 8 servings**

TIME **Active 25 min; Total 45 min**

- 1 **lb. spaghetti**
- 3 **Tbsp. extra-virgin olive oil**
- 3 **Tbsp. all-purpose flour**
- 3 **cups whole milk**
  Kosher salt
  Freshly ground pepper
- 1 **cup grated white cheddar cheese**
- 1 **cup grated Monterey Jack cheese**
- 3 **cups shredded cooked chicken (from a rotisserie chicken)**
- ¼ **cup finely grated Parmesan cheese**

1 Preheat the oven to 400°. In a large pot of salted boiling water, cook the pasta until al dente, then drain.

2 While pasta is cooking, in a large, heavy pot, heat oil over medium-high heat until hot. Whisk in flour and cook, whisking, until flour is fragrant, about 3 minutes. Whisk in milk and ½ teaspoon each salt and pepper, then bring to a boil, whisking. Boil until milk is slightly thickened, about 8 minutes. Remove from the heat and whisk in the cheddar and Monterey Jack cheeses until melted, then whisk in the chicken. Season the sauce with salt and pepper to taste.

3 Toss the pasta with the sauce and transfer to a 3-quart baking dish. Sprinkle evenly with the Parmesan cheese. Bake the casserole until the filling is bubbling and the cheese is browned on top, 20 to 25 minutes. Serve. —*Ian Knauer*

MAKE AHEAD

The baked casserole can be refrigerated overnight and reheated before serving.

SOUTHERN BAKED CHICKEN CASSEROLE

MAKES   **8 servings**

TIME   **Active 45 min;**
Total 1 hr 45 min

- 2 **Tbsp. unsalted butter**
- 1 **Tbsp. vegetable oil**
- 1 **small onion, finely chopped**
- 1 **red bell pepper, finely chopped**
- 1 **celery rib, finely chopped**
- ¼ **cup all-purpose flour**
- 1½ **cups milk**
  Kosher salt
  Freshly ground pepper
  Tabasco
- ½ **cup mayonnaise**
- 4 **cups shredded rotisserie chicken**
- ½ **cup finely chopped pimentos (from a 4-oz. jar)**
- 1 **sleeve Ritz crackers, crushed (4 oz.)**

1 Preheat the oven to 350°. In a large saucepan, melt butter in oil. Add onion, bell pepper and celery and cook over moderately high heat, stirring, until softened, about 6 minutes. Add flour and cook, stirring, for 2 minutes. Add milk and whisk until combined. Simmer until thickened, about 3 minutes. Season the mixture with salt, pepper and Tabasco. Remove from the heat and stir in the mayonnaise, chicken and pimentos.

2 Transfer the chicken mixture to a 1½-quart shallow baking dish. Scatter the crushed crackers on top. Bake for about 45 minutes, until the casserole is golden and bubbling. Let rest for 15 minutes before serving. —*Jennifer Nettles*

"Sometimes it's just hard to beat a tried-and-true classic chicken casserole topped with buttery Ritz crackers. In this one, a white sauce replaces canned soup and Tabasco adds a kick." —ANNE CAIN, BOOKS EDITOR

GREEN CHILE-CHICKEN ENCHILADAS

MAKES **10 to 12 servings**

TIME **Active 1 hr 15 min;
Total 3 hr**

4 skin-on, bone-in chicken breast
halves (4½ lbs.)

1 qt. chicken stock or low-sodium
broth

1 qt. water

Kosher salt

Freshly ground pepper

6 Tbsp. unsalted butter plus
more for greasing

⅓ cup all-purpose flour

1½ cups whole milk

18 corn tortillas

12 oz. sharp white cheddar cheese,
shredded (3 cups)

12 oz. jarred or canned chopped
roasted Hatch chiles

½ cup minced white onion

Cilantro leaves and thinly sliced
jalapeño, for garnish

1 In a large saucepan, cover the chicken breast halves with the stock and 1 quart of water and bring to a boil. Simmer over moderately low heat, turning the chicken occasionally, until an instant-read thermometer inserted in the thickest part of each piece registers 160°, 30 to 35 minutes. Using tongs, transfer the chicken to a plate to cool. Discard the skin and bones. Shred the meat and season generously with salt and pepper. Transfer 2 cups of the chicken cooking broth to a large heatproof measuring cup and reserve the remaining broth for another use.

2 Wipe out the saucepan and melt the 6 tablespoons of butter in it. Whisk in the flour and cook over moderate heat, whisking constantly, until bubbling and just starting to change color, about 2 minutes. Gradually whisk in the milk and the 2 cups of cooking broth and bring to a boil. Simmer over moderately low heat, whisking frequently, until the sauce is thickened and no floury taste remains, about 10 minutes. Remove the sauce from the heat and season generously with salt and pepper. Let cool slightly.

3 Preheat the oven to 375°. Grease a 9-by-13-inch baking dish. Line the dish with 6 slightly overlapping tortillas. Spread one-third of the sauce over the tortillas, then top with 1 cup of the cheese and half each of the chicken, chiles and onion. Repeat the layering with 6 more tortillas, one-third of the sauce, 1 cup of the cheese and the remaining chicken, chiles and onion. Lay the remaining 6 tortillas on top and spread the remaining sauce over them.

4 Bake the enchiladas for about 45 minutes, until the filling is bubbling. Sprinkle remaining 1 cup of cheese on top and bake for 15 minutes longer. Turn on the broiler and broil for 1 to 2 minutes, until lightly browned in spots. Let the enchiladas stand for 20 minutes. Garnish with cilantro leaves and jalapeño slices and serve. —*Jesse Tyler Ferguson*

MAKE AHEAD

The assembled, unbaked enchiladas can be refrigerated overnight. Bring to room temperature before baking.

ROSEMARY CHICKEN WITH CORN
AND SAUSAGE FRICASSEE

(GF)

MAKES   **6 servings**

TIME   **Active 1 hr;**
       Total 2 hr 55 min

CHICKEN

- **½ cup kosher salt**
- **6 cups cold water**
- **12 chicken drumsticks**
- **½ cup extra-virgin olive oil**
- **4 large garlic cloves, chopped**
- **2 Tbsp. finely chopped rosemary**
- **1 Tbsp. finely grated lemon zest**
- **1 tsp. crushed red pepper**

FRICASSEE

- **6 scallions**
- **3 Tbsp. extra-virgin olive oil**
- **1 medium sweet onion, halved and thinly sliced lengthwise**
- **Kosher salt**
- **4 oz. hot Italian sausage, casings removed**
- **3 cups fresh corn kernels (from 4 ears)**
- **2 cups cherry tomatoes (10 oz.), halved**
- **¼ lb. sugar snap peas, halved lengthwise**
- **½ cup basil leaves**

1 MAKE THE CHICKEN In a large bowl, whisk the salt with 6 cups of cold water until dissolved. Add the chicken and refrigerate for 45 minutes. Remove the chicken and pat dry with paper towels. Wipe out the bowl.

2 In the same bowl, whisk the olive oil with the garlic, rosemary, lemon zest and crushed red pepper. Add the chicken and turn to coat, rubbing some of the marinade under the skin. Marinate the chicken at room temperature for 45 minutes.

3 Light a grill or preheat a grill pan. Grill the chicken over moderate heat, turning occasionally, until lightly charred and an instant-read thermometer inserted in the thickest part of each leg registers 165°, about 25 minutes.

4 MEANWHILE, MAKE THE FRICASSEE In a large cast-iron skillet, cook the scallions over high heat until charred on the bottom, about 3 minutes. Transfer to a work surface and cut into 1-inch lengths. In the same skillet, heat olive oil. Add onion and a generous pinch of salt and cook over moderately high heat, stirring occasionally, until softened and lightly browned, about 6 minutes. Add sausage and cook, breaking up meat with a wooden spoon, until nearly cooked through, 6 to 8 minutes. Add corn and tomatoes and cook, stirring occasionally, until corn is crisp-tender and tomatoes are softened, about 5 minutes. Stir in the snap peas and cook until crisp-tender, about 2 minutes longer. Stir in the basil and scallions and season with salt. Transfer the fricassee to a platter, top with the chicken and serve. —*Nina Compton*

MAKE AHEAD

You can grill the chicken and make the fricassee ahead and store in the refrigerator in separate containers. Before serving, reheat broth, top the fricassee with the chicken and garnish with basil.

CHICKEN POTPIE

MAKES   **One 9-inch pie**

TIME   **Active 1 hr 20 min;
Total 3 hr 40 min**

CRUST

2½ cups all-purpose flour

2 Tbsp. sugar

1 tsp. kosher salt

**1 stick unsalted butter, cubed
and chilled**

**½ cup schmaltz (see Note),
scooped into tablespoons
and frozen**

¼ cup plus 2 Tbsp. cold buttermilk

FILLING

**2 lbs. skin-on, bone-in chicken
parts**

Kosher salt

White pepper

¼ cup canola oil

**6 cups chicken stock or
low-sodium broth**

½ stick unsalted butter

1 medium onion, finely chopped

**1 large carrot, cut into ⅓-inch
pieces**

**1 celery rib, cut into ⅓-inch
pieces**

2 garlic cloves, minced

¼ cup all-purpose flour

1¼ cups whole milk

¼ cup minced parsley

2 Tbsp. minced chives

2 tsp. minced thyme

1 Tbsp. apple cider vinegar

**1 large egg beaten with 1 Tbsp.
of water**

1 MAKE THE CRUST In a food processor, pulse the flour with the sugar and salt. Add the butter and schmaltz and pulse until the mixture resembles a coarse meal. Drizzle the buttermilk over the top and pulse until the dough just starts to come together. Turn out onto a work surface, gather any crumbs and gently knead the dough 2 or 3 times until smooth. Divide in half and flatten each piece into a disk. Wrap in plastic and refrigerate until firm, 1 hour.

2 Preheat the oven to 375°. On a floured work surface, roll out 1 disk of dough to a 12-inch round, about ¼ inch thick. Ease the round into a 9-inch deep-dish pie plate. Trim the overhang to ½ inch. Line the crust with parchment paper and fill with pie weights or dried beans. Bake for about 20 minutes, until the crust is just set. Remove the parchment paper and bake for 5 to 7 minutes longer, until lightly browned. Let cool completely.

3 MEANWHILE, MAKE THE FILLING Season the chicken with salt and pepper. In a large saucepan, heat 2 tablespoons of the oil until shimmering. Add the chicken and cook over moderately high heat, turning occasionally, until browned, about 7 minutes. Add the chicken stock and bring to a boil. Simmer over moderately low heat, turning the chicken occasionally, until an instant-read thermometer inserted in the thickest piece registers 160°, about 15 minutes. Using tongs, transfer the chicken to a plate and let cool. Boil the stock over high heat until reduced to 1 cup, 15 to 20 minutes more; transfer the stock to a small heatproof bowl. Discard the chicken skin and bones, then cut the meat into 1-inch pieces. Wipe out the saucepan.

4 In the saucepan, melt the butter in the remaining 2 tablespoons of oil. Add the onion, carrot, celery, garlic and a generous pinch of salt. Cook over moderate heat, stirring occasionally, until softened, about 10 minutes. Add the chicken and flour and cook, stirring, until the vegetables and chicken are evenly coated. Gradually stir in the milk and reduced stock and bring to a boil. Simmer over moderately low heat, stirring occasionally, until thickened, 5 to 7 minutes. Stir in the parsley, chives, thyme and vinegar and season with salt and pepper. Let cool completely, about 30 minutes.

5 On a floured work surface, roll out the other disk of dough to a 12-inch round. Scrape the filling into the cooled pie shell and cover with the top crust. Trim the overhang to 1 inch and crimp the edge decoratively, sealing it to the bottom crust. Brush with the egg wash and cut slits in the top to vent steam. Bake the potpie for 40 minutes, until the crust is browned and the filling is bubbling. Let stand for 10 minutes before serving. —*Matt Bolus*

NOTE

Schmaltz, rendered chicken fat, can be found in the freezer or refrigerated section of the grocery store or at your local butcher.

"A hearty strata is often my choice to take to a brunch or potluck dinner. It's a versatile dish because you can use whatever leftover bread you have on hand and substitute other types of meat and cheese."

—ANNE CAIN, BOOKS EDITOR

HAM AND SAUSAGE STRATA

MAKES **12 servings**

TIME **Active 1 hr;**
Total 6 hr 30 min

Two ½-lb. baguettes,
cut into ½-inch dice

2 **Tbsp. unsalted butter, plus**
more for greasing

2 **Tbsp extra-virgin olive oil**

1 **large onion, finely chopped**

3 **celery ribs, peeled and cut into**
½-inch pieces

1 **jalapeño, seeded and minced**

¾ **lb. sweet Italian sausages**
(about 4), casings removed

1 **lb. smoked baked ham, cut into**
⅓-inch pieces

1 **andouille sausage (about**
4 oz.), finely diced

1 **Tbsp. thyme leaves**

1 **Tbsp. kosher salt**

½ **tsp. freshly ground pepper**

½ **lb. Gruyère cheese, cut into**
⅓-inch pieces

½ **cup freshly grated Parmesan**
cheese

2 **large eggs, lightly beaten**

4 **cups chicken stock**

1½ **cups half-and-half or whole milk**

1 Preheat the oven to 375°. Spread the bread on 2 large baking sheets and bake in the upper and lower thirds of the oven for 10 minutes, or until golden and crisp; shift the pans from top to bottom and front to back halfway through.

2 In a large enameled cast-iron casserole, melt the butter in the olive oil. Add the onion, celery and jalapeño and cook over moderate heat, stirring, until softened, 6 minutes. Add the Italian sausages and cook, breaking up any large pieces, until no longer pink, 8 minutes. Stir in the ham, andouille, thyme and salt and pepper. Transfer to a large bowl to cool.

3 Add the Gruyère, Parmesan and bread to the meat. In another bowl, whisk the eggs, stock and half-and-half and add to the meat and bread mixture; toss until evenly mixed and moistened. Cover the strata with plastic wrap and refrigerate for at least 4 hours or overnight.

4 Preheat the oven to 350°. Butter a 4-quart glass or ceramic baking dish. Transfer the strata to the prepared baking dish and smooth the surface. Butter a large sheet of foil and cover the baking dish with it. Bake the strata in the center of the oven for 30 minutes, or until barely set. Remove the foil and bake for 45 minutes longer, or until the strata is bubbling and the top is golden and crusty. Let cool for 15 minutes before serving. —*Grace Parisi*

MAKE AHEAD

The baked strata can be kept at room temperature for up to 2 hours. Reheat before serving.

SESAME BAGEL BREAKFAST CASSEROLE

MAKES 8 to 10 servings

TIME Active 45 min;
          Total 6 hr 30 min

- 2 Tbsp. extra-virgin olive oil plus more for greasing
- 10 large eggs
- 2½ cups half-and-half
- 6 oil-packed Calabrian chiles—drained, seeded and minced
- Kosher salt
- Freshly ground pepper
- 1 lb. day-old sesame bagels (3 large), cut into 1-inch pieces (9 cups)
- 10 oz. button mushrooms, stemmed and sliced ¼ inch thick
- 1 small bunch of curly kale, stemmed and chopped (5 cups)
- 1 pint cherry tomatoes, quartered
- ¼ cup finely chopped basil leaves
- 2 Tbsp. minced rosemary
- 2 scallions, thinly sliced
- 8 oz. fresh mozzarella cheese, shredded
- 1 cup shredded Parmigiano-Reggiano cheese (2 oz.)

1 Lightly grease a 3-quart oval baking pan. In a large bowl, whisk the eggs with half-and-half, chiles, 2 teaspoons of salt and 1 teaspoon of pepper. Stir in the bagel pieces and let stand at room temperature for 20 minutes.

2 Meanwhile, in a large skillet, heat the 2 tablespoons of olive oil. Add the mushrooms and kale and season with salt and pepper. Cook over moderately high heat, stirring occasionally, until tender and wilted, about 7 minutes. Stir in the cherry tomatoes, basil and rosemary and cook until the tomatoes start to soften, about 3 minutes. Remove the skillet from the heat and stir in the scallions; season with salt and pepper. Let cool slightly.

3 Fold the vegetables and shredded cheeses into the bagel mixture, then transfer to the prepared baking pan. Cover with plastic wrap and refrigerate for at least 4 hours or overnight.

4 Preheat the oven to 350°. Remove the plastic wrap and cover the baking pan with foil. Bake for 40 minutes, remove the foil and bake for 45 minutes more, or until the top is puffed and golden and a toothpick inserted in the center comes out clean. Let stand for 20 minutes before serving. —*Anna Painter*

MAKE AHEAD

The casserole can be prepared through Step 3 and refrigerated overnight.

CHRISTMAS-MORNING CASSEROLE

MAKES **8 servings**

TIME **Active 40 min;
Total 1 hr 40 min plus
overnight soaking**

Butter, for greasing

2 Tbsp. extra-virgin olive oil

½ cup finely diced pepperoni
(2 oz.)

½ lb. shiitake mushrooms, stems
discarded and caps cut into
¾-inch pieces

1 medium onion, minced

1 red bell pepper, cut into ½-inch
pieces

2 tsp. kosher salt plus more
for seasoning

8 large eggs

3 cups whole milk

1 Tbsp. Dijon mustard

1 Tbsp. soy sauce

½ tsp. freshly ground pepper

¾ lb. day-old challah, sliced 1 inch
thick and cut into 1-inch dice
(10 cups)

6 oz. Black Forest ham, finely
diced (1¼ cups)

1 cup shredded Monterey Jack
cheese (¼ lb.)

1 cup shredded aged white
cheddar cheese (¼ lb.)

½ cup finely chopped scallions
plus thinly sliced scallions
for garnish

Hot sauce, for serving

1 Butter a 9-by-13-inch baking dish. In a large skillet, heat olive oil. Add pepperoni; cook over moderate heat until fat is rendered, about 3 minutes. Add the shiitake and cook until lightly browned and tender, about 5 minutes. Add the onion, bell pepper and a generous pinch of salt and cook, stirring occasionally, until softened and browned, about 7 minutes; let cool completely.

2 In a large bowl, beat the eggs with the milk, mustard, soy sauce, pepper and 2 teaspoons of salt. Add the cooled vegetable mixture, challah, ham, both cheeses and the chopped scallions and mix well. Scrape the mixture into the prepared baking dish, cover with plastic wrap and refrigerate overnight.

3 Preheat the oven to 350°. Uncover the casserole and bake for about 50 minutes, until it's just set and the top is browned. Let casserole stand for 10 minutes, then top with thinly sliced scallions and serve with hot sauce.
—*Bryan Voltaggio*

"Not just for Christmas and not just for breakfast. This classic egg and cheese casserole is packed with veggies and ham and good for breakfast, brunch or dinner anytime." —CAITLIN MURPHREE MILLER, MANAGING EDITOR

BAKED RIGATONI WITH MILK-BRAISED PORK, RICOTTA AND LEMON

MAKES   **8 servings**

TIME   **Active 45 min;**
Total 4 hr 30 min

¼ cup extra-virgin olive oil, plus
    more for greasing

One 4-lb. boneless pork
    shoulder roast

Kosher salt

Freshly ground pepper

12 garlic cloves

½ cup dry white wine

3 qts. whole milk

6 rosemary sprigs plus chopped
    rosemary for garnish

1 bay leaf

Five 3-inch strips of lemon zest

1 lb. rigatoni

2 cups fresh ricotta cheese (1 lb.)

Freshly grated pecorino cheese,
    preferably Pecorino di Fossa

1 Preheat the oven to 375°. In a large enameled cast-iron casserole, heat 2 tablespoons olive oil. Rub pork all over with remaining 2 tablespoons oil and season with salt and pepper. Add to casserole and cook over moderately high heat until browned all over, about 8 minutes; transfer to a plate. Add garlic to casserole and cook, stirring, until golden, 1 to 2 minutes. Add wine; cook until almost evaporated, about 2 minutes.

2 Add milk, rosemary sprigs, bay leaf and lemon zest to the casserole and bring to a simmer. Add pork and braise in the oven for about 3 hours, until meat is very tender. Let pork cool in the casserole to room temperature.

3 Transfer cooled pork to a work surface and cut in half. Coarsely chop 1 piece; reserve the remaining pork for another use. Working in 2 batches, puree the cooking liquid in a blender until smooth. Strain through a fine sieve, pressing down on the solids. Discard solids.

4 Increase oven temperature to 425°. Lightly grease a 3½- to 4-quart baking dish. In a pot of salted boiling water, cook pasta until barely al dente. Drain and transfer to a large bowl. Add chopped pork and 3 cups of the strained cooking liquid, season with salt and pepper and toss to coat. Transfer pasta to the prepared baking dish and dollop ricotta on top. Cover with foil and bake for about 20 minutes, until the pasta is tender. Uncover and bake for about 15 minutes longer, until golden on top. Garnish with pepper and chopped rosemary. Serve with grated pecorino. —*Ryan Hardy; Tim Caspare*

MAKE AHEAD

You can make the casserole ahead and reheat gently before serving. Sprinkle with pecorino cheese just before serving.

HARISSA-SPICED CASSOULET

MAKES **10 to 12 servings**

TIME **Active 1 hr 30 min;
Total 3 hr plus
overnight soaking**

½ lb. **thick-cut bacon, finely
chopped**

1 **large onion, finely diced**

1 **celery rib, finely diced**

2 **medium carrots, finely diced,
plus 2 large carrots, cut into
2½-inch lengths**

14 oz. **dried cannellini beans
(2 cups), soaked overnight
and drained**

Kosher salt

1½ tsp. **cumin seeds**

1½ tsp. **coriander seeds**

1½ tsp. **yellow mustard seeds**

1 tsp. **smoked paprika**

¾ tsp. **crushed red pepper**

¼ cup plus 1 Tbsp. **extra-virgin
olive oil**

Twelve 2-oz. merguez sausages

2 **large sweet potatoes (1¼ lbs.),
peeled and cut into 2½-inch
pieces**

3 **turnips (¾ lb.), peeled and cut
into 2½-inch pieces**

Freshly ground black pepper

4 oz. **rustic peasant bread, crusts
removed, bread cut into ¼-inch
dice (2 cups)**

2 Tbsp. **minced parsley**

1 tsp. **grated lemon zest**

Plain yogurt, for serving

1 In a large enameled cast-iron casserole, cook the bacon over moderately high heat, stirring occasionally, until the fat is rendered. Add the onion, celery and diced carrots and cook, stirring occasionally, until beginning to soften, about 8 minutes. Add the beans, cover with water and bring to a boil. Reduce heat to moderately low and simmer beans until al dente, about 20 minutes. Remove from the heat, add a generous pinch of salt and let stand for 30 minutes. Drain the beans, bacon and vegetables and transfer to a bowl; reserve 2 cups of the cooking liquid.

2 Meanwhile, preheat the oven to 350°. In a small skillet, toast the cumin, coriander and mustard seeds over moderate heat, shaking the pan, until fragrant and the mustard seeds begin to pop, 3 to 5 minutes. Transfer to a spice grinder and let cool. Add the smoked paprika and crushed red pepper and grind the harissa blend into a powder.

3 Wipe out the casserole and heat 2 tablespoons of the olive oil in it. Add the merguez and cook over moderate heat, until lightly browned all over, about 5 minutes. Transfer to a plate. Do not wipe out the casserole.

4 Add the sweet potatoes, turnips and large carrots to the casserole. Season with salt and black pepper and cook over moderately high heat, stirring occasionally, until the vegetables begin to soften, 5 minutes. Add the harissa spice blend and cook until fragrant, about 2 minutes. Stir in the bean mixture and the reserved 2 cups of cooking liquid and bring just to a simmer. Arrange the merguez on top. Cover and bake the cassoulet for about 1 hour, until the beans are tender and most of the liquid has been absorbed. Remove from the oven and uncover the cassoulet.

5 Preheat the broiler. In a bowl, toss the bread, parsley, lemon zest and the remaining 3 tablespoons of olive oil; season with salt and black pepper. Sprinkle the bread over the cassoulet and broil until golden and crisp. Let the cassoulet stand for 10 minutes before serving. Pass yogurt at the table.
—*Gavin Kaysen*

NOTE

Harissa is a North African blend of cumin, coriander and other spices.

MAKE AHEAD

You can make the cassoulet ahead through Step 4 and refrigerate overnight. Bring to room temperature, then top with bread and broil just before serving.

GARLICKY LAMB AND RICE PILAF

(GF)

MAKES **6 to 8 servings**

TIME **Total 1 hr 45 min**

- 6 oz. lamb fat, cut into ½-inch strips (see Note)
  Kosher salt
  Freshly ground pepper
- 2 lbs. boneless leg of lamb, cut into ¾-inch cubes
- 2 large yellow onions, chopped
- 20 garlic cloves
- 3 medium carrots, shredded
- 2 Tbsp. cumin seeds
- 2 Tbsp. za'atar
- 7 cups low-sodium beef broth
- 2 cups long-grain white rice
  Chopped parsley, for serving

1 In a large enameled cast-iron casserole, cook the lamb fat over moderately low heat until rendered and the cracklings are golden brown, about 10 minutes. Remove the cracklings with a slotted spoon and drain on paper towels. Season with salt. Leave the fat in the casserole.

2 In a medium bowl, season the lamb with 2 teaspoons of salt and 1 teaspoon of pepper. Add one-third of the lamb to the casserole and cook over moderate heat until browned, 5 to 7 minutes. Using a slotted spoon, transfer the browned meat to a plate. Repeat with the remaining lamb.

3 Add the onions to the casserole and season with salt and pepper. Cook, stirring occasionally, until golden brown, 8 to 10 minutes. Stir in the garlic and cook until fragrant and lightly browned, 2 to 3 minutes. Add the shredded carrots to the casserole along with the cumin and za'atar and cook, stirring occasionally, until the carrots are just softened, about 2 minutes.

4 In a saucepan, bring the beef broth to a simmer. Return the lamb and any accumulated juices to the casserole along with the rice. Add 2 cups of the broth to the rice and cook, stirring, until it is absorbed, about 4 minutes. Repeat with another 2 cups of broth, cooking until absorbed. Stir in the remaining broth. Cover and simmer over moderately low heat until the rice is tender, about 10 minutes. Remove the casserole from the heat and let stand uncovered for 10 minutes before serving. Garnish with the cracklings and parsley and serve. —*Andrew Zimmern*

NOTE

Ask your butcher for lamb fat.

MAKE AHEAD

You can make the casserole ahead and reheat gently before serving.

"The homemade spice mix and crème fraîche in the topping are the keys to updgrading a savory taco pie. You can make it up to two days ahead and serve with a red wine that has substantial body, like a Washington state Syrah." —RAY ISLE, EXECUTIVE WINE EDITOR

TACO PIE

MAKES	One 9-inch pie
TIME	Active 25 min; Total 2 hr 10 min

CRUST

5½ Tbsp. cold unsalted butter, cut into ½-inch cubes

2½ cups plus 1 Tbsp. all-purpose flour

1½ tsp. baking powder

1 tsp. kosher salt

½ cup plus 1 Tbsp. milk

FILLING

2 Tbsp. chili powder

1 Tbsp. ground cumin

Kosher salt

1 tsp. onion powder

1 tsp. cornstarch

½ tsp. cayenne

½ tsp. ground coriander

1 Tbsp. unsalted butter

1 lb. ground beef

⅔ cup water

1¼ cups crème fraîche

4½ oz. cheddar cheese, grated

1 large egg, beaten

2 Tbsp. mayonnaise

Freshly ground pepper

1 MAKE THE CRUST In a food processor, combine the butter, flour, baking powder and salt and pulse just until the mixture resembles coarse meal. Add the milk and pulse just until the dough comes together. Press the dough evenly over the bottom and halfway up the side of a 9-inch springform pan. Cover with plastic wrap and refrigerate until firm, about 45 minutes.

2 MAKE THE FILLING In a small bowl, whisk the chili powder with the cumin, 2 teaspoons of salt, the onion powder, cornstarch, cayenne and coriander. In a medium skillet, melt the butter. Add the ground beef and cook over moderately high heat, stirring, until browned and cooked through, about 5 minutes. Add the spice blend and ⅔ cup of water and cook, stirring occasionally, until the water has evaporated, about 3 minutes. Remove from the heat.

3 Preheat the oven to 350°. In a medium bowl, whisk the crème fraîche with the cheddar, egg and mayonnaise. Season with a pinch each of salt and pepper. Set the crust on a rimmed baking sheet. Using a slotted spoon, spread the ground meat evenly over the crust and cover with the cheddar topping. Bake until the topping is set and the crust is golden brown, about 45 minutes. Let cool for 15 minutes before serving. —*Magnus Nilsson*

MAKE AHEAD

The taco pie can be refrigerated for up to 2 days. Rewarm before serving.

SHREDDED BEEF TACO BAR

BEEF SHANK TACO FILLING

- 5 **dried guajillo chiles, stemmed and seeded**
- 5 **dried ancho chiles, stemmed and seeded**
- ¼ **cup extra-virgin olive oil**
- **One 4 lb. bone-in beef shank, trimmed and tied by the butcher**
- **Kosher salt**
- **Freshly ground pepper**
- 1 **yellow onion, finely chopped**
- 5 **garlic cloves, thinly sliced**
- 2 **tsp. dried oregano**
- 2 **tsp. ground cumin**
- **Two 12-oz. bottles light Mexican beer**
- **One 28-oz. can crushed tomatoes**
- 2 **cups chicken stock or low-sodium broth**
- 2 **Tbsp. apple cider vinegar**
- 2 **Tbsp. unsalted butter**

PICKLED ONION

- 1 **cup red wine vinegar**
- ¾ **cup sugar**
- 1 **tsp. kosher salt**
- 1 **medium red onion, halved and thinly sliced**

LIME CREMA

- 1 **cup sour cream**
- 1 **tsp. finely grated lime zest plus 2 Tbsp. fresh lime juice**

SLAW

- ½ **cup mayonnaise**
- 2 **Tbsp. hot sauce**
- 1¼ **lbs. red cabbage (½ medium head), cored and very thinly sliced (6 cups)**
- **Canola oil, for brushing**
- **Warm flour tortillas, chopped cilantro and lime wedges, for serving**

1 MAKE THE FILLING Preheat the oven to 325°. In a mortar, pound chiles until finely ground. In a large enameled cast-iron casserole, heat oil. Season shank with salt and pepper. Add shank to casserole and cook over moderately high heat until browned on all sides, about 25 minutes. Transfer shank to a plate.

2 Add onion, garlic and a pinch of salt to casserole and cook over moderately high heat, stirring occasionally, until onion is beginning to brown, about 8 minutes. Add chiles, oregano and cumin and cook, stirring, until fragrant, about 1 minute. Add beer and bring to a boil, scraping up any browned bits with a wooden spoon. Cook until beer is reduced by half, about 6 minutes. Add crushed tomatoes and chicken stock and return to a boil. Return shank and any accumulated juices to casserole. Cover and braise in oven for about 3½ hours, basting with sauce every hour, until meat is very tender. Remove casserole from oven and let beef stand at room temperature in braising liquid, uncovered, until ready to grill, at least 2 hours.

3 MAKE THE PICKLED ONION In a medium bowl, whisk red wine vinegar with the sugar and salt until the sugar is dissolved. Add sliced onion, cover and let stand at room temperature, stirring occasionally, for at least 1 hour.

4 MAKE THE LIME CREMA In a small bowl, whisk sour cream, zest and juice and season with salt and pepper. Refrigerate until ready to serve.

5 MAKE THE SLAW In a large bowl, whisk mayonnaise with hot sauce; season with salt and pepper. Add red cabbage; toss to coat. Refrigerate until ready to serve.

6 Remove shank from braising liquid and transfer to a plate. Transfer braising liquid to a medium saucepan; bring to a simmer over low heat, skimming off any accumulated fat. Stir in apple cider vinegar and butter; season with salt and pepper. Keep warm.

7 Light a grill. Fold a 24-inch sheet of foil in half and brush lightly with canola oil. Set the foil oiled side up on grill. Place cooled shank on foil, cover and grill over moderately high heat, basting with warm braising liquid every 10 minutes, until shank is lightly charred and warmed through, 35 to 40 minutes. Transfer to a platter and let rest for 10 minutes. Discard strings and shred; serve warm with pickled onion, crema, slaw, flour tortillas, cilantro, lime wedges and remaining braising liquid. —*Rob Levitt*

MAKE AHEAD

The braised shank can be refrigerated in the braising liquid in the casserole for up to 4 days. Rewarm gently over moderately low heat, covered, before proceeding. The pickled red onion can be refrigerated for up to 2 weeks.

> "Setting up a taco bar is a fun dinner party idea. Grill the meat and then just set out a platter of flour tortillas and bowls of fresh veggies and salsa for the toppings." —JUSTIN CHAPPLE, CULINARY DIRECTOR

PEKING-STYLE SHORT RIB TACOS

MAKES **6 servings**

TIME **Total 45 min plus 2 hr marinating**

½ **large onion, grated on a box grater**

¼ **cup soy sauce**

2 **Tbsp. finely grated peeled fresh ginger**

1½ **Tbsp. sugar**

2 **garlic cloves, finely grated**

Kosher salt

Freshly ground pepper

3½ **lbs. flanken-style beef short ribs, cut ⅓ inch thick**

Warm small flour tortillas, for serving

Hoisin sauce, julienned cucumbers, grilled yellow squash, sliced hot red chiles, sliced scallions and lime wedges, for serving

1 In a large resealable plastic bag, mix the onion with the soy sauce, ginger, sugar, garlic and 1 teaspoon each of salt and pepper. Add the short ribs, seal the bag and turn to coat all the ribs well. Let marinate in the refrigerator for at least 2 hours or overnight.

2 Light a grill. Scrape some of the marinade off the meat. Season the ribs with salt and pepper. Grill over high heat, turning once, until lightly charred in spots, about 5 minutes total. Transfer to a platter and let rest for 2 minutes. Use scissors to snip off the bones and cut the meat into bite-size pieces. Serve in tortillas with hoisin sauce, julienned cucumbers, grilled yellow squash, sliced chiles and scallions, and lime wedges for squeezing. —*Justin Chapple*

MAKE AHEAD

You can grill the ribs and prepare the toppings ahead of time and refrigerate overnight. Reheat the meat, then assemble the tacos just before serving.

BACON-CHEESEBURGER SLIDERS
WITH HICKORY SAUCE

MAKES 12 servings

TIME Active 1 hr; Total 1 hr 30 min

HICKORY SAUCE

- 2 Tbsp. canola oil
- 1 cup finely chopped yellow onion
- ¾ cup ketchup
- ⅓ cup apple cider vinegar
- ¼ cup light brown sugar
- 2 Tbsp. Worcestershire sauce
- 2 tsp. freshly ground black pepper
- ½ tsp. crushed red pepper
  Kosher salt

SLIDERS

- 12 slices of bacon
- 1 sweet onion, thinly sliced
- ¼ cup cane or apple cider vinegar
  Kosher salt
- 4 Tbsp. unsalted butter, melted
- 2¼ lbs. ground beef, formed into twelve ½-inch-thick patties
  Freshly ground pepper
- 1½ cups shredded sharp cheddar cheese (6 oz.)
  Mayonnaise
- 12 slider buns, toasted
  Sliced tomatoes, pickles and shredded lettuce, for serving

 MAKE THE HICKORY SAUCE In a medium saucepan, heat the oil. Add the onion and cook over moderate heat, stirring occasionally, until golden brown, about 10 minutes. Add the ketchup, vinegar, sugar, Worcestershire sauce, black pepper and red pepper and cook, stirring occasionally, until thick, about 5 minutes. Transfer the sauce to a blender and puree until smooth; season with salt. Transfer to a medium bowl and let cool to room temperature.

2 MAKE THE SLIDERS Preheat the oven to 400°. Arrange the bacon on a rack set over a baking sheet. Bake until golden and crisp, 25 minutes. Transfer to a paper towel-lined plate to drain, then break the slices in half. In a medium bowl, toss the onion with the vinegar and a pinch of salt.

3 In a large ovenproof skillet, heat 2 tablespoons of the butter. Season the beef patties with salt and pepper and add half of them to the skillet. Cook until browned on the bottom, about 2 minutes. Flip, then top each with 1 tablespoon of the hickory sauce and 2 tablespoons of the cheese. Transfer the skillet to the oven and cook until the cheese melts and the patties are just cooked through, 1 to 2 minutes. Transfer the burgers to a work surface, cover with foil and repeat with the remaining butter, patties, hickory sauce and cheese.

4 Spread mayonnaise on the buns and top with the sliders, tomatoes, bacon, pickled onion, pickles and shredded lettuce. Close the sliders and serve with the remaining hickory sauce on the side. —*John Besh; Chris Lusk*

MAKE AHEAD

If you're taking the sliders to a potluck, prepare recipe through Step 3, and reheat before serving. Place bowls of mayonnaise, tomatoes, pickles and lettuce on the table and let guests top their own sliders.

FLATBREAD LASAGNA

MAKES **6 to 8 serving**

TIME **Active 20 min;**
       Total 1 hr 40 min

- 1 **lb. hot Italian sausages,
  casings removed**
- 1 **Tbsp. extra-virgin olive oil**
- 1½ **cups ricotta cheese**
  Kosher salt
  Freshly ground pepper
- 3 **cups jarred marinara sauce**
- 4 **pocketless pitas or naan**
- 2 **cups shredded mozzarella
  (12 oz.)**

1 Preheat the oven to 350°. In a skillet, cook sausages in oil over moderately high heat, breaking up meat, until browned. Season ricotta with salt and pepper. Spread ½ cup of marinara sauce in a deep-dish pie plate. Top with 1 flatbread, one-third of the sausage and ½ cup each of the ricotta and mozzarella. Repeat layering twice. Add ½ cup of sauce and the last flatbread. Top with remaining 1 cup sauce and ½ cup mozzarella.

2 Cover the lasagna with foil and bake for 30 minutes. Uncover and bake 30 minutes longer. Let cool for 20 minutes and serve. —*Grace Parisi*

GROUND BEEF LASAGNA

MAKES **6 to 8 servings**

TIME **Active 30 min;**
       Total 1 hr 55 min

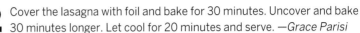 PAGE 146

- 2 **Tbsp. extra-virgin olive oil,
  plus more for greasing**
- 1 **medium onion, chopped**
- 5 **garlic cloves, minced**
  Kosher salt
  Freshly ground pepper
- 1½ **lbs. ground beef**
- ¼ **cup tomato paste**
- 1 **(28-to 32-oz.) can whole
  tomatoes in juice**
- 2 **tsp. dried oregano, crumbled**
- 12 **no-boil lasagna noodles**
- 2 **cups ricotta cheese**
- 1 **lb. fresh mozzarella balls, sliced**
  Fresh oregano, for garnish

1 Preheat the oven to 375°F. Grease a 9-by-13-inch baking dish and set aside. In a large pot, heat oil over medium-high heat until hot, then stir in onion, garlic, 1 teaspoon salt and ¾ teaspoon pepper and cook, stirring occasionally, until golden, about 6 minutes. Stir in beef, breaking up lumps with a spatula and cook, until browned, about 6 minutes. Stir in tomato paste and cook, stirring, 3 minutes. Stir in tomatoes with their juice and oregano, and boil, breaking up tomatoes with a spatula until sauce is slightly thickened, about 10 minutes. Remove sauce from the heat. Season with salt and pepper.

2 Spread 1 cup sauce in bottom of prepared dish; top with 3 noodles and another layer of sauce. Add 3 noodles and top evenly with sauce. Dollop half of ricotta and half of mozzarella evenly over sauce. Top with another layer of 3 noodles, then sauce, then remaining 3 noodles and sauce. Top with remaining ricotta and mozzarella.

3 Cover dish with foil and bake until filling is bubbling, about 45 minutes. Uncover and continue to bake until cheese is browned in places, about 30 minutes longer. Let stand 10 minutes before serving. Garnish with fresh oregano. —*Ian Knauer*

MAKE AHEAD

The unbaked lasagna can be refrigerated overnight. Bring to room temperature before baking.

LEMON-GARLIC-MARINATED FLANK STEAK

MAKES 6 to 8 servings

TIME Active 40 min; Total 2 hr 15 min

- **20 garlic cloves, peeled**
- **2¼ cups extra-virgin olive oil**
- **Kosher salt**
- **Freshly ground pepper**
- **Two 1¼-lb. flank steaks**
- **1½ cups fresh lemon juice (from about 8 lemons)**
- **2 Tbsp. dried oregano**

1 In a small saucepan, cover garlic with 1½ cups olive oil and cook over low heat until garlic is tender and golden brown, 35 to 40 minutes. Strain the garlic through a fine sieve set over a small bowl; reserve the garlicky olive oil for another use. In a small bowl, mash the garlic with 1½ tablespoons of salt and 1½ teaspoons of pepper. Rub 3 tablespoons of the garlic paste all over the flank steaks.

2 In a medium bowl, whisk the lemon juice with the remaining ¾ cup of olive oil and the oregano. Place the steaks in a 9-by-13-inch baking dish and coat with 1½ cups of the lemony marinade. Let stand at room temperature for 1 hour.

3 Light a grill. Remove the steaks from the marinade, pat dry and season with salt and pepper. Discard the marinade. Grill the steaks over moderately high heat, turning once, until lightly charred and an instant-read thermometer inserted in the thickest part registers 125°, 8 to 10 minutes. Dip the grilled steaks in the remaining marinade in the bowl and transfer to a carving board. Spread the remaining garlic paste on the steaks and let stand for 5 minutes. Thinly slice the meat against the grain and serve. —*Jimmy Bannos, Jr.*

MAKE AHEAD

Both the garlic rub and the marinade can be refrigerated overnight. Bring to room temperature before using.

GRILLED AND CHILLED BEEF
WITH BUTTERMILK-HORSERADISH SAUCE

(GF)

MAKES **8 servings**

TIME **Active 45 min;
Total 2 hr 50 min plus
overnight chilling**

- 2 **Tbsp. extra-virgin olive oil**
- 3 **garlic cloves, minced**
- 1 **Tbsp. ground fennel**
- 1 **Tbsp. minced thyme leaves**
  Kosher salt
  Freshly ground pepper
  **One 3½-lb. center-cut beef
  tenderloin roast, tied**
- 1 **cup buttermilk**
- ½ **cup mayonnaise**
- 2 **Tbsp. freshly grated horseradish
  plus more for serving**

1 In a small bowl, whisk the oil, garlic, fennel, thyme, 1 tablespoon of salt and 2 teaspoons of pepper. Rub the paste over the beef and bring to room temperature, 1 hour.

2 Light a grill. Grill the roast over moderate heat, turning often, until charred and an instant-read thermometer inserted in the thickest part registers 118°, 35 to 40 minutes. Transfer to a carving board, tent with foil and let cool for 30 minutes. Wrap the roast tightly in foil and let cool completely, then refrigerate overnight.

3 In a bowl, whisk the buttermilk, mayonnaise and the 2 tablespoons of horseradish. Season with salt and pepper. Carve the roast into ¼-inch-thick slices and serve cold with the buttermilk sauce and more freshly grated horseradish. —*Justin Chapple*

MAKE AHEAD

Grill the roast, make the sauce and refrigerate both overnight. Carve the beef just before serving and serve with the sauce.

"Everyone usually thinks about serving grilled beef tenderloin hot, but it's also perfect for refrigerating and serving cold, especially during the summer. I like to serve it with a cool, creamy horseradish–spiked buttermilk sauce." —JUSTIN CHAPPLE, CULINARY DIRECTOR

GRILLED FLANK STEAK SANDWICHES

MAKES **8 servings**

TIME **Total 40 min plus overnight marinating**

One 1¾-lb. flank steak
1 **Tbsp. Dijon mustard**
¼ **cup dry red wine**
¼ **cup olive oil**
4 **large garlic cloves**
½ **tsp. finely chopped thyme**
½ **cup mayonnaise**
1 **tsp. fresh lemon juice**
Kosher salt
Freshly ground pepper
8 **rosemary focaccia or other rolls, split**
½ **lb. sliced imported provolone or Fontina cheese**
8 **lettuce leaves**

1 Brush the flank steak on both sides with the mustard. Put the steak in a sturdy resealable plastic bag and add the wine. Seal the bag, pressing out any air, and refrigerate overnight. Drain the steak, pat dry and bring to room temperature before grilling.

2 Meanwhile, in a small saucepan, combine the olive oil and garlic and cook over low heat until the garlic is golden and soft, about 15 minutes. Using a slotted spoon, transfer the garlic to a small bowl; reserve the garlic oil. Add the thyme to the garlic and mash to a paste. Stir in the mayonnaise and lemon juice and season with salt and pepper.

3 Light a charcoal grill or preheat a cast-iron grill pan. Brush the steak with the reserved garlic oil, season liberally with salt and pepper and grill over moderate heat for about 15 minutes, turning once, for medium-rare meat. Transfer the steak to a cutting board to rest for 5 minutes. Thinly slice the meat across the grain on the diagonal.

4 Spread the garlic mayonnaise on the rolls and top with the flank steak, cheese and lettuce. Cut the sandwiches in half and serve. —*Michael Kramer*

MAKE AHEAD

The sandwiches can be made 6 hours ahead.

GRILLED SKIRT STEAK
WITH GREEN SRIRACHA

(GF)

MAKES **20 servings**

TIME **Active 25 min; Total 1 hr**

- 3 **large poblano chiles**
- 2 **serrano chiles, stemmed**
- 3 **large peeled garlic cloves, smashed**
- 2 **loose cups basil leaves**
- 2 **loose cups mint leaves**
- 1½ **cups snipped chives**
- 1 **cup shredded unsweetened coconut**
- ½ **cup chopped cilantro**
- ½ **cup thinly sliced fresh ginger**
- ½ **tsp. ground turmeric**
- 4 **kaffir lime leaves, shredded**
- 1 **lemongrass stalk—tender inner bulb, bottom 4 inches peeled and thinly sliced**
- 1 **cup canola oil plus more for brushing**
- ¼ **cup plus 2 Tbsp. fresh lime juice**
  Kosher salt
- 5 **lbs. skirt steak, cut into 4-inch pieces**

1 Roast the poblanos directly over a gas flame, turning, until charred and tender. Transfer to a bowl, cover with plastic wrap and let cool. Peel, core and seed the poblanos, then transfer to a blender. Add the serranos, garlic, basil, mint, chives, coconut, cilantro, ginger turmeric, lime leaves, and lemongrass and pulse to chop. With the machine on, add 1 cup of oil and puree. Add the lime juice and season with salt.

2 Light a grill. Brush the steaks with oil and season with salt. Oil the grill grates and grill the steaks in batches over high heat, turning once or twice, until the meat is lightly charred and medium-rare, 5 to 6 minutes. Transfer the steaks to a carving board and let rest for 5 minutes before slicing across the grain. Serve the steak with the green Sriracha. —*Susan Feniger*

MAKE AHEAD

The steak can be grilled earlier in the day and refrigerated. The green Sriracha can be refrigerated for up to 3 days.

desserts

CARAMEL LAYER CAKE

Ⓥ

MAKES **16 to 20 servings**

TIME **Active 1 hr 10 min;**
Total 3 hr 55 min

CAKE

- **2 sticks unsalted butter, softened, plus more for greasing**
- **4 cups all-purpose flour plus more for dusting**
- **2 Tbsp. baking powder**
- **2 tsp. kosher salt**
- **½ tsp. baking soda**
- **2½ cups sugar**
- **1 vanilla bean, split and seeds scraped**
- **4 large eggs**
- **3 cups buttermilk**

CARAMEL FROSTING

- **3 sticks unsalted butter**
- **3 cups sugar**
- **1½ cups buttermilk**
- **1 Tbsp. baking soda**
- **1 tsp. pure vanilla extract**

1 MAKE THE CAKE Preheat the oven to 350°. Butter and flour two 10-inch round cake pans and line the bottoms with parchment paper. In a bowl, whisk the flour, baking powder, salt and baking soda. In the bowl of a stand mixer fitted with the paddle, beat the 2 sticks of butter with the sugar and vanilla seeds at medium speed until fluffy, 3 minutes. Beat in the eggs 1 at a time until incorporated, then beat until very pale and billowy, 3 minutes. At low speed, alternately beat in the dry ingredients and buttermilk until just combined.

2 Divide the batter between the pans. Bake for 35 minutes, until the cakes are golden and a toothpick inserted in the centers comes out clean. Transfer to a rack; let cool in the pans for 30 minutes. Unmold the cakes, peel off the parchment and let cool. Place 1 cake layer on a cake stand or serving platter.

3 MAKE THE FROSTING In a large, heavy-bottomed Dutch oven, melt the butter over moderately high heat. Stir in the sugar, buttermilk and baking soda. Cook, stirring constantly, as the mixture foams up, about 5 to 7 minutes. Continue cooking, stirring steadily, until the caramel mixture is very dark brown and reaches 240° on a candy thermometer, about 15 to 20 minutes. Carefully pour the mixture into the bowl of a stand mixer fitted with the paddle, add the vanilla and beat at low speed for 3 minutes, until thickened but still pourable. Use the frosting immediately.

4 Working quickly, scrape about 1 cup of the Caramel Frosting onto the cake on the stand and spread it to the edge. Top with the second cake layer. Pour the remaining frosting on top; quickly spread it over and around the cake to cover completely. Let the frosting cool for at least 2 hours before serving. —Lisa Donovan

VARIATION

Caramel-Buttercream Frosting Combine 1 cup granulated sugar and ⅓ cup water in a small saucepan over medium-high heat. Cook, stirring often, until sugar dissolves. Bring to a boil; cook, without stirring, but swirling pan occasionally, until mixture is deep amber, about 10 minutes. Remove from heat and quickly add ⅓ cup heavy cream in a thin, steady stream, stirring constantly with a wooden spoon. Add ¼ cup chilled unsalted butter cut into ½-inch pieces, stirring until smooth. Transfer caramel to a bowl to cool completely, about 2 hours.

Using a hand mixer, beat 1½ cups softened unsalted butter at medium speed until creamy, about 3 minutes. Stir in 1 teaspoon vanilla and ¼ teaspoon salt. Gradually add 2 cups powdered sugar, beating on low until smooth, about 2 minutes. Add the caramel, beating on medium speed until mixture is combined, about 2 minutes. Reduce speed to low and gradually add 2 more cups powdered sugar, beating until combined. Proceed with frosting the cake as directed above. —F&W Test Kitchen 📷 PAGE 203

PUMPKIN LAYER CAKE
WITH MASCARPONE FROSTING

Ⓥ

MAKES **10 to 12 servings**

TIME **Active 50 min; Total 3 hr**

CAKE

- **Unsalted butter, for greasing**
- **3 cups all-purpose flour plus more for dusting**
- **2 Tbsp. ground cinnamon**
- **1½ Tbsp. ground ginger**
- **1½ tsp. baking soda**
- **1 tsp. baking powder**
- **1½ tsp. kosher salt**
- **4 large eggs**
- **1½ cups packed light brown sugar**
- **One 15-oz. can pumpkin puree**
- **1 cup canola oil**

FROSTING

- **1½ sticks unsalted butter, softened**
- **3 cups confectioners' sugar**
- **1½ tsp. pure vanilla extract**
- **Kosher salt**
- **1½ cups mascarpone cheese**

1 MAKE THE CAKE Preheat the oven to 350°. Butter two 9-inch round cake pans and line the bottoms with parchment paper. Butter the paper and dust with flour, tapping out the excess.

2 In a medium bowl, whisk the 3 cups of all-purpose flour with the cinnamon, ginger, baking soda, baking powder and salt.

3 In a large bowl, using a hand mixer, beat the eggs with the brown sugar, pumpkin and oil at medium-high speed until blended. At low speed, beat in the dry ingredients.

4 Scrape the batter into the prepared pans and bake in the center of the oven for about 40 minutes, until a toothpick inserted in the center of the cakes comes out clean. Let the cakes cool in the pans for 30 minutes, then invert onto a rack to cool completely. Peel off the parchment paper.

5 MEANWHILE, MAKE THE FROSTING In a large bowl, using a hand mixer, beat the butter with the confectioners' sugar, vanilla and a pinch of salt until smooth. Add the mascarpone and beat at high speed just until smooth; do not overbeat. Refrigerate the frosting until just set, about 30 minutes.

6 Set 1 cake layer on a platter. Spread ¾ cup of the frosting on top and cover with the second cake layer. Spread a thin layer of frosting all over the cake and refrigerate until set, about 15 minutes. Spread the remaining frosting over the top and side of the cake. Refrigerate until firm, at least 30 minutes, before serving. —*Justin Chapple*

MAKE AHEAD

The cake can be refrigerated for up to 3 days.

APPLESAUCE-CHOCOLATE CHIP BUNDT CAKE

MAKES **12 servings**

TIME **Active 15 min; Total 2 hr**

1 **stick unsalted butter, melted, plus more for greasing**

2½ **cups all-purpose flour, plus more for dusting**

1½ **cups granulated sugar**

2 **tsp. baking soda**

2 **tsp. cinnamon**

1 **tsp. ground cardamom**

1 **tsp. salt**

½ **tsp. ground cloves**

½ **tsp. pepper**

2 **cups unsweetened applesauce**

2 **large eggs, lightly beaten**

½ **cup vegetable oil**

One 12-oz. bag semisweet chocolate chips

Confectioners' sugar, for dusting

Crème fraîche, for serving

1 Preheat the oven to 350°. Butter and flour a 12-cup Bundt pan. In a large bowl, whisk the 2½ cups of flour with the granulated sugar, baking soda, cinnamon, cardamom, salt, cloves and pepper. Whisk in the applesauce, eggs, oil and melted butter. Fold in the chocolate chips.

2 Scrape the batter into the prepared pan. Bake for 1 hour and 15 minutes, until a toothpick inserted in the center comes out with a few crumbs attached.

3 Transfer the pan to a rack and let the cake cool for 10 minutes, then invert it onto the rack and let cool completely, about 20 minutes. Sift confectioners' sugar over the cake, slice and serve with crème fraîche. —*Kristen Donnelly*

MAKE AHEAD

The cake can be stored in an airtight container at room temperature for up to 3 days.

DEVIL'S FOOD SNACKING CAKE

(v)

MAKES	One 9-by-13-inch cake
TIME	Active 30 min; Total 2 hr 35 min

CAKE

Nonstick baking spray, for greasing

2¼ cups all-purpose flour

1⅛ tsp. baking soda

¾ tsp. kosher salt

¾ cup unsweetened Dutch-process cocoa powder

1 Tbsp. instant coffee

1½ cups boiling water

1 cup packed dark brown sugar

¾ cup buttermilk

2½ tsp. pure vanilla extract

12 Tbsp. salted butter, softened

1¾ cups granulated sugar

3 large eggs, at room temperature

GANACHE FROSTING

8 oz. bittersweet chocolate, finely chopped

1 cup heavy cream

1½ Tbsp. light corn syrup

Crispy chocolate pearls, for topping (optional; see Note)

1 MAKE THE CAKE Preheat the oven to 350°. Grease a 9-by-13-inch baking pan with baking spray and line the bottom with parchment paper.

2 In a medium bowl, whisk the flour with the baking soda and salt. In a large heatproof bowl, whisk the cocoa powder with the instant coffee, then whisk in 1½ cups of boiling water. Stir in the brown sugar and buttermilk until no lumps remain. Let cool for 5 minutes, then stir in the vanilla.

3 In a stand mixer fitted with the paddle, beat the butter at medium-high speed until lightened, about 1 minute. Beat in the granulated sugar in 3 additions, beating well after each one, until light and fluffy, about 5 minutes. Add the eggs 1 at a time, beating well after each addition. At low speed, beat in the dry ingredients and the cocoa mixture in 3 alternating additions, scraping down the side and bottom of the bowl as necessary, until just combined.

4 Scrape the batter into the prepared pan. Bake for about 35 minutes, until a toothpick inserted in the center comes out clean; rotate the pan halfway through baking. Transfer the cake to a rack and let cool for 1 hour. Run a knife around the edge of the pan, then invert the cake and remove the parchment. Let cool completely, about 30 minutes.

5 MEANWHILE, MAKE THE FROSTING Put the chocolate in the bowl of a stand mixer. In a small saucepan, bring the cream and corn syrup to a simmer. Pour the hot cream over the chocolate; let stand for 2 minutes, then whisk until smooth. Let the ganache cool until barely warm, 45 minutes. In the stand mixer fitted with the whisk, beat the ganache at medium-high speed until light and spreadable, about 2 minutes. Spread the ganache frosting over the top of the cake, top with pearls (if using) and serve. —*Umber Ahmad; Shelly Acuña Barbera*

NOTE

Crispy chocolate pearls are available at specialty food shops and from amazon.com.

MAKE AHEAD

If you're making the cake to take to a potluck, use a 9-by-13-inch baking pan with a lid. You can make the cake ahead and store covered at room temperature.

GLUTEN-FREE CHOCOLATE CHILE CAKES

(GF) (V)

MAKES 1 dozen small cupcakes

TIME Active 30 min; Total 4 hr plus 24 hr draining

- 2 cups full-fat plain probiotic yogurt
- 2 Tbsp. honey
- 1 Tbsp. plus ½ tsp. pure vanilla extract
- ½ lb. Medjool dates, pitted
- 5 oz. cooked beets, chopped (2 cups)
- 4 Tbsp. unsalted butter, melted and cooled
- ½ tsp. tamari (optional)
- ½ tsp. baking soda
- ½ cup unsweetened cocoa powder
- 1 tsp. ground cinnamon
- ⅛ tsp. cayenne

   Pinch of sea salt
- 3 large eggs

   Grated dark chocolate and crushed red pepper, for garnish

1 Line a sieve with cheesecloth and place it over a bowl. Add the yogurt, cover with plastic wrap and refrigerate for 24 hours to drain until thick. Transfer the yogurt to a medium bowl and stir in the honey and ½ teaspoon of the vanilla; refrigerate.

2 Preheat the oven to 350°. Line 12 muffin cups with paper liners. In a food processor, combine the dates, beets, butter, tamari (if using), baking soda and the remaining 1 tablespoon of vanilla and puree until smooth. Scrape down the side of the bowl. Add the cocoa powder, cinnamon, cayenne, salt and eggs and puree until well blended and smooth.

3 Spoon the batter into the muffin cups and bake for about 30 minutes, until a cake tester inserted in the center of a cake comes out clean. Transfer cakes to a rack to cool completely, then refrigerate them until cold, at least 3 hours or overnight.

4 Peel the paper liners off the cakes. Dollop the yogurt frosting on top of the cakes; garnish with grated chocolate and crushed red pepper. Serve cold.
—*Melissa Hemsley; Jasmine Hemsley*

MAKE AHEAD

The cakes and frosting can be refrigerated separately for up to 4 days.

MIXED-BERRY SPOON CAKE

Ⓥ

MAKES **8 to 10 servings**

TIME **Active 20 min;**
Total 2 hr 20 min

FILLING

4 pints strawberries (2 lbs.),
hulled and quartered

2 pints blackberries (12 oz.)

2 pints raspberries (12 oz.)

¾ cup sugar

2 Tbsp. cornstarch

CAKE

1½ cups all-purpose flour

1 cup sugar

2 tsp. finely grated lemon zest

1½ tsp. baking powder

1 tsp. kosher salt

2 large eggs

½ cup milk

1 tsp. pure vanilla extract

1½ sticks unsalted butter, melted

1 MAKE THE FILLING In a large bowl, toss the strawberries, blackberries and raspberries with the sugar and cornstarch and let stand for 10 minutes.

2 MAKE THE CAKE Preheat the oven to 375°. In a medium bowl, whisk the flour with the sugar, lemon zest, baking powder and salt. In a small bowl, whisk the eggs with the milk and vanilla. Whisk the liquid into the dry ingredients until evenly moistened, then whisk in the melted butter until smooth.

3 Spread the filling in a 9-by-13-inch baking dish. Spoon the batter on top, leaving small gaps. Bake in the center of the oven for 1 hour, until the fruit is bubbling and a toothpick inserted into the topping comes out clean. Let cool for 1 hour before serving. —*Grace Parisi*

VARIATION

Stone-Fruit Spoon Cake Use 4 pounds of stone fruit (peaches, nectarines and apricots) cut into large wedges or 4 pounds of plums, cut into 1-inch cubes in place of the berries and proceed with recipe as directed.

> "Because of the yogurt and the fresh lemon juice, this blueberry loaf cake is not overly sweet and is a nice option for a brunch menu or a light dessert."
>
> —JUSTIN CHAPPLE, CULINARY DIRECTOR

LEMON-BLUEBERRY YOGURT LOAF CAKE

(v)

MAKES One 9-by-4-inch loaf

TIME Active 30 min; Total 3 hr

- ¾ cup refined coconut oil, melted and cooled slightly, plus more for greasing
- 2 cups all-purpose flour
- 1¼ tsp. baking powder
- ½ tsp. baking soda
  - Kosher salt
- 1 cup granulated sugar
- 3 large eggs
- 1¼ cups whole-milk Greek yogurt
- 2 Tbsp. finely grated lemon zest
- ¾ tsp. pure vanilla extract
- ¼ cup plus 2 Tbsp. fresh lemon juice
- 1 cup blueberries
- ¾ cup confectioners' sugar

1 Preheat the oven to 350°. Grease a 9-by-4-inch metal loaf pan and line with parchment paper, allowing at least 2 inches of overhang on the 2 long sides.

2 In a medium bowl, whisk the flour with the baking powder, baking soda and ¾ teaspoon of salt. In a large bowl, using a hand mixer, beat the ¾ cup of coconut oil with the granulated sugar at medium speed until very smooth, about 1 minute. Beat in the eggs 1 at a time, then beat in the yogurt, lemon zest, vanilla and ¼ cup of the lemon juice. Scrape down the side and bottom of the bowl, then beat in the dry ingredients in 3 additions until just incorporated. Using a rubber spatula, fold in the blueberries.

3 Scrape the batter into the prepared pan and spread in an even layer. Bake for about 1 hour and 15 minutes, until a cake tester inserted in the center of the cake comes out clean. Transfer the pan to a rack and let the cake cool completely, about 1 hour.

4 In a small bowl, whisk the confectioners' sugar with remaining 2 tablespoons of lemon juice and a pinch of salt. Using the overhanging parchment paper, lift the cake out of the pan. Drizzle the glaze over the top and let stand until set, about 15 minutes. Cut into slices and serve. —*Justin Chapple*

MAKE AHEAD

The cake can be kept in an airtight container for up to 3 days.

CHOCOLATE, CINNAMON AND ALMOND LOAF CAKE

MAKES One 9-by-5-inch loaf

TIME Active 20 min; Total 2 hr

Nonstick baking spray, for greasing

2½ **cups superfine almond meal**

½ **cup unsweetened Dutch-process cocoa powder, sifted**

2 **tsp. baking powder**

½ **tsp. kosher salt**

2½ **tsp. ground cinnamon**

6 **large eggs, separated**

1 **cup coconut palm sugar**

½ **stick unsalted butter, melted and cooled slightly**

½ **cup cooled brewed coffee**

2 **tsp. pure vanilla extract**

1 **cup heavy cream**

1 Preheat the oven to 350°. Grease a 9-by-5-inch loaf pan with baking spray and line it with parchment paper, allowing 2 inches of overhang on the short sides.

2 In a medium bowl, whisk the almond meal with the cocoa powder, baking powder, salt and 1½ teaspoons of the cinnamon. In a large bowl, whisk the egg yolks with the coconut sugar, melted butter, coffee and vanilla. Stir the dry ingredients into the wet ingredients until the batter is smooth.

3 In a stand mixer fitted with the whisk, beat the egg whites at medium-high speed until stiff peaks form, 1 to 2 minutes. Fold one-third of the beaten egg whites into the batter to lighten it, then fold in the remaining egg whites until no streaks remain.

4 Scrape the batter into the prepared pan and bake for 45 to 50 minutes, until a toothpick inserted in the center comes out with a few crumbs attached. Transfer to a rack to cool for 20 minutes, then unmold and let cool completely.

5 Meanwhile, in a medium bowl, beat the heavy cream with the remaining 1 teaspoon of cinnamon until soft peaks form. Cut the cake into slices and serve with a dollop of the cinnamon cream. —*Julia Turshen*

MAKE AHEAD

The cake can be stored in an airtight container at room temperature overnight.

CHOCOLATE-COOKIE CRUNCH TRIFLE

Ⓥ

MAKES 8 servings

TIME Active 50 min;
Total 4 hr 15 min

PUDDING

- 2 **cups heavy cream**
- 2 **cups whole milk**
- 1 **cup granulated sugar**
- ¼ **cup cornstarch**
- ¼ **cup unsweetened cocoa powder**
- 2 **large eggs**
- 6 **oz. bittersweet chocolate, coarsely chopped (1½ cups)**
- 1 **Tbsp. unsalted butter**
- ¼ **tsp. kosher salt**

WHIPPED CREAM

- 2 **cups heavy cream, chilled**
- ½ **cup confectioners' sugar**
- 1 **tsp. pure vanilla extract**
  Pinch of kosher salt
- 4 **cups coarsely chopped crunchy cookies, such as Oreos, Thin Mints, shortbread, biscotti, Nutter Butters, or Samoas**

 MAKE THE PUDDING In a medium saucepan, combine 1¾ cups of the heavy cream with the milk and granulated sugar and bring to a bare simmer over moderately low heat, stirring occasionally, about 12 minutes. Meanwhile, sift the cornstarch and cocoa powder into a medium bowl, then whisk in the eggs and the remaining ¼ cup of heavy cream to form a smooth paste. Gradually whisk 1 cup of the hot milk into the cornstarch mixture, then scrape the mixture into the saucepan and cook over moderately low heat, stirring constantly, until the pudding is thick enough to coat the back of a spoon, about 30 minutes.

 Put the chopped chocolate in a heatproof medium bowl and set a fine sieve over it. Strain the pudding over the chocolate and let stand for 3 minutes. Whisk until smooth, then whisk in the butter and salt. Press a sheet of plastic wrap directly on the surface of the pudding and refrigerate until chilled, about 3 hours.

3 **MAKE THE WHIPPED CREAM** In a medium bowl, using a hand mixer, beat the heavy cream with the confectioners' sugar, vanilla and salt until firm, about 5 minutes.

4 In a 3-quart trifle bowl, make 4 layers each of the pudding, whipped cream and crushed cookies. —*Tiffany MacIsaac*

MAKE AHEAD

The recipe can be prepared through Step 2 and refrigerated for up to 4 days. Make the whipped cream and layer the pudding, whipped cream and cookies before taking to the potluck.

HAZELNUT CHOCOLATE BARS

MAKES **12 bars**

TIME **Active 25 min; Total 1 hr 10 min**

- 2 cups peeled toasted hazelnuts
- 1 cup confectioners' sugar
- 1 tsp. pure vanilla extract
- ½ tsp. pure almond extract
- ¼ tsp. kosher salt
- ½ cup light corn syrup
- 8 oz. dark chocolate, finely chopped

  Sprinkles, for garnish

1 In a food processor, pulse the hazelnuts just until finely ground. Add the sugar, vanilla, almond extract and salt and pulse to combine. With the machine on, drizzle in the corn syrup and blend until the mixture comes together. Turn the mixture out onto a parchment paper-lined baking sheet and form into a 12-by-2-inch bar. Cut the bar crosswise into 12 equal pieces and freeze until firm, at least 15 minutes.

2 In a microwave-safe medium bowl, melt the chocolate in 30-second intervals, stirring, until smooth. Let cool to room temperature.

3 Using a fork, dip the hazelnut candy into the chocolate to evenly coat, letting the excess drip off. Arrange the bars on the baking sheet and top with sprinkles. Refrigerate until firm, at least 30 minutes. Serve cold. —*Molly Yeh*

MAKE AHEAD

The bars can be refrigerated for 5 days.

"These supersimple little nutty homemade candy bars are satisfyingly chewy and sweet. They're great for a potluck dessert because you can make them quickly in a food processor and keep them in the refrigerator up to five days." —MARY-FRANCES HECK, SENIOR FOOD EDITOR

CHOCOLATE ESPRESSO PIE BARS

MAKES **48 bars**

TIME **Active 45 min;
Total 3 hr 45 min,
plus cooling**

CRUST

4 sticks unsalted butter, melted,
plus more for brushing

4½ cups all-purpose flour

¾ cup packed light brown sugar

¾ tsp. kosher salt

FILLING

3 sticks unsalted butter, cut into
large dice

1 cup dark chocolate chips

1 Tbsp. pure vanilla extract

3 cups granulated sugar

1 Tbsp. instant espresso powder

1 tsp. ground cinnamon

½ tsp. kosher salt

6 large eggs

Confectioners' sugar, for
dusting

1 MAKE THE CRUST Preheat the oven to 350°. Brush a large rimmed baking sheet with melted butter. Line the baking sheet with parchment paper, leaving a 1-inch overhang.

2 In a large bowl, using your fingers, combine the flour with the brown sugar and salt. Drizzle in the 4 sticks of melted butter and stir with a fork until a lumpy dough forms. Press the dough evenly over the bottom and up the sides of the prepared baking sheet. Refrigerate until firm, about 15 minutes.

3 Line the pie shell with parchment paper and fill to the top with pie weights or dried beans. Bake in the center of the oven for about 20 minutes, until lightly browned. Remove the pie weights and parchment paper. Transfer the crust to a wire rack to cool, about 1 hour.

4 MEANWHILE, MAKE THE FILLING Reduce the oven temperature to 325°. In a heatproof medium bowl set over a saucepan of simmering water, melt the diced butter with the chocolate chips, stirring occasionally, until smooth, about 3 minutes. Stir in the vanilla and remove the bowl from the heat. Whisk in the granulated sugar, espresso, cinnamon and salt until blended. Whisk in the eggs 1 at a time. Pour the filling into the cooled crust. Bake for about 45 minutes, until the center is set and the top begins to crack. Transfer the pie to a wire rack to cool completely, about 2 hours.

5 Cut the pie into 2-inch-square bars. Dust the top with confectioners' sugar and serve. —*Cheryl Day*

MAKE AHEAD

The bars can be stored in an airtight container at room temperature for up to 2 days.

> "The F&W staff loves these deeply dark-chocolatey brownies from our friend Gail Simmons. They have a sophisticated touch of salt, plus notes of molasses and anise from black licorice, and the combo makes a brilliant treat that is irresistibly chewy and not too sweet." —JORDANA ROTHMAN, RESTAURANT EDITOR

CHEWY BLACK LICORICE-CHOCOLATE BROWNIES

(v)

MAKES 12 brownies

TIME Active 30 min;
Total 1 hr 10 min
plus cooling

1½ sticks unsalted butter, melted, plus more for brushing

1 cup all-purpose flour

½ cup unsweetened cocoa powder

2 Tbsp. licorice root powder

2 tsp. ground anise seeds

½ tsp. kosher salt

1 cup granulated sugar

1 cup packed brown sugar

3 large eggs

1 tsp. pure vanilla extract

2 oz. bittersweet chocolate, chopped

½ cup chopped soft black licorice chews (3 oz.)

1 Preheat the oven to 350°. Line a 9-inch-square baking pan with paper or foil, leaving 2 inches of overhang on 2 sides. Brush the paper with butter.

2 In a medium bowl, whisk the flour with the cocoa powder, licorice root powder, anise and salt. In a large bowl, whisk the melted butter with both sugars, then whisk in the eggs and vanilla. Stir in the dry ingredients, then three-fourths of the chocolate and licorice chews. Scrape the batter into the prepared pan and smooth the top. Gently press the remaining chocolate and licorice chews into the batter.

3 Bake the brownies for about 40 minutes, until a toothpick inserted in the center comes out clean, with a few moist crumbs attached. Let the brownies cool completely, then lift them out of the pan using the paper. Cut the brownies into 12 rectangles and serve. —*Gail Simmons*

RASPBERRY LINZER BARS

(v)

MAKES **24 bars**

TIME **Active 25 min;
Total 3 hr plus
overnight chilling**

1½ **cups all-purpose flour**

¾ **cup rye flour**

6 **Tbsp. hazelnut flour**

1½ **tsp. baking powder**

1 **tsp. ground cinnamon**

¾ **tsp. kosher salt**

2 **sticks unsalted butter,
at room temperature**

1½ **cups granulated sugar**

4 **tsp. grated lemon zest**

1 **tsp. pure vanilla extract**

3 **large egg yolks**

Nonstick cooking spray

1¼ **cups raspberry jam**

**Confectioners' sugar, for
dusting**

1 In a medium bowl, whisk the 3 flours with the baking powder, cinnamon and salt. In a stand mixer fitted with the paddle, beat the butter with the granulated sugar, lemon zest and vanilla at medium speed until smooth, about 5 minutes. Beat in the egg yolks 1 at a time, scraping down the side of the bowl, until incorporated. Beat in the dry ingredients at low speed until the dough just comes together. Press one-third of the dough and two-thirds of the dough into 2 disks and wrap in plastic. Refrigerate overnight until firm.

2 Preheat the oven to 350°. Coat a 9-by-13-inch metal baking pan with cooking spray. Line with parchment paper, leaving a 2-inch overhang on the 2 long sides, and coat with cooking spray. Using the large holes of a box grater, shred the larger disk of dough evenly in the pan.

3 Spread the jam over the shredded dough, leaving a ½-inch border. Shred the smaller disk over the jam. Bake, rotating the pan halfway through, for 35 to 45 minutes, until the top is deep golden brown. Transfer to a wire rack and let cool. Refrigerate in the pan until firm, at least 2 hours.

4 Using the paper, transfer the pastry to a work surface. Dust with confectioners' sugar, cut into 2-inch bars and serve cold or at room temperature. —*Della Gossett*

MAKE AHEAD

The bars can be stored in an airtight container at room temperature for up to 4 days.

SALTY-SWEET CHOCOLATE CHIP-PRETZEL BARS

Ⓥ

MAKES 12 bars

TIME Active 40 min;
Total 1 hr plus cooling

- 14 oz. graham crackers (28 whole crackers), finely ground
- 1½ sticks unsalted butter, melted
- 3 Tbsp. sugar
- Pinch of kosher salt
- One 14-oz. can sweetened condensed milk
- One 10-oz. bag bittersweet chocolate chips
- 6 oz. thin hard pretzels (4 cups), broken
- Flaky sea salt, for sprinkling

1 Preheat the oven to 350°. Line a 9-inch-square baking pan with foil, allowing 2 inches of overhang on 2 sides. In a medium bowl, using a fork, mix the graham cracker crumbs with the butter, sugar and the kosher salt until evenly moistened. Press the crumbs evenly into the bottom of the prepared pan.

2 In a medium saucepan, combine the condensed milk with the chocolate chips and cook over low heat, stirring, until melted and smooth, about 5 minutes.

3 Scrape the mixture onto the crust and smooth the top. Scatter the pretzels evenly on top, gently pressing them into the chocolate. Sprinkle with flaky sea salt and bake for 15 to 20 minutes, until the edges are set. Let cool completely, then refrigerate until chilled, about 45 minutes. Unmold and cut into bars. —*F&W*

MAKE AHEAD

The bars can be stored in an airtight container at room temperature for up to 3 days.

CHOCOLATE-PEPPERMINT-MARSHMALLOW COOKIES

Ⓥ

MAKES **4 dozen cookies**

TIME **Active 1 hr 15 min;
Total 3 hr 30 min**

MARSHMALLOWS

Nonstick cooking spray

¼ **cup powdered gelatin**

1¾ **cups water**

2 **large egg whites, at room temperature**

2¼ **cups sugar**

1 **Tbsp. light corn syrup**

2 **tsp. pure vanilla extract**

1 **cup crushed peppermint candies (10 oz.) plus more for sprinkling**

8 **to 12 drops of red food coloring**

COOKIES

1¼ **cups bread flour**

1 **cup pastry flour**

½ **tsp. kosher salt**

2 **sticks unsalted butter, at room temperature**

1 **cup sugar**

½ **vanilla bean, split lengthwise and seeds scraped**

1 **large egg**

1 **large egg yolk**

2 **tsp. pure vanilla extract**

Neutral oil, such as grapeseed, for brushing

GLAZE

28 **oz. dark chocolate (65% to 70% cocoa), chopped**

4 **oz. cocoa butter**

1 MAKE MARSHMALLOWS Coat a 13-by-18-inch rimmed baking sheet with cooking spray. Line with parchment paper and coat with cooking spray. In a microwavable bowl, whisk gelatin with ¾ cup of the water. Microwave on high in 10-second increments, stirring after each one, until gelatin is melted, about 50 seconds.

2 In a stand mixer fitted with the whisk, beat egg whites at medium-low speed until foamy. In a medium saucepan, combine sugar with corn syrup and remaining 1 cup water. Bring to a boil, stirring occasionally. Cook over moderate heat, without stirring, until syrup registers 260° on a candy thermometer, about 10 minutes. Remove pan from heat; stir in gelatin until melted. Drizzle hot syrup into egg whites down side of bowl, beating at medium speed. Add vanilla and beat at high speed until thick and glossy, about 10 minutes. Using a rubber spatula, fold in 1 cup peppermint candies. Sprinkle in food coloring, then scrape marshmallow mixture onto baking sheet, swirling food coloring, and smooth surface. Let stand at room temperature until set, at least 2 hours or overnight.

3 MAKE COOKIES In a medium bowl, whisk flours and salt. In a stand mixer fitted with the paddle, beat butter with sugar and vanilla bean seeds at medium speed until fluffy, about 5 minutes. Beat in egg, egg yolk and vanilla. Beat in dry ingredients at low speed until just combined. Divide dough in half and press into disks. Wrap in plastic; refrigerate until firm, at least 1 hour or overnight.

4 On a floured sheet of parchment paper, roll out 1 disk of dough into a rectangle, ¼ inch thick. Transfer on parchment paper to a baking sheet and refrigerate until firm, about 30 minutes. Repeat with second disk of dough.

5 Preheat oven to 325°. Using a square cookie cutter, cut 2-inch squares from dough and arrange on baking sheets 1 inch apart. Reroll scraps and cut more squares. Bake for 10 to 12 minutes, until golden brown. Transfer baking sheets to wire racks and let cool.

6 Lightly brush cookie cutter with oil, repeating as needed. Cut forty-eight 2-inch marshmallows. Place 1 marshmallow on top of each cookie and transfer to baking sheets. Freeze until cold, at least 15 minutes.

7 MAKE GLAZE In a microwavable bowl, combine chocolate with cocoa butter. Microwave on high in 20-second increments, stirring after each one, until mixture is smooth.

8 Coat 2 rimmed baking sheets with cooking spray. Line with parchment paper and coat with cooking spray. Using a fork, dip each cookie in glaze, then set on a baking sheet and sprinkle with peppermint candy. Refrigerate until set, at least 15 minutes, and serve cold. —*Della Gossett*

ALMOND SHORTBREAD COOKIES (V)

MAKES   **About 2 dozen cookies**

TIME   **Active 25 min;
Total 45 min plus cooling**

- ½ cup sliced almonds
- 1¼ cups all-purpose flour
- ½ cup almond meal
- ½ tsp. kosher salt
- ½ cup smooth unsalted roasted almond butter
- ½ cup refined coconut oil, melted
- ½ cup granulated sugar
- ¼ cup turbinado sugar
- 1 tsp. pure vanilla extract

1 Preheat the oven to 350°. Line a baking sheet with parchment paper. Spread the sliced almonds in a pie plate and bake for about 8 minutes, until golden. Let cool, then coarsely chop.

2 In a medium bowl, whisk the flour with the almond meal and salt. In a large bowl, using a hand mixer at medium speed, beat the almond butter with the coconut oil, both sugars and the vanilla until well blended, about 1 minute. Beat in the flour mixture and chopped almonds just until combined.

3 Scoop 2-tablespoon-size mounds of dough onto the prepared baking sheet 1 inch apart and flatten to a ¼-inch thickness. Bake the cookies for 15 to 18 minutes, until golden. Transfer to a rack and let cool completely. —*Kay Chun*

MAKE AHEAD

The cookies can be refrigerated in an airtight container for 1 week.

EINKORN SHORTBREAD (V)

MAKES   **20 cookies**

TIME   **Active 25 min;
Total 2 hr 25 min**

- 6 Tbsp. confectioners' sugar
- ⅓ cup packed dark brown sugar
- 2 sticks unsalted butter, cubed, at room temperature
- 1¼ cups whole-grain Einkorn flour
- 1 cup all-purpose flour
- 1¾ tsp. kosher salt

1 Preheat the oven to 300°. In a food processor, pulse confectioners' sugar with brown sugar until combined. Add butter and pulse to combine. Add both flours and salt and pulse until dough comes together. Divide in half and press into disks. Wrap in plastic and refrigerate for 30 minutes.

2 Roll out each disk of dough between 2 sheets of parchment paper into a ¼-inch-thick round. Peel off top layer of parchment. Using a 2½-inch round cookie cutter, stamp out cookies and transfer to 2 baking sheets, spaced ½ inch apart. Using a small star-shaped cookie cutter, stamp out a star in the top of each cookie. Transfer stars to a separate baking sheet. Reroll scraps and cut out more cookies.

3 Bake the cookies and stars until deep golden brown, 25 to 30 minutes for the cookies and 10 to 12 minutes for the stars. Transfer the baking sheets to wire racks and let cool completely. —*Roxana Jullapa*

MAKE AHEAD

The cookies can be stored in an airtight container at room temperature for up to 3 days.

Almond Shortbread Cookies

Finnish Sticks (bottom row): Slightly Chewy
Ginger Cookies (second row from bottom)

FINNISH STICKS

(v)

MAKES **24 cookies**

TIME **Active 30 min;
Total 1 hr 45 min
plus cooling**

1¼ cups cake flour plus more
for dusting

7 Tbsp. unsalted butter, at room
temperature

¼ cup granulated sugar

½ tsp. pure almond extract

3 Tbsp. whole milk

1 large egg, beaten

1 Tbsp. finely chopped roasted
almonds

1 Tbsp. pearl sugar

1 In a food processor, combine 1¼ cups flour with butter, granulated sugar and almond extract and pulse until a dough forms. Shape into a ball and flatten into a 1-inch-thick disk. Cover with plastic wrap and refrigerate for 1 hour.

2 Preheat the oven to 350°. In a small bowl, beat the milk with the egg. Divide the cookie dough in half. On a lightly floured work surface, roll each piece of dough into a ¾-inch-thick log. Brush the logs with the milk-egg wash and sprinkle with almonds and pearl sugar. Cut logs into 2-inch pieces and arrange on a parchment paper-lined baking sheet. Bake cookies for 12 to 14 minutes, until barely golden. Transfer to a rack to cool before serving. —*Magnus Nilsson*

MAKE AHEAD

The cookies can be stored in an airtight container at room temperature for up to 3 days.

SLIGHTLY CHEWY GINGER COOKIES

(v)

MAKES **24 cookies**

TIME **30 min**

1¼ cups whole-wheat flour

1 tsp. ground ginger

½ tsp. baking soda

Pinch of kosher salt

1 stick plus 2 Tbsp. unsalted
butter, at room temperature

⅓ cup plus 1 Tbsp. sugar

2 Tbsp. Lyle's Golden Syrup

1 Preheat the oven to 350°. Sift the whole-wheat flour with the ginger, baking soda and salt into a small bowl. In a medium bowl, using a hand mixer, beat the butter with the sugar and syrup at medium speed until pale yellow and fluffy, about 3 minutes. Beat in the flour mixture just until incorporated. Knead the dough a few times in the bowl and divide in half.

2 On a parchment paper-lined baking sheet, roll each piece of dough into a 12-inch log, about 1 inch wide. Arrange the logs on the prepared baking sheet 6 inches apart and bake for about 15 minutes, until golden; they will spread a lot. Transfer to a rack to cool until warm. On a work surface, cut the logs crosswise into 1¼-inch slices. Transfer the cookies to a rack to cool before serving. —*Magnus Nilsson*

MAKE AHEAD

The cookies can be stored in an airtight container at room temperature for up to 3 days.

FORGOTTEN COOKIES

MAKES	**18 cookies**
TIME	**Active 20 min;**
	Total 8 hr 30 min

- 2 **large egg whites**
- ½ **tsp. cream of tartar**
- ¾ **cup sugar**
- ½ **tsp. vanilla bean paste**
- ¼ **tsp. ground cardamom**
- ¾ **cup bittersweet chocolate chips**
- ¾ **cup chopped toasted pecans**
- ¼ **cup dried cherries**
- **Coarse sea salt**

1 Preheat the oven to 350°. In a stand mixer fitted with the whisk, beat egg whites with the cream of tartar at medium speed until soft peaks start to form form, 1 to 2 minutes. With the machine on, gradually add the sugar. Add the vanilla bean paste and cardamom and beat at high speed until stiff peaks form, about 3 minutes. Using a spatula, scrape down the side and bottom of the bowl and fold in the chocolate chips, pecans and cherries.

2 Using 2 spoons, drop 2-inch balls of the meringue mixture onto a large foil-lined baking sheet. Sprinkle the cookies with sea salt and bake for 5 minutes. Turn the oven off and leave the cookies in for at least 8 hours or overnight before serving. —*Sarah Grueneberg*

MAKE AHEAD

Make these cookies the day before you need to serve them since they need to stand in the oven overnight.

"These classic Southern egg white cookies are barely baked, then left in the oven overnight to develop their wonderful crispy-chewy texture."
—NINA FRIEND, EDITORIAL ASSISTANT

APPLE AND PEAR GALETTE
WITH WALNUT STREUSEL

ⓥ

MAKES	12 servings
TIME	Active 45 min; Total 2 hr 45 min plus cooling

CRUST

- **2 cups all-purpose flour plus more for rolling**
- **¾ tsp. kosher salt**
- **1½ sticks cold unsalted butter, cubed**
- **½ cup ice water**

STREUSEL

- **⅔ cup walnuts**
- **½ cup all-purpose flour**
- **½ cup packed light brown sugar**
- **½ tsp. kosher salt**
- **6 Tbsp. cold unsalted butter, cubed**

FILLING

- **2 Granny Smith apples—halved, cored and thinly sliced lengthwise**
- **2 firm Bartlett pears—halved, cored and sliced lengthwise ¼ inch thick**
- **¼ cup granulated sugar plus more for sprinkling**
- **¼ tsp. kosher salt**
- **2 tsp. fresh lemon juice**
- **1 large egg beaten with 1 tsp. water**
- **Confectioners' sugar, for dusting (optional)**

1 MAKE THE CRUST In a food processor, pulse the 2 cups of flour with the salt. Add the butter and pulse until the pieces are the size of small peas. Sprinkle the water on top and pulse until the dough just comes together. Turn the dough out onto a work surface, gather up any crumbs and pat into a disk. Wrap in plastic and refrigerate until well chilled, 1 hour.

2 MEANWHILE, MAKE THE STREUSEL Preheat the oven to 400°. Spread the walnuts in a pie plate and bake for about 8 minutes, until lightly browned. Let cool, then chop.

3 In a medium bowl, whisk the flour with the brown sugar and salt. Add the butter and, using your fingers, pinch it into the dry ingredients until the mixture resembles coarse meal. Add the walnuts and pinch the streusel into clumps. Refrigerate until chilled, about 15 minutes.

4 MAKE THE FILLING Line a rimmed baking sheet with parchment paper. In a large bowl, toss the apples with the pears, ¼ cup of granulated sugar, the salt and lemon juice. On a lightly floured work surface, roll out the dough to a 13-by-19-inch oval. Ease the dough onto the prepared baking sheet. Mound the filling in the center of the oval, leaving a 2-inch border. Sprinkle the streusel evenly over the fruit and fold the edge of the dough up and over the filling.

5 Brush the crust with the egg wash and sprinkle evenly with granulated sugar. Bake the galette for 45 to 50 minutes, until the fruit is tender and the streusel and crust are golden brown. Let the galette cool. Dust with confectioners' sugar, if using, before serving. —*Justin Chapple*

"Free-form galettes are simpler to make than fruit pies. Using unpeeled apples and pears adds texture and flavor while cutting down on prep time and ingredient waste." —JUSTIN CHAPPLE, CULINARY DIRECTOR

PEAR AND CRANBERRY SLAB PIE

(V)

MAKES **8 to 10 servings**

TIME **Active 50 min;
Total 3 hr plus cooling**

2¾ **cups all-purpose flour, plus
more for rolling**

½ **cup plus 1 Tbsp. granulated
sugar**

Kosher salt

2 **sticks unsalted butter, cubed
and chilled**

½ **cup ice water**

4 **firm Bartlett or Anjou pears—
peeled, cored and cut into
¾-inch wedges**

1½ **cups frozen cranberries**

1 **tsp. ground ginger**

1 **large egg beaten with 1 Tbsp.
water**

Turbinado sugar, for sprinkling

Vanilla ice cream, for serving

1 In a food processor, combine 2½ cups of the flour with 1 tablespoon of the granulated sugar and 1 teaspoon of kosher salt and pulse to mix. Add the butter and pulse in 1-second bursts until the mixture resembles coarse meal. Drizzle the ice water over the mixture and pulse in 1-second bursts until the dough just comes together. Turn the dough out onto a work surface, gather any crumbs and pat into 2 squares. Wrap the squares in plastic and refrigerate until chilled, about 45 minutes.

2 On a floured work surface, roll out 1 piece of the dough to a 12-inch square. Slide the dough onto a large sheet of parchment paper, then slide onto a large baking sheet. Repeat with the second piece of dough. Refrigerate for 15 minutes.

3 Slide 1 square of dough onto a work surface. In a large bowl, toss the pears with the cranberries, ginger, ½ teaspoon of salt and the remaining ½ cup of granulated sugar and ¼ cup of flour. Spread the fruit evenly on the dough square on the baking sheet, leaving a 1-inch border. Ease the other square of dough on top of the fruit. Fold over the edge and crimp decoratively all around to seal. Brush the pie with the egg wash and sprinkle with turbinado sugar. Cut 16 small slits in the top and freeze for 15 minutes.

4 Preheat the oven to 400°. Bake the pie for about 50 minutes, until golden and the pears are tender; rotate halfway through baking. Let cool. Cut the pie into squares and serve with vanilla ice cream. —*Justin Chapple*

MAKE AHEAD

The slab pie can be stored in an airtight container at room temperature for up to 2 days.

HAZELNUT-ROSEMARY CARAMEL TART

(v)

MAKES	One 10-inch tart
TIME	Active 1 hr; Total 4 hr

CRUST

- 1 cup plus 2 Tbsp. all-purpose flour, plus more for rolling
- ¼ cup confectioners' sugar
- ¾ tsp. baking powder
- ½ tsp. fine sea salt
- 1½ sticks cold unsalted butter, cubed
- 2 large egg yolks
- Ice water

FILLING

- 1½ sticks unsalted butter
- 1 Tbsp. chopped rosemary
- 1½ cups hazelnuts
- 3 large eggs
- 3 large egg yolks
- 1 cup packed light brown sugar
- ¾ cup brown rice syrup
- ¼ cup honey
- 1 tsp. fine sea salt
- 2 Tbsp. heavy cream
- 1 Tbsp. all-purpose flour
- 1 tsp. pure vanilla extract
- Flaky sea salt, for sprinkling
- Whipped crème fraîche, for serving

1 MAKE THE CRUST In a food processor, pulse flour with confectioners' sugar, baking powder and fine sea salt. Add the butter and pulse until the mixture resembles coarse meal. Add the egg yolks and 1 tablespoon of ice water and pulse until the dough just comes together; add another tablespoon of ice water if it seems dry. Turn the dough out onto a work surface and pat into a disk. Wrap in plastic and refrigerate until chilled, 1 hour.

2 On a floured work surface, roll out the dough to a 12-inch round. Ease the round into a 10-inch fluted tart pan with a removable bottom, pressing it into the corners and up the side, patching any tears. Trim off any overhang. Freeze tart shell for 30 minutes.

3 Preheat the oven to 375°. Line the tart shell with parchment paper and fill it with pie weights or dried beans. Bake in the center of the oven for 20 minutes. Remove the parchment and weights. Bake the shell for 10 to 15 minutes longer, until lightly browned. Let cool completely. Leave the oven on.

4 MEANWHILE, MAKE THE FILLING In a small saucepan, melt the butter over moderate heat. Remove from the heat, add the rosemary and let steep for 20 minutes. Strain the butter into a small bowl and let cool.

5 Spread the hazelnuts on a rimmed baking sheet and toast in the oven until fragrant and golden and skins are splitting, about 12 minutes. Let cool slightly, then transfer to a kitchen towel and rub together to remove skins; let cool. Coarsely chop hazelnuts and spread them in cooled tart shell. Put tart shell on a rimmed baking sheet. Reduce oven temperature to 300°.

6 In a large bowl, beat the whole eggs and yolks with the brown sugar, brown rice syrup, honey and fine sea salt. Gradually whisk in the rosemary butter, then whisk in the cream, flour and vanilla. Pour the filling into the tart shell and sprinkle flaky sea salt on top. Bake the tart for 50 minutes, until the filling is set at the edge but slightly jiggly in the center. Let cool completely. Serve at room temperature or slightly chilled, topped with a dollop of whipped crème fraîche alongside. —*Meadow Ramsay*

MAKE AHEAD

The tart can be refrigerated for up to 3 days.

CRANBERRY-WALNUT TART
WITH BUCKWHEAT CRUST

(GF) (V)

MAKES **One 14-inch tart**

TIME **Active 30 min;
Total 2 hr 30 min**

CRUST

- 1 cup buckwheat flour
- 1 Tbsp. tapioca flour
- 1 stick plus 2 Tbsp. cold unsalted butter, cubed, plus more for greasing
- 1 tsp. kosher salt
- 2 large egg yolks plus 1 large egg, lightly beaten
- 1 Tbsp. water

FRANGIPANE

- ½ cup walnut halves
- ¼ cup sugar
- ½ stick unsalted butter, softened
- 1 large egg
- 1 Tbsp. tapioca flour
- 1 Tbsp. heavy cream
- 1 Tbsp. Grand Marnier
- Finely grated zest of 1 clementine or small orange
- Pinch of kosher salt

TOPPING

- 2 cups fresh or thawed frozen cranberries
- ¼ cup sugar
- 3 Tbsp. fresh clementine or orange juice
- Greek yogurt, for serving

1 MAKE THE CRUST In a food processor, pulse the two flours with the butter and salt until the mixture is the texture of wet sand. Add the egg yolks and 1 tablespoon of water and pulse until the dough just comes together in a ball. Transfer to a work surface and pat into a 3-by-6-inch rectangle. Wrap in plastic and refrigerate until firm, at least 30 minutes.

2 Butter a 4-by-14-inch fluted rectangular tart pan with a removable bottom. Set the dough between 2 sheets of plastic wrap; roll out to a 6-by-16-inch rectangle. Discard the top sheet of plastic wrap and invert the dough into the prepared pan. Gently press into the corners and up the sides of the pan. Discard the plastic wrap and trim the overhanging dough flush with the rim. Refrigerate until firm, at least 15 minutes.

3 Preheat the oven to 375°. Line the tart shell with parchment paper and fill with pie weights or dried beans. Bake for 15 minutes. Remove parchment and pie weights and brush tart shell with beaten egg. Bake for about 5 more minutes, until set. Let cool slightly. Reduce oven temperature to 350°.

4 MEANWHILE, MAKE THE FRANGIPANE In a food processor, combine the walnuts and sugar; process until finely chopped. Add the butter, egg, tapioca flour, cream, Grand Marnier, clementine zest and salt and pulse until smooth. Scrape the frangipane into a bowl; chill until firm, 30 minutes.

5 MAKE THE TOPPING In a food processor, combine the cranberries, sugar and clementine juice and pulse just until the cranberries begin to break up.

6 Spread the frangipane in the tart shell and top with the cranberries. Set the tart on a rimmed baking sheet and bake, rotating once, until the frangipane is puffed and lightly browned at the edges, 30 to 35 minutes. Transfer to a rack and let cool. Unmold and serve with Greek yogurt. —*Claire Ptak*

CUMIN-AND-JAGGERY-GLAZED APPLE PIE

(V)

MAKES   One 9-inch pie

TIME   Active 1 hr;
Total 3 hr 15 min
plus cooling

CRUST

3 cups all-purpose flour plus
more for dusting

1½ tsp. kosher salt

½ tsp. baking powder

2 sticks plus 2 Tbsp. unsalted
butter, cubed and chilled

7 oz. cream cheese, cubed
and chilled

¼ cup ice water

FILLING

6 Granny Smith apples—peeled,
cored and cut into 1-inch-thick
wedges

½ cup finely grated jaggery
(see Note)

2 Tbsp. all-purpose flour

1 tsp. ground cinnamon

½ tsp. cumin seeds

GLAZE

4 Tbsp. unsalted butter

1 tsp. cumin seeds

⅓ cup finely grated jaggery

2 Tbsp. water

1 MAKE THE CRUST In a food processor, pulse the 3 cups of flour with the salt and baking powder until combined. Add the butter and cream cheese and pulse to form coarse crumbs. With the machine on, drizzle in the water until the dough starts to come together. Transfer to a work surface, gather any crumbs and press into a ball. Divide the dough into 2 equal pieces and pat into disks. Wrap in plastic and refrigerate until firm, 1 hour.

2 MAKE THE FILLING Preheat the oven to 350°. In a large bowl, combine apples, jaggery, flour, cinnamon and cumin.

3 On a lightly floured work surface and using a lightly floured rolling pin, roll out each piece of dough to a 14-inch round, about ⅛ inch thick. Ease 1 dough round into a 9-inch cast-iron skillet or deep-dish pie plate. Scrape the filling into the skillet and top with the second dough round. Press the edges of the dough together, then trim the overhang to about 1 inch, fold it under itself and crimp decoratively. Cut 4 slits in the top of the pie and bake for about 1 hour and 15 minutes, until golden brown. Transfer to a rack and let cool completely.

4 MEANWHILE, MAKE THE GLAZE In a small saucepan, melt the butter. Add the cumin and cook over moderately low heat, stirring, until fragrant, about 1 minute. Add the jaggery and 2 tablespoons of water and cook until the jaggery dissolves and the mixture is slightly thickened, 2 to 3 minutes. Brush some of the glaze over the pie and serve, passing the remaining glaze at the table. —*Asha Gomez*

NOTE

Jaggery is an unrefined cane sugar popular in Asia and Africa and is made from cane juice and either date or palm sap. The molasses and crystals in the sugar are not separated out so the color ranges from golden to dark brown. It's slightly less sweet than maple syrup, a little thicker than honey and has a rich, brown sugar-like flavor.

> "Cutting small circles out of the rye crust looks dramatic and also allows moisture to evaporate from the fruit filling as it cooks, deepening the flavor."
> —JUSTIN CHAPPLE, CULINARY DIRECTOR

BLUEBERRY PIE WITH RYE CRUST ⓥ

MAKES	One 9-inch pie
TIME	Active 45 min; Total 3 hr 30 min plus 5 hours cooling

CRUST

- 1¼ cups all-purpose flour, plus more for rolling
- 1 cup dark rye flour
- 1½ tsp. kosher salt
- 1 stick plus 6 Tbsp. cold unsalted butter, cubed
- ⅔ cup ice water

FILLING

- 1 vanilla bean, split and seeds scraped
- ¾ cup granulated sugar
- ½ tsp. kosher salt
- 2 lbs. blueberries (6 cups)
- ½ cup all-purpose flour
- 1 Tbsp. finely grated lemon zest plus 2 Tbsp. fresh lemon juice
- 1 large egg beaten with 2 tsp. water
- Turbinado sugar, for sprinkling

1 MAKE THE CRUST In a food processor, pulse both flours with the salt to mix. Add the butter and pulse until it is the size of small peas. Sprinkle the water over the flour and pulse just until a dough starts to form. Turn the dough out onto a work surface, gather up any crumbs and knead gently until the dough comes together. Cut the dough in half and pat each piece into a disk. Wrap the disks in plastic and refrigerate until well chilled, about 1 hour.

2 On a lightly floured work surface, roll out 1 disk of dough to a 12-inch round. Ease the dough into a 9-inch glass pie plate and trim the overhang to ½ inch. Freeze for 15 minutes.

3 PREPARE THE FILLING In a large bowl, rub the vanilla seeds into the granulated sugar and salt. Add the blueberries, flour, lemon zest and lemon juice and toss well. Scrape the filling into the pie plate.

4 On a lightly floured work surface, roll out the remaining disk of dough to a 12-inch round. Using three sizes of small round cutters, stamp out decorative holes in the dough, leaving a 2-inch border. Lay the dough over the filling and trim the overhang to ½ inch. Press the overhang together to seal, then fold it under itself. Freeze the pie for 1 hour.

5 Preheat the oven to 375°. Brush the pie with the egg wash and sprinkle with turbinado sugar. Bake for about 1 hour and 15 minutes, until the filling is bubbling and the crust is browned; cover the edge of the pie with foil if it browns too quickly. Let the pie cool completely before serving, at least 5 hours or overnight.
—*Justin Chapple*

BUTTERSCOTCH PUDDING PIE

Ⓥ

MAKES One 9-inch pie

TIME Active 1 hr 15 min;
Total 5 hr 50 min
plus cooling

CRUST

½ cup plus 1 Tbsp. chopped pecans

1¼ cups all-purpose flour

½ tsp. kosher salt

6 Tbsp. unsalted butter, cubed and chilled

¼ cup ice water

FILLING

1¾ cups whole milk

1½ cups heavy cream

6 Tbsp. unsalted butter, cubed

1 cup packed dark brown sugar

2 large eggs

3 Tbsp. cornstarch

¾ tsp. kosher salt

2 Tbsp. Scotch whisky

2 tsp. pure vanilla extract

Turbinado sugar, for garnish

1 Preheat the oven to 350°. Spread the pecans on a baking sheet and toast for about 8 minutes, until fragrant and lightly browned. Let cool.

2 MAKE THE CRUST In a food processor, pulse ½ cup of the pecans until finely ground. Add the flour and salt and pulse to mix. Add the butter and pulse until pea-size pieces form. Add the ice water and pulse until a dough starts to come together. Transfer the dough into a 9-inch round fluted tart pan with a removable bottom and press it evenly over the bottom and up the side. Prick the piecrust all over with a fork, then freeze it for 30 minutes.

3 Preheat the oven to 375°. Put the piecrust on a large baking sheet and bake for about 35 minutes, until the edge is lightly browned and the crust is firm. Let cool completely.

4 MEANWHILE, MAKE THE FILLING In a small saucepan, bring the milk and ½ cup of the cream to a simmer over medium heat. Remove from the heat. In a medium saucepan, melt the butter over moderately high heat. Add the brown sugar and cook, whisking constantly, until the mixture is bubbling and smooth, about 2 minutes. Remove from the heat and gradually whisk in the milk mixture.

5 In a medium bowl, beat the eggs with the cornstarch and salt. Very gradually whisk in ½ cup of the milk mixture. Scrape the mixture into the medium saucepan and cook over moderate heat, stirring constantly, until very thick, about 7 minutes. Strain the pudding into a medium bowl and stir in the Scotch and vanilla. Let cool slightly, then press a piece of plastic directly on the surface and refrigerate until well chilled, at least 4 hours or overnight.

6 Scrape the butterscotch filling into the piecrust and smooth the top. In a large bowl, using a hand mixer, beat the remaining 1 cup of cream until stiff peaks form. Mound the whipped cream on the pie and garnish with turbinado sugar and the remaining 1 tablespoon of pecans. Cut the pie into wedges and serve.
—*Gail Simmons*

NOTE

Use the bottom of a metal measuring cup to help press the dough into an even layer in the tart pan.

MAKE AHEAD

The pie can be refrigerated overnight.

CLASSIC PUMPKIN PIE

(v)

MAKES	One 9-inch pie
TIME	Active 30 min; Total 2 hr 30 min plus cooling

CRUST

1¼ cups all-purpose flour plus
   more for dusting

   Pinch of salt

 1 stick cold unsalted butter,
   cubed

¼ cup ice water

FILLING

 4 large eggs

¾ cup sugar

 1 Tbsp. cornstarch

 2 tsp. ground cinnamon

¼ tsp. ground cloves

   Pinch of salt

   One 15-oz. can pumpkin puree

½ cup heavy cream

1 MAKE THE CRUST In a food processor, pulse 1¼ cups of flour with salt. Add butter and pulse until it is the size of peas. Drizzle in water and pulse until crumbs are moistened; turn out onto a work surface. Gather dough into a ball, flatten, wrap in plastic and refrigerate for 30 minutes.

2 Preheat the oven to 350°. On a lightly floured surface, roll out the dough to a 13-inch round, a scant ¼ inch thick. Fit the dough into a 9-inch glass pie plate and trim the overhang to ¾ inch. Fold the dough under itself and crimp decoratively; refrigerate the pie shell for 10 minutes.

3 Line pie shell with foil and fill with pie weights or dried beans. Bake in center of the oven until nearly set, about 25 minutes. Remove foil and weights and bake until crust is pale golden, about 10 minutes. Let cool slightly.

4 MAKE THE FILLING In a medium bowl, whisk the eggs with the sugar, cornstarch, cinnamon, cloves and salt until smooth. Whisk in the pumpkin puree, then the cream. Working near the oven, pour the filling into the crust. Bake for about 45 minutes, until the custard is set. Let the pie cool on a rack.
—*Grace Parisi*

"When you're taking a pie to a holiday dinner, there's just no point in messing with the classics. This pumpkin pie is what everyone will be expecting."
—WINSLOW TAFT, CREATIVE DIRECTOR

drinks

POTLUCK WINE GUIDE

Use these tips for selecting wines for a potluck dinner where there will be a wide variety of foods and flavors.

Choose a wine with bright acidity

Use potlucks as a test run for Thanksgiving, the only other time of the year where we take a whole bunch of dishes that have nothing to do with one another and try to come up with a wine that will be perfect for them all. Acidity is your friend here; it will help the wine align with lighter dishes and salads and will cut through richer, meatier ones. Look for salty white Albariño or fresh red Mencía from northwest Spain, minerally Chablis from Burgundy and cool-climate reds from northern Italy.

Stick to light to medium–bodied reds

Unless you're going to a steak cookout or pot roast party where everyone's bringing sides, super tannic or higher alcohol reds aren't the right move for a potluck; they'll overwhelm things like citrusy salads, fried chicken and vegetable pastas. When it comes to reds, choose more versatile, light- to medium-bodied wines, like Barbera from Italy's Piedmont, Beaujolais from France and País from Chile.

Think outside the bottle

More and more wineries are packaging their wines in bag-in-boxes and screwcap bottles that don't require a corkscrew to open them. These are ideal for picnic potlucks. There's even been an uptick in great canned wines, which are lightweight and easy to discard. Just know that these canned wines are not single-serve; a 16-ounce can of wine contains about three glasses.

Think seasonally

Spring and summer potlucks will be plentiful with lighter dishes that put to use fresh fruits and vegetables, whereas fall and winter ones will be much heartier (think: mac and cheese and meatballs). Choose a wine that pairs with the flavors of the seasons.

Spring Flavors Green vegetables, goat cheese, herbs

Spring Wines Citrusy, lightly vegetal Grüner Veltliner from Austria; fragrant, dark-berried Cabernet Franc from France's Loire Valley

Summer Flavors Peaches, corn, tomatoes, grilled meats

Summer Wines Lemony, vibrant Vermentino from Italy's coastal Liguria; fruity, full-bodied California rosé

Fall Flavors Roast chicken and squash, apples

Fall Wines Ripe, concentrated German Riesling; tangy, red-fruited Chianti Classico

Winter Flavors Hearty greens and root vegetables, slow-cooked meats

Winter Wines Juicy, fruit-forward Dolcetto from Piedmont; cherry-rich Grenache-based Côtes du Rhone

Everyone loves bubbles

No one has ever been sad to hear a cork pop out of a bottle of sparkling wine and bubbles—like acidity—will help wines better pair with a wider variety of dishes. There are so many great options for affordable sparkling wines these days; try a cremant de Bourgogne from France's Burgundy (made from the same grapes as Champagne, at a lower cost); a pet nat (Petillant Naturel) from California; or a fizzy red Lambrusco in cooler months.

Don't bring a wine that you'll be sad not to drink

This isn't the moment to break out that Pinot Noir you've been hanging on to ever since you visited the Sonoma Coast a few years ago. Undoubtedly, someone you don't really know will open the bottle when you're not looking and pour themselves a larger serving than you deem necessary before you have a chance to taste it. Bring a wine that you like, but don't have sentimental attachments to.

Go big

If you really want to be the star of a potluck, bring a bigger bottle. More and more retailers are stocking large-format wines, especially magnums (double the size of a standard bottle) and they're not necessarily expensive. Look for oversized rosé or Beaujolais. So too, the Austrians have hung their hats on liter-sized bottles, many of which are super affordable like Grüner Veltliner and Zweigelt, both of which are great for potlucks.

Pick a wine that goes with your dish

Don't overthink this. A potluck is meant to be a compendium of flavors. Choosing a wine that pairs well with your dish is an easy way to make sure that it has at least one good match on the table; just bring a wine you like.

PINEAPPLE-SAKE SANGRIA
WITH JALAPEÑO

(GF) (V)

MAKES **8 servings**

TIME **Active 15 min;**
     Total 1 hr 40 min

¾ **cup water**

¾ **cup sugar**

1 **jalapeño, thinly sliced crosswise**

4½ **cups pineapple juice**

One 750-ml bottle dry filtered sake

Ice

Pineapple slices and mint sprigs, for garnish

1 In a small saucepan, bring the water to a boil with the sugar and jalapeño, stirring to dissolve the sugar. Let cool completely, then strain the syrup; discard the jalapeño.

2 In a large pitcher, combine the jalapeño syrup, pineapple juice and sake and stir well. Refrigerate until well chilled, about 1 hour. Serve the sangria over ice in tumblers, garnished with pineapple and mint. —*Helene Henderson*

MAKE AHEAD

The sangria can be refrigerated overnight.

NEGRONIS WITH FRESH OREGANO

(GF) (V)

MAKES **8 servings**

TIME **10 min**

16 **oz. Plymouth Gin**

8 **oz. sweet vermouth**

8 **oz. Campari**

Ice

8 **oregano sprigs**

1 In a large pitcher, stir the gin, vermouth and Campari; pour into 8 rocks glasses filled with ice. Garnish with the oregano. —*Zakary Pelaccio*

"Don't let the drinks be an afterthought at your next potluck dinner. I love to offer a signature cocktail such as a pitcher of negronis garnished with fresh oregano." —KELSEY YOUNGMAN, TEST KITCHEN MANAGER

Pineapple-Sake Sangria
with Jalapeño

> "With warming flavors of pear, cinnamon and citrus, this aromatic punch is my go-to drink if I'm having folks over during the holidays for appetizers or desserts." —KAREN SHIMIZU, EXECUTIVE EDITOR

ANJOU PUNCH

(GF) (V)

MAKES 12 servings

TIME 40 min

Three 3-inch cinnamon sticks, broken into pieces plus whole cinnamon sticks for garnish

1 cup water

½ cup sugar

Crushed ice

Orange and lemon wheels

12 oz. Cognac

12 oz. Belle de Brillet (pear liqueur)

9 oz. fresh lemon juice

6 oz. triple sec

12 oz. chilled Champagne

1 In a small saucepan, cover the broken cinnamon sticks with 1 cup of water and bring to a boil. Simmer over moderately low heat until reduced by half. Stir in the sugar until dissolved. Let cool, then strain through a fine sieve into a bowl; refrigerate until chilled. Discard solids.

2 Mound crushed ice in the middle of a large punch bowl. Using a long stirrer or spoon, slide orange and lemon wheels against the inside of the punch bowl, then push the crushed ice back to keep the fruit in place.

3 In a cocktail shaker, combine one-fourth each of the cinnamon syrup, Cognac, Belle de Brillet, lemon juice and triple sec; shake well. Add one-fourth of the Champagne and shake once, then add to the punch bowl. Repeat the shaking 3 more times with the remaining ingredients. Serve the punch in glasses filled with crushed ice; garnish with cinnamon sticks and orange and lemon wheels.
—*Leo Robitschek*

> "Instead of simply serving bottles of bubbly, I like to make the menu more special with this sparkly punch made with Prosecco, sparkling pear juice, and club soda." —CAITLIN MURPHREE MILLER, MANAGING EDITOR

POMELDER PROSECCO PUNCH

MAKES **12 servings**

TIME **20 min plus 2 hr chilling**

- 2 **cups pure pomegranate juice**
- **One 3-inch piece of peeled fresh ginger, thinly sliced**
- 20 **green cardamom pods, crushed**
- **One chilled 750-ml bottle extra-dry Prosecco**
- **One chilled 750-ml bottle sparkling pear juice**
- ½ **cup St.-Germain elderflower liqueur**
- 2 **cups club soda or sparkling water**
- **Ice**

1 In a medium saucepan, combine the pomegranate juice, ginger and cardamom and bring to a boil. Simmer briskly until reduced to 1¼ cups, about 10 minutes. Remove from the heat and let cool to room temperature. Strain the syrup into a bowl. Cover and refrigerate for 2 hours.

2 In a pitcher or large punch bowl, combine the pomegranate syrup, Prosecco, sparkling pear juice, St.-Germain and club soda. Serve the punch over ice.
—*Food52 member hardlikearmour*

MAKE AHEAD

The pomegranate syrup can be refrigerated for up to 2 weeks.

ROSÉ SANGRIA WITH A MIXED-BERRY ICE RING

(GF) (V)

MAKES **8 to 10 servings**

TIME **Active 30 min;
Total 1 hr 15 min
plus 8 hr freezing**

📷 PAGE 245

- 1 **cup blueberries**
- 1 **cup raspberries**
- 1 **cup sliced strawberries**
- 1 **cup blackberries**
- ½ **cup fresh currants (optional)**
- **Distilled water**
- **Two 750-ml bottles rosé**
- 8 **oz. light rum**
- 8 **oz. simple syrup (see Note)**
- 4 **oz. Campari**
- 2 **oz. fresh lemon juice**
- **Ice cubes (optional)**

1 Layer the berries in a Bundt pan. Gradually add just enough distilled water to cover. Freeze until solid, 8 hours or overnight.

2 In a large punch bowl, stir the wine with the rum, simple syrup, Campari and lemon juice. Refrigerate until chilled, about 45 minutes.

3 Fill a large bowl with very hot water. Dip the bottom of the Bundt pan in the water to loosen the ice ring and invert it onto a plate. Add the ice ring to the sangria. Serve in wineglasses, with or without ice. —*Justin Chapple*

NOTE

To make 8 ounces of simple syrup, combine ¾ cup each of water and sugar in a saucepan. Boil, stirring to dissolve the sugar. Let cool before using.

MAKE AHEAD

The mixed-berry ice ring can be frozen for up to 3 days. The sangria can be refrigerated overnight.

Spicy Margarita Punch

SPICY MARGARITA PUNCH

MAKES	10 servings
TIME	Active 15 min; Total 1 hr 15 min

📷 PAGE 244

- 1 **English cucumber, thinly sliced, plus more for garnish**
- 1 **small jalapeño, thinly sliced, plus more for garnish**
- ¼ **cup lightly packed cilantro**
- ¼ **cup lightly packed mint**
-    **One 750-ml bottle silver tequila**
- 2 **cups fresh lime juice**
- 1 **cup light agave nectar**
- ½ **cup fresh orange juice**
-    **Ice, lime slices and kosher salt, for serving**

1 In a punch bowl, muddle the cucumber with the jalapeño, cilantro and mint. Add the tequila, lime juice, agave and orange juice and stir well. Refrigerate until well chilled, about 1 hour.

2 Using a fine sieve, remove and discard the solids from the punch. Garnish with more thinly sliced cucumber and jalapeño. Serve ice, jalapeño slices and lime slices alongside, as well as salt for rimming glasses. —*Justin Chapple*

MAKE AHEAD

The punch can be refrigerated overnight.

SUNSET PUNCH

MAKES	8 servings
TIME	10 min

- 8 **oz. bourbon**
- 8 **oz. white vermouth**
- ½ **cup fresh lemon juice plus lemon slices for garnish**
- ¼ **cup simple syrup (see Note)**
- 2 **oz. chilled ginger beer**

1 In a punch bowl, combine the bourbon, vermouth, lemon juice and syrup. Add the ginger beer and lemon slices and serve over ice. —*Ethan Stowell*

NOTE

To make simple syrup, combine ¼ cup of sugar and ¼ cup of water in a saucepan. Boil, stirring, until the sugar is dissolved. Let cool before using.

CARDAMOM-ROSEWATER ICED TEA

MAKES 8 servings

TIME Active 10 min; Total 25 min plus chilling

- ½ cup green cardamom pods (2 oz.)
- 12 black tea bags
- 8 cups hot water
- ½ cup honey
- Ice
- ¾ cup heavy cream
- 8 drops of rosewater

1 In a small skillet, toast the cardamom pods over moderate heat, stirring, until very fragrant and deep golden, about 5 minutes. Transfer to a heatproof bowl. Add the tea bags and 8 cups of hot water and let steep for 15 minutes. Strain the tea into a bowl and stir in the honey. Cover and refrigerate until cold.

2 Pour the tea into 8 ice-filled glasses. Top each serving with 1½ tablespoons of heavy cream and 1 drop of rosewater. —*Eli Sussman; Max Sussman*

MAKE AHEAD

The strained cardamom tea can be refrigerated for 3 days.

"It's a good idea to offer at least one nonalcoholic beverage, and this tea with cardamom, rosewater and cream is way better than just pouring up a pitcher of plain iced tea." –JORDANA ROTHMAN, RESTAURANT EDITOR

bonus section

EASY PARTY APPETIZERS

SUGAR AND SPICE NUTS

MAKES	**5 cups**
TIME	**Active 10 min; Total 1 hr**

Nonstick cooking spray,
for coating

¾ cup sugar

1 Tbsp. kosher salt

1 Tbsp. chile powder

2 tsp. cinnamon

2 tsp. cayenne

1 large egg white

2 cups raw cashews (9 oz.)

2 cups raw almonds (9 oz.)

1 Preheat the oven to 300°. Coat a rimmed baking sheet with nonstick cooking spray.

2 In a small bowl, whisk the sugar with salt, chile powder, cinnamon and cayenne.

3 In a large bowl, beat egg white until frothy. Add cashews, almonds and spiced sugar and toss. Spread out nuts on prepared baking sheet and bake for about 45 minutes, stirring once, until browned. Let nuts cool on baking sheet, stirring occasionally. —*F&W*

MAKE AHEAD

The spiced nuts can be stored in an airtight container for up to 2 days.

ASIAN SNACK MIX
WITH NORI

MAKES	**6 cups**
TIME	**Active 10 min; Total 30 min plus cooling**

½ cup pecans, broken into large pieces (2 oz.)

6 cups rice-flake cereal, such as Special K (6 oz.)

5 sheets seasoned nori, crumbled (from one .74-oz. bag; see Note)

3 Tbsp. shinshu (yellow) or shiro (white) miso

2 Tbsp. agave nectar

1 Tbsp. wasabi powder or 1½ tsp. wasabi paste

1 tsp. kosher salt

¼ cup canola oil

1 Preheat the oven to 350°. Spread pecans in a pie plate and toast for about 6 minutes, until fragrant. Transfer to a large bowl and let cool slightly. Add cereal and nori and toss well.

2 In a mini food processor, combine miso, agave nectar, wasabi and salt. Add oil and process until smooth. Dollop mixture over flakes, pecans and nori and toss with your hands to coat evenly.

3 Spread mix evenly on a parchment paper-lined rimmed baking sheet. Toast for about 18 minutes, stirring and tossing 2 or 3 times, until browned; the mix will crisp as it cools. Transfer to a bowl and serve. —*Grace Parisi*

NOTE

If seasoned nori is unavailable, use plain nori and add 1 teaspoon of toasted sesame oil to the food processor in Step 2.

MAKE AHEAD

The cooled snack mix can be stored in an airtight container for up to 5 days.

CHILE-TOASTED MARCONA ALMONDS   (GF) (V)

MAKES 3 cups

TIME 15 minutes

📷 PAGE 258

2 **Tbsp. unsalted butter**

1 **Tbsp. minced garlic**

1 **tsp. crushed red pepper**

3 **cups roasted marcona almonds**

  Kosher salt

  Black pepper

1 **Tbsp. minced chives**

1 In a large skillet, melt the butter. Add the garlic and crushed red pepper and cook over moderate heat, stirring, until the garlic is softened, about 2 minutes. Add the almonds and cook, stirring occasionally, until coated and hot, about 2 minutes. Season with salt and pepper. Let cool completely; stir in the chives. —*Martha Wiggins*

MAKE AHEAD

The almonds can be stored at room temperature overnight; stir in the chives before serving.

POPCORN WITH SESAME-GLAZED PISTACHIOS

MAKES 18 cups

TIME Active 15 min; Total 30 min

📷 PAGE 258

⅓ **cup vegetable oil**

½ **cup popping corn**

  Kosher salt

3 **Tbsp. extra-virgin olive oil**

2 **Tbsp. sugar**

2 **Tbsp. toasted sesame seeds**

2 **tsp. soy sauce**

½ **tsp. garlic powder**

2 **cups shelled unsalted pistachios (8 oz.)**

1 Preheat the oven to 350° and line a baking sheet with parchment paper. In a large saucepan, combine the vegetable oil and popping corn, cover and cook over moderate heat until the corn starts to pop. Cook, shaking the pan until the popping stops, 3 to 5 minutes. Transfer the popcorn to a large bowl and season lightly with salt.

2 Wipe out the saucepan. Add the olive oil, sugar, sesame seeds, soy sauce, garlic powder and 2 teaspoons of salt and cook over moderate heat, stirring, until the sugar dissolves, about 3 minutes. Add the pistachios and cook, stirring, for 1 minute. Scrape the pistachios onto the prepared baking sheet and bake for about 10 minutes, until bubbling. Scrape the pistachio mixture into the popcorn and toss well. Let cool before serving. —*Martha Wiggins*

MAKE AHEAD

The mix can be made early in the day and stored in an airtight container at room temperature.

MARINATED OLIVES
WITH ORANGE

(GF) (V)

MAKES **1 quart**

TIME **15 min**

📷 PAGE 259

2 Tbsp. extra-virgin olive oil

1 Tbsp. thinly sliced garlic

1½ tsp. finely grated orange zest

1 tsp. crushed red pepper

1 qt. mixed olives

⅓ cup fresh orange juice

1 In a large skillet, heat the oil. Add the garlic, orange zest and crushed red pepper and cook over moderate heat, stirring, until the garlic is softened, about 2 minutes. Add the olives and cook, stirring, until hot, about 5 minutes. Remove from the heat and stir in the orange juice. Let cool completely, stirring occasionally. Serve at room temperature. —*Martha Wiggins*

MAKE AHEAD

The olives can be refrigerated for up to 1 week. Bring to room temperature before serving.

CHILE OIL-MARINATED GOAT CHEESE

(V)

MAKES **6 servings**

TIME **10 min plus 3 days marinating**

9 dried chiles de árbol

One 11-oz. log of semifirm goat cheese, cut into 6 pieces

3 to 4 cups extra-virgin olive oil

Toasted sliced baguette or sourdough bread, for serving

1 Scatter 3 of the chiles in the bottom of a small bowl at least 3 inches deep. Arrange cheese in a single layer over chiles; top with 3 more chiles. Pour in enough oil to submerge cheese. Crumble remaining 3 chiles into oil. Cover and marinate in the refrigerator for at least 3 days.

2 Bring to room temperature before serving with bread. (Once the cheese is marinated, strain the chile oil and use in other dishes.) —*Adapted from Les Arcades, Biot, Frances*

MAKE AHEAD

The cheese can be refrigerated for up to 1 week.

Chile Oil-Marinated
Goat Cheese

PISTACHIO AND YELLOW LENTIL DIP

(V)

MAKES 3 cups

TIME Active 15 min; Total 35 min

- 1 cup yellow lentils (7 oz.), rinsed and picked over
- 1²/₃ cups unsalted pistachios (8 oz.)
- 2 garlic cloves, coarsely chopped
- ½ cup extra-virgin olive oil
- ½ cup water
- ¼ cup plus 2 Tbsp. fresh lemon juice
- 2 Tbsp. ground coriander
  Kosher salt
- ¼ cup chopped flat-leaf parsley
  Warm pita bread, for serving

1 Cook lentils in a medium saucepan of boiling water until lentils are tender, 12 to 15 minutes. Drain well.

2 Meanwhile, in a large skillet, toast pistachios over moderate heat, stirring, until deep golden, 4 to 5 minutes. Let cool completely.

3 In a food processor, pulse pistachios with garlic until nuts are finely chopped. With the machine on, slowly drizzle in the olive oil, then drizzle in water and lemon juice and puree until smooth. Add coriander and lentils and pulse until smooth. Season with salt. Scrape dip into a bowl, stir in parsley and serve with pita bread. —*Eli Sussman; Max Sussman*

MAKE AHEAD

The dip can be refrigerated for 2 days.

SOUR CREAM AND SHALLOT DIP

(GF) (V)

MAKES 2¾ cups

TIME Active 10 min; Total 2 hr 10 min

- 1 large shallot, sliced
- 2 Tbsp. extra-virgin olive oil
- 2 cups sour cream
- ½ cup mayonnaise
- ¼ cup SparCs dehydrated vegetable powder (See Note)
  Kosher salt
  Crudités or chips, for serving

1 In a small skillet, cook shallot in olive oil over moderate heat, stirring, until softened and caramelized, about 10 minutes.

2 Transfer shallot to a medium bowl. Stir in sour cream, mayonnaise and SparCs powder; season with salt. Cover and refrigerate until chilled, about 2 hours. Serve with crudités or chips. —*Emily Tylman*

NOTE

In the fight against food waste, chefs are leading the charge. Last year Dan Barber asked Baldor, a produce wholesaler, for carrot peels and celery tops to use for his wastED pop-up dinners at NYC's Blue Hill. Inspired, Baldor has introduced SparCs (scraps backward), a vegetable-peel powder that can add a healthy kick to anything. The powder is available at baldorfood.com.

SPINACH AND CARAMELIZED ONION DIP

MAKES **2 cups**

TIME **30 min**

3 Tbsp. extra-virgin olive oil

1 large onion, thinly sliced

4 oz. curly spinach (4 packed cups), stemmed

1 cup nonfat Greek yogurt

¼ cup chopped chives

½ tsp. freshly grated nutmeg

Kosher salt

Freshly ground pepper

Crackers, for serving

1 In a large nonstick skillet, heat 2 tablespoons olive oil. Add onion and cook over moderate heat, stirring occasionally, until deeply golden, about 15 minutes. Stir in the remaining 1 tablespoon of oil and spinach and stir until wilted. Transfer to a medium bowl and let cool to room temperature.

2 Stir yogurt, chives and nutmeg into spinach and onion and season with salt and pepper. Serve with crackers. *—Kay Chun*

MAKE AHEAD

The dip can be refrigerated overnight.

CHARRED EGGPLANT DIP

MAKES **1½ cups**

TIME **Active 25 min; Total 1 hr 30 min**

One 1¼-lb. eggplant

2 large shallots, halved lengthwise

3 large garlic cloves

1 Tbsp. extra-virgin olive oil

Kosher salt

Freshly ground pepper

½ cup plain Greek yogurt

2 Tbsp. fresh lemon juice

2 Tbsp. minced parsley

2 Tbsp. minced cilantro

2 Tbsp. minced mint

Pita chips and crudités, for serving

1 Preheat the oven to 375°. Roast eggplant over an open flame or under a broiler until softened and charred, 12 minutes. Transfer to a baking dish. Add shallots and garlic to the eggplant, drizzle with oil and season with salt and pepper; roast for 35 minutes, until very tender. Let cool completely. Scrape eggplant flesh into a colander to drain for 15 minutes; discard skin.

2 Mince eggplant, garlic and shallots; transfer to a bowl. Stir in yogurt, lemon juice and herbs. Season with salt and pepper and serve at room temperature with pita chips and crudités. *—Serge Madikians*

MAKE AHEAD

The dip can be refrigerated overnight. Bring to room temperature before serving.

Caramelized White
Chocolate Spread

CARAMELIZED WHITE CHOCOLATE SPREAD

(V)

MAKES **1¼ cups**

TIME **3 hr 20 min**

½ lb. Valrhona Ivoire white baking chocolate, chopped (see Note)

½ cup heavy cream, warmed

Sea salt

Toasted rustic bread, sliced apples, sliced pears and strawberries, for serving

1 Preheat the oven to 225°. In a medium stainless steel bowl, bake chocolate for 3 hours, stirring every 15 minutes, until golden. Gradually whisk in warm cream and a generous pinch of salt. Let cool completely, then refrigerate until just spreadable, about 10 minutes. —*Justin Chapple*

NOTE

Valrhona Ivoire is available at specialty food shops and from amazon.com.

MAKE AHEAD

The spread can be refrigerated for up to 5 days. Soften in the microwave at 10-second intervals, stirring between intervals, until just spreadable.

BACON CANDY

(GF)

MAKES **20 strips**

TIME **Active 10 min; Total 30 min**

½ cup packed light brown sugar

1½ tsp. chile powder

20 slices of thick-cut bacon (1½ lbs.)

1 Preheat the oven to 400°. Line 2 rimmed baking sheets with foil. In a small bowl, whisk brown sugar with chile powder. Arrange bacon strips on foil and coat tops with chile sugar. Bake for 20 to 25 minutes, until caramelized and almost crisp. Transfer bacon to a rack set over a sheet of foil to cool completely; serve. —*F&W*

MAKE AHEAD

The bacon candy can be made earlier in the day; store at room temperature.

PEPPER-GLAZED GOAT CHEESE GRATIN

(v)

MAKES 8 servings

TIME 20 min

- 1 lb. creamy fresh goat cheese, softened
- 6 Tbsp. apricot preserves
- 4 Peppadew peppers, finely chopped
- 1 pickled jalapeño, seeded and finely chopped
- 2 Tbsp. minced cocktail onions
- 2 tsp. Dijon mustard
- 1½ tsp. dry sherry
- Pita chips and toasted baguette slices, for serving

1 Preheat the oven to 400°. Spread goat cheese in an even layer in a 5-by-8-inch gratin dish.

2 In a small bowl, whisk preserves with Peppadews, jalapeño, onions, mustard and sherry. Spread mixture over goat cheese and bake on the top rack of oven for about 5 minutes, until warm. Turn on broiler and broil for about 2 minutes, until topping is bubbling and lightly browned at the edges. Serve hot, with pita chips and toasted baguette slices. —*Grace Parisi*

MAKE AHEAD

You can assemble the gratin a day ahead and bake just before serving.

HOGS IN A BLANKET

MAKES 36 appetizers

TIME Active 20 min; Total 50 min

- 7 oz. all-butter puff pastry, thawed and cut into four 5-inch squares
- 1 large egg yolk mixed with 1 Tbsp. of water
- 4 andouille sausages (3 oz. each)
- ¼ cup Major Grey's chutney
- 2 Tbsp. whole-grain mustard

1 Preheat the oven to 375° and position a rack in the center. Arrange puff pastry squares on a work surface and brush top edges with the egg wash. Place sausages on bottom edges and roll up pastry, pressing edges to seal. Freeze logs for 10 minutes, or until firm.

2 Cut logs into ½-inch slices and place them cut side up in 3 mini muffin pans. Bake for 25 minutes, until golden and sizzling. Turn out onto a paper towel-lined rack to cool.

3 Meanwhile, in a mini food processor, pulse chutney and mustard just until chutney is chopped. Spoon a dollop of chutney mustard on each slice and serve. —*Grace Parisi*

MAKE AHEAD

The unbaked sliced rounds can be frozen for up to 1 month. Thaw before baking.

Pepper-Glazed Goat
Cheese Gratin

SPICY PICKLED BEETS

MAKES **6 cups**

TIME **Active 30 min; Total 2 hr plus overnight chilling**

📷 PAGE 258

- **3 lbs. medium beets**
- **1 cup water**
- **Kosher salt**
- **1½ cups water**
- **1½ cups apple cider vinegar**
- **1½ cups sugar**
- **3 bay leaves**
- **One 2-inch cinnamon stick**
- **2 tsp. whole allspice berries**
- **2 tsp. black peppercorns**
- **¾ tsp. whole cloves**

1 Preheat the oven to 375°. Put the beets in a large baking dish. Add 1 cup of water and a generous pinch of salt. Cover tightly with foil and bake for about 1 hour, until the beets are tender. Uncover and let cool. Peel the beets and cut them into ¾-inch wedges. Transfer to a large heatproof bowl.

2 In a medium saucepan, combine 1½ cups of water with the vinegar, sugar, bay leaves, cinnamon stick, allspice, peppercorns, cloves and 2 teaspoons of salt. Bring to a boil over high heat, then simmer over moderately low heat until reduced to 3 cups, about 12 minutes. Pour the liquid over the beets and let cool; refrigerate overnight. Drain the following day, before serving. —*Martha Wiggins*

MAKE AHEAD

The drained pickled beets can be refrigerated for up to 5 days.

FIG AND STILTON SQUARES ⓥ

MAKES **4 dozen**

TIME **Active 20 min; Total 3 hr 15 min**

- **One 14-oz. package all-butter puff pastry, thawed if frozen but still cold**
- **½ cup fig preserves**
- **¾ cup crumbled Stilton cheese (4 oz.)**

1 On a lightly floured work surface, roll out puff pastry to a 11½-by-16-inch rectangle. Trim to form a 10½-by-15-inch rectangle. Transfer pastry to a large rimmed baking sheet and cut into 1¾-inch squares; you should have about 48. Freeze squares until firm, about 30 minutes.

2 Preheat the oven to 375°. Line a large rimmed baking sheet with parchment paper. Arrange 12 squares on sheet and cover with more parchment paper. Top squares with another baking sheet, bottom side down. If you have another pair of baking sheets, repeat with 12 more squares. Bake squares for about 35 minutes, until pastry is golden. Transfer squares to a rack to cool. Repeat to bake remaining squares.

3 Return as many cooled squares as will fit to a baking sheet. Top each square with ½ teaspoon of fig preserves. Sprinkle with Stilton and bake for about 5 minutes, until Stilton is melted. Serve warm or at room temperature. —*Melissa Rubel Jacobson*

MAKE AHEAD

The unbaked frozen pastry squares can be frozen in an airtight container for up to 1 month.

TOMATO TARTLETS

Ⓥ

MAKES	**5 dozen**
TIME	**Active 30 min; Total 45 min**

All-purpose flour, for rolling

½ lb. **all-butter puff pastry**

30 **cherry tomatoes (about 1 lb.), halved crosswise**

2 Tbsp. **extra-virgin olive oil**

2 tsp. **thyme leaves plus more for garnish**

Kosher salt

Freshly ground pepper

½ lb. **fresh ricotta**

1 Preheat the oven to 425° and line a large baking sheet with parchment paper. Position racks in the middle and upper thirds of the oven.

2 On a lightly floured surface, roll out puff pastry to a 9½-by-17½-inch rectangle. Using a straight edge, trim pastry to a 9-by-17-inch rectangle. Transfer pastry to prepared baking sheet and poke all over with a fork. Top with another sheet of parchment and another baking sheet and bake for 25 minutes on middle rack, until golden. Remove top sheet and parchment paper and bake pastry until lightly browned and dry, about 10 minutes longer. Slide paper and pastry onto a rack and let cool.

3 Meanwhile, in a large bowl, toss the tomatoes with olive oil and 2 teaspoons of thyme and season with salt and pepper. Place tomatoes on a baking sheet, cut side up, and bake on upper rack for about 15 minutes, until softened slightly. Let cool.

4 In a food processor, puree ricotta until very creamy. Spread ricotta over pastry and season with salt and pepper. Arrange tomatoes cut side up on the ricotta in 5 rows of 12. Sprinkle lightly with fresh thyme. Using a long knife, cut pastry between the tomatoes into 60 squares. Transfer tartlets to platters and serve.
—*Grace Parisi*

MAKE AHEAD

The recipe can be prepared through Step 2 and kept at room temperature for up to 8 hours.

Smoked-Trout Crackers
with Broken Tapenade

BOILED SHRIMP WITH
SPICY MAYONNAISE

MAKES 8 servings

TIME 15 min

- 2 very fresh organic egg yolks
- 1½ Tbsp. Colman's hot mustard powder
- 1 tsp. fresh lemon juice
- 1 cup canola oil
- Kosher salt
- Freshly ground white pepper
- 1 Tbsp. water
- 2 lbs. medium shrimp, peeled and deveined

1 In a medium bowl, whisk together egg yolks, mustard powder and lemon juice. Whisking constantly, slowly dribble in canola oil. Season with salt and white pepper to taste. Whisk in 1 tablespoon water to thin out mayonnaise if necessary.

2 Bring a large saucepan of water to a boil. Add shrimp and boil until pink, about 3 minutes. Drain and let cool. Serve shrimp with the spicy mayonnaise.
—*Eugenia Bone*

MAKE AHEAD

You can make the mayonnaise and boil the shrimp a day ahead and refrigerate until ready to serve.

SMOKED-TROUT CRACKERS
WITH BROKEN TAPENADE

MAKES 8 servings

TIME 30 min

- ¼ cup pitted kalamata olives
- 3 Tbsp. extra-virgin olive oil
- 8 oz. feta cheese, crumbled
- Seeded crackers
- 12 oz. smoked-trout fillets, skin and bones discarded and flesh flaked
- Baby arugula, for garnish

1 In a food processor, pulse olives with olive oil until finely chopped. Scrape into a small saucepan and cook over moderately low heat, stirring occasionally, until oil separates and mixture looks broken, 2 to 3 minutes. Transfer tapenade to a small bowl. Clean food processor.

2 In food processor, puree feta until smooth. Transfer to a small bowl. To serve, spread feta on crackers and top with smoked trout, broken tapenade and arugula. —*Eli Dahlin*

MAKE AHEAD

The feta puree and the broken tapenade can be refrigerated separately overnight. Bring to room temperature before serving.

TIPS FOR A SUCCESSFUL POTLUCK

Planning a Potluck

If you're organizing the potluck, consider coordinating dishes among attendees so that you don't end up with, say, four pasta salads. If you're hosting, offer to provide the main course, and invite guests to round out the meal with sides and desserts.

Provide serving utensils, serving bowls, hot pads and trivets. Most people will bring their food item in a serving dish, but it's a good idea to pull out extra bowls, platters, and serving spoons just in case. Set out plenty of plates, napkins, and cups.

Set up a drinks and appetizer station in a different area from where mains and sides are being served, where guests can enjoy drinks and snacks while the rest of the food is being set out.

Transporting

Select foods that travel well instead of saucy meats, soups, stews and delicate desserts. (All of the recipes in this book will work.)

To keep hot food hot and cold food cold en route to a potluck, cover food tightly with heavy-duty plastic wrap or foil, or use an insulated casserole carrier or tote.

Potluck Protocol

Bring your food in its own serving dish, and bring a serving utensil.

Don't leave your platter or bowl behind with the host.

Bring dishes that need minimal preparation or reheating since the kitchen and oven space will likely be limited. If you do want to bring something that will require some on-site cooking, ask in advance if the oven or stovetop will be available for reheating or last-minute assembly.

Bring a bottle of wine that can be served at the meal or enjoyed later by the host. (See page 246 for potluck-friendly wine suggestions.)

Dietary Restrictions

Whether you're hosting or attending a potluck, ask ahead of time if there will be guests with dietary restrictions.

Vegetarian Be sure to provide several vegetarian dishes if there will be guests who do not eat meat. If you're serving a dish where the meat is not visible, put out a card or a tag to let guests know that the dish contains meat.

We've flagged meat-free recipes that will please carnivores and vegetarians alike throughout this book with Ⓥ, but you may also modify recipes to make them meat-free:

- Replace beef or chicken broth with vegetable broth.
- Omit the meat in salads or soups, and serve it in a separate bowl so that guests can add it if they wish.

Gluten-Free To accommodate guests on gluten-free diets, select from among the recipes in the book identified with ⒼⒻ, or modify recipes using gluten-free products:

- Substitute gluten-free pasta in casseroles and salads.
- Offer gluten-free crackers and fresh veggies as dippers.
- Serve croutons for salads in a separate bowl.
- Make or purchase a loaf of gluten-free bread to serve with the meal.

Food Safety

Until it's time to serve, keep hot dishes at a temperature higher than 140°, and cold dishes at a temperature of 40° or colder.

Consider serving hot foods from a slow cooker or a chafing dish, and placing chilled foods over a shallow baking dish of ice.

Remember the "two-hour rule." Do not let potentially hazardous foods such as dairy, eggs, meat, fish, or diced fruits sit at room temperature for more than two hours. (And if the room temperature is above 90°, do not let it sit out more than one hour.) Include transportation time in the "two-hour rule."

Don't partially cook food at home to finish at the potluck. The best method would be to completely cook all potentially hazardous foods, such as meat, at the meal site.

To reheat a casserole, keep it covered and reheat at a moderate temperature, 250° to 350°, for 20 to 30 minutes.

Use separate serving utensils for each dish on the table.

PARTY-PLANNING ESSENTIALS

The best potluck dinners are fun and relaxing; the worst are chaotic and unsatisfying. The key to success? "You have to have some form of organization," says Marco Flavio Marinucci, founder of the blog *Cook Here and Now* (cookhereandnow.com), which organizes San Francisco-based potluck dinners. Marinucci spoke with *Food & Wine* to divulge his five best tips.

Create a Theme

"I don't believe in hodgepodge potlucks. It's important to create a theme; it can really surprise and delight guests and get them excited about cooking. Try to move beyond generic themes, like Italian or Cantonese; instead, choose a specific ingredient, like sustainable seafood or heirloom tomatoes. That way, you get really different approaches that reflect each cook's background, and you end up with dishes you might never have expected. Try to finalize the theme two weeks before the dinner so guests have time to come up with great recipes."

Plot out the Courses

"Potluck should include every course—appetizers, soups or salads, entrées, desserts—as well as alcoholic and nonalcoholic beverages. Always plan more than one for each course: Someone with the best intentions may bring an appetizer that does not work well, and you don't want that to be the only choice on the table. Or someone may have to cancel at the last minute. For that reason, I think it's important that the host always makes the main dish—because then it's guaranteed to show up!"

Give Portion Guidelines

"If you have 20 guests and two of them are making desserts, they should each prepare something that serves 10 people. The good thing with potlucks is that you don't need to be exact—people generally will not eat a full portion of something when there are other options on the table. We usually have a lot of leftovers, which is great. Encourage people to bring their own to-go containers and to ask each cook for permission to bring home extras of his or her dish."

Limit Last–Minute Preparations

"For potlucks, cooks usually prepare dishes three hours before they are served, but not all dishes can wait that long. Try to find out which guests will need a stove burner or oven space, but encourage them to make as much of the dish in advance as they can. For example, vegetables can be grilled at home and then tossed into a salad on-site."

Stress the Importance of Presentation

"There is a tendency not to think about the way a dish will look when it's served at potlucks. But presentation is a big part of the meal. Even if you're with a group of good friends, don't just put everything out in the containers they came in. Have everyone bring a nice serving dish, and garnish dishes with a sprig of rosemary or a slice of lemon, or whatever is appropriate to the dish."

—*Emily Carrus*

RECIPE INDEX

Page numbers in **bold** indicate photographs.

Clockwise from top right:
Chicken and Wild Rice Casserole,
p. 170; Root Vegetable Hot Dish
with Parsnip Puree, p. 123;
Harissa-Spiced Cassoulet, p. 187

Pumpkin Layer Cake with
Mascarpone Frosting, p. 207

PHOTO CREDITS